Fit Citizens

Fit Citizens

A History of Black Women's Exercise from

Post-Reconstruction to Postwar America

AVA PURKISS

THE UNIVERSITY OF NORTH CAROLINA PRESS   Chapel Hill

This book was published with the assistance of the Lilian R. Furst Fund of the University of North Carolina Press.

Designed by Richard Hendel
Set in Utopia and Klavika types by codeMantra
Manufactured in the United States of America

A version of Chapter 3 first appeared in *Journal of Women's History*, Volume 29, Issue 2, Summer 2017, pages 14–37. Published with permission by Johns Hopkins University Press. Copyright © 2017 Journal of Women's History.

Cover illustration courtesy of National Archives.
Frontispiece: "Girls Physical Education, Hampton Institute." Girls Physical Education Photographs Collection, Hampton University's Archival and Museum Collection, Hampton University, Hampton, Virginia.

Library of Congress Cataloging-in-Publication Data
Names: Purkiss, Ava, author.
Title: Fit citizens : a history of Black women's exercise from post-Reconstruction to postwar America / Ava Purkiss.
Other titles: History of Black women's exercise from post-Reconstruction to postwar America | Gender & American culture.
Description: Chapel Hill : The University of North Carolina Press, 2023. | Series: Gender and American culture | Includes bibliographical references and index.
Identifiers: LCCN 2022033515 | ISBN 9781469670485 (cloth ; alk. paper) | ISBN 9781469672724 (paperback ; alk. paper) | ISBN 9781469670492 (ebook)
Subjects: LCSH: African American women—Health and hygiene—United States—History—20th century. | Body image in women—United States—History—20th century. | Physical fitness for women—United States. | Citizenship—United States.
Classification: LCC RA778.4.A36 P87 2023 | DDC 613.7/045—dc23/eng/20220722
LC record available at https://lccn.loc.gov/2022033515

For my sister, mother, and father

Contents

Illustrations

Acknowledgments

I conceived of, drafted, and completed this book with the continuous love, support, and generosity of many people. This project took root during a conversation with Tiffany Gill, and her insights and mentorship greatly shaped its development. I am forever grateful to her, as well as to Daina Ramey Berry, Jackie Jones, and Janet Davis, for support in the early iterations of this undertaking. Interlocutors at the Carter G. Woodson Institute for African-American and African Studies at the University of Virginia also contributed to the formation of the project, and I thank Deborah McDowell, Maurice Wallace, Talitha LeFlouria, Tammy C. Owens, Taneisha Means, Nicole Burrowes, Laura Helton, and La TaSha Levy for their careful reading and comments on my work. The University of North Carolina Press showed interest in the project from its early stages. I thank Mark Simpson-Vos, María Garcia, and the anonymous reviewers for helping to bring this book to fruition.

At the University of Michigan, colleagues enthusiastically supported this book as it developed. LaKisha Simmons and Stephen Berrey read the entire manuscript and offered constructive feedback that broadened my historical imagination for the project. I greatly benefited from Allison Alexy's keen eye for clarity, argumentation, and organization. Several colleagues, including Mary Kelley, Kristin Hass, Abby Stewart, Liz Wingrove, Alex Stern, Matthew Countryman, and Jesse Hoffnung-Garskof, provided brilliant insights that sharpened the book's analysis. Comments from and conversations with colleagues Jessica Kenyatta Walker, Jennifer Dominique Jones, and Diana Louis improved the book significantly, reinvigorated my love for the subject matter, and kept me going while on the tenure track. Several colleagues offered me sage advice and genuine kindness that were critical to completing the project, especially Victor Mendoza, Sara McClelland, and Reginald Jackson. I also thank Valerie Traub, Ruby Tapia, Anna Kirkland, Colin Gunckel, Leela Fernandes, and Rosario Ceballo for their comments on my burgeoning work and their general support as senior faculty and administrative leaders. I am also grateful for the support of colleagues Charlotte Karem Albrecht, Sandra Gunning, Magda Zaborowska, Clare Croft, Manan Desai, Anna Watkins Fisher, William Calvo-Quirós, and Michelle Segar. Graduate students

Casidy Campbell, Eshe Sherley, and Jallicia Jolly (now assistant professor) provided inspiration, encouragement, and critical note-taking that pushed the project along. Andrea "Andy" Holman's exceptional generosity helped sustain me as I worked on the manuscript.

I heartily thank staff members of the Departments of Women's and Gender Studies and American Culture, including Donna Ainsworth, Sarah Ellerholz, Kevin O'Neill, Mary Freiman, and Judy Gray. A yearlong fellowship at the Institute for the Humanities at the University of Michigan was critical for me in making progress on the book, and I sincerely thank Peggy McCracken and the faculty and graduate student fellows of the 2018–19 cohort for their comments on an early chapter draft. I am also grateful for funding from the Institute for Research on Women and Gender at the University of Michigan that allowed me to perform essential archival research for the book.

Scholars, archivists, and institutions outside of my university community proved crucial to the research and writing process, especially Ula Taylor, LaShawn Harris, Deboleena Roy, Mary-Elizabeth Murphy, Olivia Affuso, Psyche Williams-Forson, Lynn Johnson, and Fidan Elcioglu. Sara Saylor, developmental editor extraordinaire, provided critical feedback that improved the book in every way. Jacob Oertel supplied critical research assistance, problem-solving virtuosity, and an energetic presence that contributed greatly to the project. The archival staffs at Tuskegee University, the Western Reserve Historical Society, Temple University, and the Grand Rapids Public Library were exceptionally helpful and kind. I am especially thankful for external fellowships and grants from the American Association of University Women, the American Council of Learned Societies, and the National Endowment for the Humanities that granted me precious time and resources to work on the project.

I could not have completed this book without a community of people who are equally smart and generous. My love and admiration for Adrienne Sockwell runs deep, and she has never failed to buoy me during my lowest moments and celebrate me during my highest. I am forever indebted to her for her unyielding support, brilliant mind, and inexhaustible benevolence. Keith Mayes read the manuscript with a critical yet gracious eye and offered invaluable comments. I thank him for his intellectual generosity, equanimity, and love. Helen Pho proved to be an amazing reader, listener, and cheerleader, and I am grateful for her consistent support and investments in me and this book. Friends and fellow historians Justene Hill Edwards, Mary Phillips, and Mónica Jimenez encouraged me and offered meaningful peer mentoring. Several others provided great support, friendship, and good humor, including Pardip Bolina (and Ana and Simone), Alice Gorham, Cristina Pérez, and Goli Bagheri.

My sister, Kim Anderson, is largely responsible for my being a scholar, and she cared for, reassured, and supported me in numerous ways as I wrote this book. My love for her is ineffable, and I thank her enormously for being the best sister I could ever ask for. My brother-in-law and nephew supported me every step of the way, and I am grateful for their presence in my life. I also thank my cousin Pauline, Aunt Eunice, and Aunt Sonia for their enduring love and encouragement. My beloved grandaunt and cousins in Maryland constantly reminded me of how proud I made them and provided immense moral support. Finally, I am grateful to my mother, from whom my ambition emanates, and my father, who gave me the gift of curiosity and a love for the life of the mind.

Prayer (both my own and others), faith, and God's grace sustained me throughout the years it took to complete this book. I am eternally grateful for His mercies.

Fit Citizens

Introduction

EXERCISING CITIZENSHIP

In the summer of 1920, ten southern Black YWCA branches organized one-week camping trips for their Colored Girl Reserves. In light of the segregated structure of outdoor recreation, the trip provided a unique exercise opportunity for the girls as well as for the Black women Y officers. Organizers sought to expose the girls to forms of exercise that they rarely experienced, such as hiking in the woods, setting up tents, and "splashing about" in streams. Y leaders expected the girls to come away with "a real gain in physical fitness" that would help them to develop "strong, vigorous bodies."[1] A YWCA secretary added that the physical nature of the trip would enable the Reserves to "[act] as American citizens in the fullest sense of the words."[2] The relationship between the camping trip's physical activities and American citizenship might seem nebulous. But "gains" in physical fitness and "vigorous bodies" indicated civic virtue at a time in the twentieth century when citizenship signaled a physical state of being and not merely a legal status.

At the beginning of the twentieth century, physical exercise became intrinsic to the socially and politically constructed idea of the "good" American citizen. This constructed citizen was based on a set of assumptions, many of which were imagined and idealized. Exercising Americans kept themselves in shape and prepared to contribute to national progress through public health recommendations, healthy reproduction, and, when needed, military enlistment. They avoided extra weight, which increasingly became a marker of gluttony, untrustworthiness, selfishness, and many other qualities that designated a "bad" citizen. American exercisers used their free time productively by engaging in intentional physical activity and not wasting precious time, energy, or money on more frivolous diversions. Exercise, Americans believed, produced physical fitness. A physically fit body became synonymous with a fit character, and both were vital to notions of the fit citizen. Presumed to be outside of this value system, many African American women, like the Black YWCA officers, adhered to these logics of fitness.

Fit Citizens: A History of Black Women's Exercise from Post-Reconstruction to Postwar America chronicles African American women's participation in the modern exercise movement and situates them within a tradition of Black physical and civic fitness. The book examines the social and political significance of Black women's exercise behaviors as the physical culture, racial uplift, and early civil rights movements placed overlapping demands on African American women's bodies. *Fit Citizens* argues that Black women used exercise to demonstrate their "fitness" for citizenship during a time when physically fit bodies garnered new political meaning. It captures how African American women made exercise instrumental to their ideas of health, ideal corporality, and civic inclusion. Through camping trips, physical education classes, in-home exercises, or simple walks, Black women, indeed, "acted" as American citizens.

"Doing" and Embodying Citizenship

When the Colored Girl Reserves and the group's Black chaperones asserted their citizenship in 1920, African Americans had been granted birthright citizenship through the Fourteenth Amendment and women had gained the right to vote through the Nineteenth Amendment. Nevertheless, they conceptualized their citizenship outside of these legislative edicts. Black women, whose civic value was confined by race and gender, often looked beyond narrow legal and political spheres for meanings of citizenship. Physical exercise served as one sociocultural modality of citizenship that Black women used to signal their civic worth absent the "substantive" status of full citizen.[3] Likewise, this book traces how African Americans enacted concepts of civic virtue through both the act of exercise and the embodiment of fitness.[4]

Because exercise "activates" citizenship in this book, its historical actors are not examined through accounts of voting, running for public office, or other typical forms of state recognition like marriage, taxes, property ownership, and legal petitioning. *Fit Citizens* does not argue that exercise granted access to the ballot box or that physical fitness enabled Black women to enter electoral politics. These are common ways that historians have, justifiably, categorized the act of "exercising citizenship." In the field of African American history, for example, "exercise" has rarely referred to physical exercise. When encountering the term in the scholarship on the Black past, "exercise" usually adopts the transitive usage, as in she "exercised her rights" or they "exercised resistance."[5] In contrast, *Fit Citizens* uses exercise in its intransitive, physical sense.[6] This book identifies

2

moments when "fitness" occupied both the physical and civic realms for Black people and when the endeavor of "exercising citizenship" called for physical exercise.[7]

Theorizations of citizenship capture the ways in which national belonging has been understood as codified legal status as well as less-defined social and physical practices. Often drawing on T. H. Marshall's tripartite understanding of citizenship as civil, political, and social in nature,[8] scholars have documented how state actors used informal understandings of citizenship to both grant and deny rights.[9] This body of scholarship posits that ideas of "good" and "bad" citizens developed outside of established law and has examined citizenship as "legal status" or "desirable activity." "Legal status" concerns "full membership in a particular political community" in which citizens are guaranteed state entitlements, such as the right to vote, assemble, and engage in political dissent.[10] "Desirable activity" attends to how "one's citizenship is the function of one's participation in that community."[11] Desirable activity involves responsibilities of citizenship, including paying taxes, serving in the military, and obeying the law.[12] In the better part of the twentieth century, African Americans failed to be fully recognized as citizens through a status-based paradigm. Nevertheless, Black people asserted their citizenship through certain practices or activities.

A deep investment in citizenship-as-activity shaped how Black people thought about and performed citizenship. Some African Americans conceived of citizenship not as who one "is" but as what one "does."[13] They believed that physical acts *produced* citizenship. For instance, in 1919, the Black publication the *Southern Workman* published an article about the virtues of physical education and its relationship to citizenship, stating, "Universal physical education . . . would have mighty results in producing men and women physically fit for whatever may be the responsibilities of citizenship."[14] Here, the author argues that the act of participating in physical education activated one's citizenship. Other African Americans believed themselves to be citizens, without the full benefit of citizen status, through their physical practices, habits, and behaviors. At times, Black assertions of citizenship involved the subtlest of negotiations and embodied encounters not connected to direct political engagement.[15] Koritha Mitchell explains that "as much as African Americans worked toward citizenship rights in terms of voting and holding political office, there is no question that citizenship was negotiated in private and corporal ways."[16] Indeed, Black people affirmed their citizenship in understated forms like making direct eye contact with white people, walking with an air of dignity and self-possession, and generally moving their bodies in ways that belied their second-class citizenship.

While the citizenship-as-activity model describes what citizens do, theories of embodied citizenship help us understand the bodies that perform the "doing."[17] Embodied citizenship draws our attention to how ideas of civic value and national belonging have hinged on bodily demarcation, perceived corporal virtue, and physical service to the nation.[18] In the first half of the twentieth century, African American women like Nannie Helen Burroughs juxtaposed "physical fit[ness]" to "contributions to American civilization" in ways that intentionally linked Black citizenship to corporality.[19] But embodied citizenship posed a problem for Black women, as hegemonic notions of corporal difference served as the "overdetermining force of political participation for those marked as different."[20] Throughout American history, marginalization from the category of "citizen" has relied on "marked" bodies that appeared ineligible for full incorporation into civil society. Scholars note, for example, that individuals perceived to have control over their bodies, as opposed to those whose bodies must be managed by government forces, have been constituted as more ideal citizens.[21] Inspired by these formulations of citizenship, *Fit Citizens* charts how Black women exercisers contested the idea that their Black and female bodies made them illegitimate citizens and instead championed their fit bodies as morally, aesthetically, and physically ideal for participation in civic life. Like the YWCA campers who tethered "vigorous bodies" to "American citizens," this book considers how African American women stitched together notions of Black physical and civic fitness even as the nation-state sought to dispute their fitness for citizenship.[22]

Black Women and American Fitness

The first half of the twentieth century was a time of extraordinary national focus on health, thinness, and physical fitness in the United States. This period also functioned as a time of intense scrutiny of Black women's bodies and character. With these realities in mind, African American women approached "fitness" as a marker of both character and physique. Poor physical health, ugliness, and immorality had served as constitutive identifiers of Black women since slavery and acquired new significance in the late nineteenth- and early twentieth-century context. In the post-Reconstruction period, southern apologists claimed that African Americans would be obliterated by disease, images of overweight mammies became ubiquitous, and slanderous claims concerning Black women's deviant natures littered newspapers and magazines. Through their engagement with the modern exercise movement, African American women contested these pejorative tropes of Black womanhood. Exercise enabled Black women to fashion themselves as "fit" citizens and wrestle with the social, physical, and representational uses of the Black female body.

Black women's fit bodies proved symbolically valuable in the late nineteenth and twentieth centuries. Several defining qualities of American citizenship, including wartime patriotism and military participation, required a demonstration of physical strength and self-restraint. The Spanish-American War and especially World War I tied physical fitness to the imperial power and superiority of the nation. During both world wars, Black writers decried the lack of physical fitness among the American citizenry (including African Americans) and its effect on the country's preparedness for battle. Fit bodies then, as now, were perceived as a boon to national security. Health and fitness composed some of the basic personal traits of twentieth-century citizenship, and Black women crafted part of their racial uplift ideology around these principles. Black women's embrace of the exercised body became entangled with the political tides of the twentieth century.

The modern American exercise movement emerged from major changes in work, health standards, and leisure during the Progressive Era. In the late nineteenth century, as parts of the country transitioned from an agrarian society to factory and desk jobs, work did not require the same kind of physical exertion it once did. Health experts and reformers grew concerned about what this change in labor would do to the bodies of Americans.[23] With increasing industrial development, new modes of transportation, sedentary employment, and encouragement from health reformers, Americans sought intentional exercise in unprecedented numbers. Opportunities to exercise expanded from the homes and private gymnasiums of the nineteenth century to the more publicly available recreational spaces and educational institutions of the twentieth century. This institutionalization marked a key development of the modern American exercise movement.[24]

The rise of American exercise culture coincided with other cognate biomedical and social movements that took place between 1890 and 1920. In the late nineteenth century, the germ theory of disease and the discovery of the bacterium that causes tuberculosis prompted a public health crusade and preoccupation with hygiene.[25] In the early twentieth century, home economists professionalized domestic work through the scientific study of food preservation and sanitation.[26] Middle-class white and Black women invested in this new discipline that combated contagious disease and ensured family health through domestic science. Similarly, health enthusiasts marketed exercise as one of a few necessary steps in living a clean and hygienic life.

The "face" of this burgeoning exercise movement was Bernarr Macfadden—the most well-known promoter of exercise who subsequently held the title of the "father of physical culture." Macfadden first published his *Physical Culture* magazine in 1899, and it was the first and most popular fitness publication of the early twentieth century. The magazine featured instructions for specific exercises that fitness hopefuls could perform to improve their health and perfect their bodies. In 1900, Macfadden targeted women with *Woman's Physical Development*, a by-product of *Physical Culture*. He created the magazine to encourage white women's fitness and place them front and center of the physical culture movement. Women responded enthusiastically—the offshoot magazine became so popular that by 1903 it accumulated a readership of over 80,000.[27]

Macfadden and other white physical culturists like John Harvey Kellogg, Eugen Sandow, and Milo Hastings built successful careers by promoting physical fitness to the American public. They seized on the commercialization of the early twentieth century by selling physical culture publications and exercise products and by organizing publicity stunts and beauty competitions. Physical culturists used these venues to offer gender-specific recommendations on exercise. Macfadden, in particular, categorized strength as a feminine quality and claimed that exercise was the best way to achieve a beautiful body and ideal white womanhood. Supporting these claims, physical educators, health experts, and purveyors of natural medicine agreed that exercise proved essential for women's health.[28]

Physical culture dovetailed with commercialized leisure and made participation in sport and exercise programs fashionable in the early twentieth century, especially for women. The purchase of gymnasium equipment and sports paraphernalia informed notions of the Progressive Era "New Woman."[29] Large numbers of upper-class women engaged in respectable, modern leisure activity, including basketball and bicycling.[30] Other social and cultural developments, such as middle-class anxieties about slimness and emergent beauty advertising, encouraged American women to exercise.[31]

Americans' newfound infatuation with exercise, however, contained deeply ingrained racial, gender, and class inequities that marginalized African Americans. Black women encountered several structural obstacles to accessing suitable fitness spaces. The Y presents a prime case in point. The Young Men's Christian Association and the Young Women's Christian Association, founded in 1844 and 1858 respectively, became instrumental spaces for exercise.[32] Both institutions adhered to firm racial and gender demarcations from their founding into the twentieth century. The first Black branches of the YMCA and YWCA were founded respectively in 1853 and 1889 and remained underfunded and under-resourced compared to their white counterparts. Accordingly, Black women levied countless complaints and launched campaigns to secure gymnasiums comparable to white YWCA facilities.

African Americans, and Black women in particular, encountered similar forms of discrimination in fitness culture in later periods. Nevertheless, they found creative ways to engage in exercise and made physical activity essential to ideas of Black health. Afflicted with high rates of tuberculosis, pneumonia, and other infectious diseases, Black women integrated exercise into their public health programming in the 1920s. Nurses like Mary E. Williams, who worked on behalf of the National Negro Health Week inaugurated by Tuskegee Institute, emphasized "exercise, diet, and air" when counseling expectant Black mothers in the rural South—a population that suffered disproportionately from high infant mortality.[33] Medical professionals and other African American public health workers used exercise to combat premature death in Black communities. They linked this health imperative to larger racial uplift campaigns and notions of racial destiny.

During the Great Depression, when exercise would seem like an afterthought, some Black women regarded exercise as a productive and valuable pastime for African Americans. In 1932, Alice Richards, a Black columnist for the *Washington Tribune*, admonished Black men at the height of the economic crisis, "The unemployed man bluffs himself into believing that he could walk right into the job he says he seeks and work satisfactorily after wasting all the many hours of leisure he has had, sitting on park benches, lamenting to his fellow victims of woe the same old fairy tale."[34] Instead of "sitting" and "lamenting," she advised Black men experiencing Depression-induced unemployment to "exercise vigorously" and "seek wholesome amusement in public swimming pools, recreational centers, and camps."[35] Throughout the first few decades of the twentieth century and especially during the lean years of the 1930s, African Americans strove to reconcile their material deprivations with the physical and civic benefits of fitness activity, and Black women remained at the center of this negotiation.

After World War II, achieving physical fitness became a pressing matter for all Americans. The U.S. government instituted a national fitness agenda by creating the first President's Council on Youth Fitness in 1956, and the connection between bodily fitness and citizenship acquired a more official tenor once "fitness" became a matter of domestic policy. Americans grew concerned about their physical unpreparedness for war, and many expressed the need for exercise, now that the number of laborsaving appliances had multiplied in the postwar era. These national pressures to exercise exacerbated Black women's fitness burdens. African American housewives, for instance, experienced intra-racial pressures to guarantee personal, family, and racial "fitness." Ensuring the physical fitness of the family through proper diet and exercise was perceived as part of Black women's homemaking duties. Other Black women felt obliged to portray "fit" bodies in light of intersecting political developments after 1945. The civil rights movement, postwar consumption trends, and increased media visibility through magazines like *Jet* and *Ebony* all placed a premium on fit bodies ready for a political struggle, bodies that did not appear *over*consumed, and bodies that helped to depict Black people as upwardly mobile. Physical fitness remained an important element in Black concepts of American citizenship from the post-Reconstruction period to the postwar era. Black women's history of exercise undergirded these concepts and compels us to consider all of the ways in which African Americans "exercised" their citizenship.

)(

Americans' fascination with exercise and fit physiques has received consistent coverage from historians over the past three decades.[36] Scholars have examined government "body projects" that sought to intervene in private citizens' decision-making regarding diet and exercise.[37] Other works cover how exercise became intertwined with consumerism and American values in the latter half of the twentieth century.[38] While we have some understanding of how the U.S. government and popular culture shaped ideas of fitness, questions about how the intersection of race and gender affected the fitness zeitgeist remain underexplored. The stories of unheralded Black women chronicled in this book, including Olivia Davidson, Amanda Falker, Madame Sara Washington, and Maryrose Reeves Allen, among many others, encourage scholars to reconsider commonplace assumptions about Black women's history of exercise, or lack thereof. This book places Black women squarely within the history of American fitness and decenters labor as the primary mode of Black mobility and physicality. In essence, *Fit Citizens* puts fitness history and Black women's history in rare conversation.

Scholarship on Black women's history has documented the ways in which African American women worked, protested, organized, and campaigned but has not yet examined how exercise operated as a part of their physical and political lives. Some of the most notable monographs about Black women in the twentieth century detail their physically exhausting wage labor, the creative social organizing they performed, and their manifold concepts of womanhood.[39] This study builds on these themes by exploring how Black women used exercise to offset the stress of work, as motivation to build community gyms and recreational outlets, and to form a new kind of "fit" Black womanhood. This book helps us to think more literally, and in effect more critically, about how African American women utilized "fitness" as an ambition, tool, and ideology.

Fit Citizens performs the difficult task of exploring a dynamic history of Black women's exercise vis-à-vis an overwhelmingly white historical record. I intervene in a historiographical tendency to examine obvious and, in effect, white-dominated source material to understand fitness movements. White Americans have a monopoly on archival health and fitness sources from the U.S. government, the YWCA, the American Medical Association, fitness enterprises, and professional sports organizations. Exercise print media from the first half of the twentieth century, including *Physical Culture, Woman's Physical Development, Outing,* and *Playground,* effectively excluded African Americans. *Fit Citizens,* alternatively, explores the history of exercise by privileging Black historical documents.

As a work of social history, this book uses Black print culture to examine the quotidian lives and discourses of Black women who otherwise would remain nameless in the annals of history. I employ an array of textual and visual primary sources to form a robust history of Black women's exercise. This assemblage is remarkable considering that no known African American print source that singularly focused on exercise, Black women's fitness contests, or African American entrepreneurs made wealthy from selling exercise goods existed in the first half of the twentieth century. But careful readings of Black newspapers, magazines, advice literature, public health documents, physical education reports, diaries, and cookbooks reveal that

African Americans engaged enthusiastically in the modern exercise movement. Photography and other images support the textual documents by offering visual evidence of Black women's efforts to present themselves as fit citizens.[40] For many African Americans, visualizing fitness, both in real life and in representations of Blackness, was central to exercising their citizenship.

)(

Over five chapters, *Fit Citizens* chronicles the rising stakes of physical fitness for Black women beginning in the late nineteenth century with the physical culture movement. "Physical culture," as a distinct movement, is not typically conceived of as a historical project of the African American past. The first chapter of the book, however, takes this movement seriously by telling the story of Black citizenship through the lens of physical culture. Chapter 1, "Making Fit Citizens: Race, Gender, and the Rise of Physical Culture," argues that in creating a *Black* physical culture, African American women linked physical fitness to civic fitness and perceived their bodies as sites of citizenship making. African American women challenged ideas about the deteriorated Black body and the race's unfitness for citizenship through Black physical culture. As a gendered project, physical culture functioned as a bodily strategy that Black women used to contest the putative inferiority and physical depravity associated with Black womanhood. Women like Mary P. Evans, editor of the Black women's magazine the *Woman's Era*, avowed that "regulated exercise" contributed to "useful" Black womanhood in 1894—around the same time that politicians like U.S. senator William Cabell Bruce argued that Black people were "wanting in all the characteristics that constitute . . . useful citizens."[41] By departing from categories of wage labor, homemaking, organizing, and other common ways that historians have classified Black women's physical movement and politics, this chapter uses exercise to offer an unconventional narrative of African American women's combined physical and civic worlds.

Within Black physical culture, health became the most exigent catalyst for Black women's exercise behaviors. Chapter 2, "Healthy Bodies: Black Women's Exercise and Public Health in the Early Twentieth Century," asserts that Black women augmented their public health campaigns by integrating exercise into their health activism. With particular attention to physical education, the YWCA, and community health programs, I reposition early twentieth-century Black public health crusades like the National Negro Health Week as

Figure 0.1. The National Negro Health Week campaign often encouraged physical exercise during its operation from 1915 to 1951. On the opposite side of this ad, a list of ten ways to "Live a Hundred Years" includes the advice "Exercise your larger muscles regularly every day." Tuskegee University Archives, Tuskegee University, Alabama.

part of the modern exercise movement (see fig. 0.1). This chapter reveals that Black women promoted exercise not only as a civic and public health good but also as a physical act that had implications for racial competition and Black eugenic advancement. Black health experts and physical educators worried about the progeny of weak, "unfit" young women and encouraged physical activity to curtail this trend. The chapter includes the perspectives of physicians, athletes, public health nurses, physical education teachers, and college deans like Lucy Diggs Slowe who used exercise to produce "physically, mentally, and spiritually fit" Black women.[42] This chapter illustrates how Black girls and women who achieved fit bodies through exercise could uplift the race and secure its future existence.

Beauty, not wholly separate from "health," also motivated Black women's exercise practices. Chapter 3, "Plenty of Good Exercise: Beauty, Fatness, and the Fit Black Female Body in the Interwar Years," contends that middle-class Black women used exercise to promote their ideals of beauty, slimness, and the respectable Black body after World War I. This chapter explains how and why thinness gained political cachet and, accordingly, how Black women used fat-shaming and exercise promotion to influence Black beauty culture. Black beauty advice often contained explicit mentions of physical exercise as a means to achieve slimness. Before advising "Frances S." to "get plenty of exercise in the fresh air," beauty columnist Madame Katherine Wilson admitted, "Personally, I admire slenderness and I think most of us favor the slim rather than the buxom type of girl."[43] Several columnists in the 1910s, 1920s, and 1930s repeated this sentiment and presented the exercised Black female body as desirable. As most studies on Black beauty trends tend to focus on hair and cosmetics, this chapter extends the discussion to the entire body and ties corporal beauty to notions of upstanding citizenship. From anonymous Black women who sought weight loss advice to relatively well-known figures like poet Alice Dunbar-Nelson and beauty entrepreneur Anthony Overton, this chapter shows that within the context of Black women's fitness history, fat stigmatization functioned as a political project—one that African American women mounted to counter racist and sexist notions about Black women's "excessive" bodies.

Chapter 4, "Never Idle: Black Women's Active Recreation during the Great Depression," explores how physical exercise shaped the implementation of Black recreation programs when "free time" became abundant and acquired new meaning in an era of joblessness. Because African Americans suffered disproportionately from work discrimination during the Depression, being productive (that is, active) during their leisure time proved critical to Black respectability politics and, oddly enough, a work ethic. As such, this chapter focuses on *active* recreation—physically intense and seemingly wholesome leisure activities that Black women reformers championed for the sake of Black civic and social uplift. Reformers repeatedly pointed to "lack of supervised recreation" as the source of juvenile delinquency and counted this delinquency as a serious challenge to citizenship. The chapter chronicles women like Janie Porter Barrett, Jane Edna Hunter, and Lucy Diggs Slowe—longtime recreation advocates who became even more invested in physically active recreation in the 1930s. Sorority members, agricultural extension agents, and community organizers shared the concerns of these advocates and creatively navigated segregationist policies that barred African Americans from active recreation sites (such as playgrounds, parks, campgrounds, and swimming pools). As Black women circumvented these restrictive statutes and organized grassroots recreation programs, activities like camping, hiking, and swimming became more than merely fun pastimes; they became synonymous with good citizenship.

After the Depression and World War II, when access to food became more available, definitions of physical fitness expanded to include both physical exercise and healthy, moderate eating. Chapter 5, "34-24-36: Black Women's Diet, Exercise, and Fitness in the Postwar Era," argues that Black women portrayed themselves as ascending, successful, and ideal Black citizens through exercise and dieting practices. Diet and exercise advice aimed at Black women appeared frequently in Black magazines and newspapers in the 1940s and 1950s, linking both behaviors to ideal corporality and upward mobility. As African American women merged food restrictions with exercise after World War II, abstemiousness came to reflect a new civic virtue in an era of food abundance. Ironically, Black women's cookbooks from the postwar era echoed this virtue around food abstention. Freda De Knight's 1948 cookbook, *A Date with a Dish: A Cook Book of American Negro Recipes*, explained, "A well-balanced diet is a 'must' in your daily routine. And if you want to keep your weight down . . . eat sparingly of starches, sugar and fats. . . . That plate of vegetables should be green. Not potatoes, macaroni, rice and spaghetti."[44] Women like De Knight endeavored to influence Black appetites and the meaning of African American food, bodies, and character. This chapter explores the historical relationship between race, gender, and food in new ways by presenting Black women as regulators and not just consumers of food.

Throughout the late nineteenth and twentieth centuries, white Americans created law, public policy, and everyday customs based on the belief that Black people were the bane of public health, were helplessly overweight, and gravitated toward wasteful leisure. These pernicious notions were predicated, in part, on assumptions about African Americans as nonparticipants in fitness culture. Omitting Black people from American fitness history helps reinforce these insidious notions that endure in our contemporary moment. *Fit Citizens* offers a corrective to this omission. This book shows that Black women aspired toward "fitness" despite social and political mandates that told them otherwise and created definitions of Black womanhood that confounded mainstream ideas about Black embodiment and physicality.

CHAPTER 1

Making Fit Citizens

RACE, GENDER, AND THE RISE

OF PHYSICAL CULTURE

In 1883, Rebecca Lee Crumpler, the first African American woman to earn a medical degree, published *A Book of Medical Discourses: In Two Parts* and dedicated it to "mothers, nurses, and all who may desire to mitigate the afflictions of the human race."[1] The book, which primarily concerned the illnesses of women and children, combined practical medical advice with commentary on gender and race. She wrote on sundry topics from bathing newborns, breastfeeding, and relieving menstrual pain to "when to marry," the immorality of lynching, and the poor labor conditions of Black people. Although mentioning it only briefly, Crumpler advocated physical exercise. She instructed parents to allow their children to exercise in the daylight while avoiding "low, dark, bad-smelling, water-soaked basement kitchens" and counseled menopausal women to "secure cheerful exercise."[2] Crumpler acknowledged the political nature of such health practices by pointing out that "diminutive, sickly, and half-dependent people care little what party governs, so long as they, themselves, barely exist."[3] She grounded progress, the "bright futures" of girls, and the production of "educated men" in proper health regimens and wholesome physical routines—critical imperatives for a post-Reconstruction generation of African Americans seeking full-fledged citizenship. By encouraging exercise in this temporal and political context, Crumpler sowed the seeds of Black physical culture. She refashioned bodily movement for a cohort of African Americans whose physical activity had once been confined to bondage and tied exercise to notions of Black civic advancement.

In cultivating a Black physical culture, African American women like Crumpler linked physical fitness to ideas of "civic fitness" and perceived their bodies as sites of citizenship making.[4] Through Black physical culture, African American women challenged old and emerging racialized ideas about indolence, the deterioration of the Black body, and Black people's supposed unfitness for citizenship. Physical culture functioned as a bodily strategy that Black women used to contest the putative inferiority and physical depravity associated with Black womanhood. By moving away from categories of labor, caretaking, and political organizing, this chapter uses exercise to offer a novel account of African American women's physical and civic aspirations.

Turn-of-the-century print media demonstrate the relationship between physical activity and citizenship for all Americans. The first sentence of the 1899 Whitley Exerciser manual states, "Alertness and Activity are the passwords for those who enter the arena of the Twentieth Century as successful contestants."[5] Civics textbooks like Waldo Sherman's 1905 *Civics: Studies in American Citizenship* warned that "physical deterioration" usually precedes "moral deterioration." Sherman argued that cities without parks, playgrounds, and athletic fields where residents could exercise caused physical and moral decline.[6] Supporters of women's sports aimed some of these sentiments directly at girls and women and made explicit pleas to include women in the new enthusiasm for physical culture. Gertrude Dudley and Frances Kellor, director of women's PE at the University of Chicago and social scientist, respectively, believed that athletics helped to activate a gendered "training for citizenship." They explained in their 1909 *Athletic Games in the Education of Women*, "It is evident that the training obtained through athletics is carried over into the business and social life after the girl leaves school. Other things being equal, she is ordinarily a fairer competitor and better citizen."[7] Exercise enthusiasts, textbook authors, and social reformers intertwined ideas of physical, moral, and civic fitness, and everyday Americans began to associate fitness of the body with fitness for the body politic. In the first few decades of the twentieth century, physical fitness became a corporal signifier of health, success, virtue, and "good" citizenship. Accordingly, through private acts and public displays of exercise, African American women demonstrated that they could meet the demands of the "strenuous life" propagated by the nation's political leaders, reformers, and health crusaders.[8]

Black women physical culturists in the Progressive Era used exercise to achieve strong but not overly developed bodies to address their real and imagined physical weakness. Only a few decades removed from slavery, intentional exercise was a welcome shift from the forced physicality of bondage that controlled how Black women's bodies moved and functioned. Exercise allowed Black women to retain a measure of freedom, however small, to control how strong their bodies could be. At the same time, aspiring-class Black people created notions of fit Black womanhood and the ideal female body for rank-and-file women to follow.[9] Although middle-class African Americans celebrated the civic and physical benefits of exercise, they also perceived risks and warned of overdevelopment and masculinization. Black advocates of physical culture toed a thin line between strength as a female characteristic and too much strength that would detract from women's femininity, thereby narrowing the autonomy that Black women held to shape their bodies in any way they pleased. During the overlapping eras of racial uplift and physical culture, "making" fit citizens became a complicated political endeavor for Black women.

This chapter analyzes conversations about Black women's bodies, strength, and character that took place precisely because of Americans' interests in fitness culture at the turn of the century. The chapter's first section, "Unfit Citizens: Physical and Ideological Cases against Black Citizenship," examines how a putative lack of physical, intellectual, and moral fitness served as a rationale for the denial of Black citizenship. This section presents the hostile ideological setting in which Black women embarked on the modern exercise movement and argued for their holistic fitness. The second section, "Still Unfit: A Racial and Gendered History of Physical Culture," explains *why* African Americans created a separate Black physical culture. It offers a rare examination of race, gender, and exercise during the Progressive Era and shows how white exercise advocates marginalized African Americans from mainstream physical culture. The final section, "The Origins of Black Women's Physical Culture," brings together the preceding sections and addresses *how* Black women created their own category of physical culture. It shows that before African American women could engage in the physical culture movement, they had to make the ideological case for Black exercise, racial uplift, and citizenship.

Unfit Citizens: Physical and Ideological Cases against Black Citizenship

At the turn of the twentieth century, African Americans were keenly aware of the legal, social, and ideological barriers to full-fledged citizenship. Despite the promises of the Thirteenth, Fourteenth, and Fifteenth Amendments, which defined African Americans as emancipated citizens with equal protection and voting rights, Black people found that these rights existed more in theory than in practice. From the end of Reconstruction in 1877 to 1901, the "nadir of race relations," African Americans experienced racial terrorism, political oppression, disenfranchisement, and the reification of Jim Crow laws through the *Plessy v. Ferguson* decision in 1896.[10] White landowners coerced Black people into exploitative farm labor contracts, while other African Americans toiled in arduous and conscribed low-wage work as convict laborers, laundresses, domestics, and cooks. To the horror of many Black families, white mobs lynched and violated Black men and women for unsubstantiated infractions during this period.

Racial ideologies about Black people's unsuitability for citizenship undergirded these daily abuses. Many white individuals argued that African Americans showed a physical, mental, and moral lack of fitness for citizenship.[11] While historians have well documented these ideologies, they are important to underscore to gain a clear understanding of racialized arguments against citizenship and to appreciate fully why Black individuals responded to this slander through physical culture.[12]

White politicians, writers, health practitioners, statisticians, and other "experts" gave African Americans good reason to lose post-Reconstruction optimism. They provided specious justifications for why Black people could not, and should not, be entirely incorporated into the body politic. In 1891, writer and eventual U.S. senator William Cabell Bruce of Maryland outlined the profound physical and character flaws he perceived in Black people. Bruce drew attention to "the wooly hair, the receding forehead, the flat nose, the thick lips and the protruding jaw of the negro" that marked the "physical lines of separation" between African Americans and white citizens.[13] These physical distinctions prefaced the intellectual and moral deficiencies Bruce outlined in his screed.[14] He argued that African Americans were "saucy, vagrant, improvident, without self-restraint, and subject to no external discipline," as well as "notoriously wanting in all the characteristics that constitute thrifty or useful citizens."[15] Black people had shown little political and intellectual progress since emancipation, a self-evident fact according to Bruce. Legislators brought these ideas into Congress and made disenfranchisement a political and material reality for African Americans.

Frederick L. Hoffman, a statistician employed by the Prudential Life Insurance Company, supported his theory on the "Negro Problem" through anthropometric analysis, vital statistics, and actuarial science in 1896. In *Race Traits and Tendencies of the American Negro*, Hoffman, who claimed to be "fortunately free from a personal bias" because of his German immigrant status, provided ostensibly objective data to support eugenics-laden ideas of white supremacy.[16] He noted that African Americans inherited racial "tendencies" toward crime, pauperism, and sexual immorality. These tendencies resulted from both moral and physical origins, as he concluded that Black populations suffered from deficiencies in weight, height, lung capacity, chest circumference, strength, and a host of other bodily measures.

Hoffman used exercise as both a rhetorical and an anthropometric device for devaluing Black physicality. Remarkably, he opined, "The mean lifting strength of the white is in excess of that of the negro. The prevailing opinion that the negro is on the whole more capable of enduring physical exercise is therefore disproved."[17] Hoffman's conclusions would have an uncritical reader believe that the end of slavery was physically ruinous for African Americans, as they now (that is, in freedom) struggled with "exercise endurance" whereas they once (that is, in slavery) performed physically demanding labor seemingly without trouble. As the chapter later shows, African Americans confronted this construction of Black weakness through physical culture. But this confrontation proved an uphill battle. Assertions of physical debility, of which exercise endurance served as an essential data point, factored into Hoffman's presentation of Black people as hopelessly unfit.

Hoffman further argued that freedom from slavery and opportunities for education had done very little to advance the race and that since emancipation, Black people had failed to lift themselves to a "higher level of citizenship."[18] Inherent "race traits," not environmental factors, he contended, explained their high mortality rates: "It is not in *the conditions of life*, but in *the race traits and tendencies* that we find the causes of the excessive mortality" (emphasis in original).[19] Eventually, the disproportionate mortality rate would lead African Americans to self-eliminate: "So long as these tendencies are persisted in, so long as immorality and vice are a habit of life of the vast majority of the colored population, the effect will be to increase the mortality by hereditary transmission of weak constitutions, and to lower still further the rate of natural increase, until the births fall below the deaths, and gradual extinction results."[20] Arguments like this framed citizenship as a wasted civic benefit for an inherently unfit race. Hoffman's ideas presumed that not only did Black "tendencies" conflict with American civic virtues, but African Americans would not need enduring political inclusion because they would not survive much longer to enjoy it.

Some writers did not rely on faulty social science to argue for Black exclusion but just stated their views plainly as fact. Newspaper reporter Henry Peck Fry wrote at length about the issue of Black enfranchisement in 1906. He proposed a surefire way to eliminate the "race problem": "The race problem will vanish into the gloom of an unpleasant memory of unpleasant events, if one thing is done by the American people, and that one thing is THE REPEAL OF THE FIFTEENTH AMENDMENT TO THE CONSTITUTION OF THE UNITED STATES."[21] The amendment, which stated, "The right of citizens of the United States to vote shall not be denied or abridged by the United States or by any State on account of race, color, or previous condition of servitude," threatened white political rule.[22] Fry called the Fifteenth Amendment "damnable" and "destructive of American happiness," as it lowered "the standard of the priceless jewel of American citizenship." Writing in all capital letters, he exclaimed further, "THE NEGRO IS UNFIT TO EXERCISE THE PRIVILEGES OF AMERICAN CITIZENSHIP. HIS BEING IN POLITICS IS A MENACE, AND, IN THE NAME OF ALL THAT'S DECENT, WILL YOU NOT ALLOW US TO BUILD UP THE BUSINESS INTERESTS OF THE SOUTH WITHOUT CONSTANTLY HAVING THE DANGER CONFRONTING US OF NEGRO SUPREMACY?"[23]

Fry supported this attack on Black "fitness" by providing the physical rationales for Black people's exclusion from the body politic. The reporter reminded his audience that Abraham Lincoln once averred that "there is a physical difference between [the white and Black races], which, in my judgement, will probably forever forbid their living together upon the footing of perfect equality."[24] He buttressed arguments about physical differences with assertions of character differences, as he classified Black people as barbaric, ignorant, and uncivilized. Perspectives like Fry's were not outliers; they permeated social, medical, academic, and political circles in the early twentieth century. These ideas captured the racial catch-22 of the time in which some whites believed that African Americans were utterly unsuited for citizenship and, at the same time, denied them the resources that would "make" them better citizens.

While white opponents of Black social and political freedom used the explicit language of "fitness" to argue against Black civil rights, Black women, in particular, pointed to the combined racialized and gendered contempt they garnered from white people as a formidable barrier to civic respect. An unnamed Black woman who wrote anonymously out of fear for her life relayed a story about this intersection in 1902:

A noble man, who has established rescue homes for fallen women all over the country, visited a Southern city. The women of the city were invited to meet him in one of the churches. The fallen women were especially invited and both good and bad went. They sat wherever they could find a seat, so long as their faces were white; but I, a respectable married woman, was asked to sit apart. A colored woman, however respectable, is lower than the white prostitute. The Southern white woman will declare that no Negro women are virtuous.[25]

The idea that a "respectable" Black woman should be considered more honorable than "the white prostitute" is fraught with class-laden presumptions. This notion represented a complex and imperfect racial uplift ideology whereby "better" classes of Black people provided proof of Black political and social worth. Nevertheless, for this anonymous woman, the anecdote illustrated that neither education nor marital status nor profession could absolve Black women of assumed depravity. Ascending to the station of the "white prostitute" functioned as a real sociopolitical barometer for some Black women.

Lacking "virtue" may seem like a tangential matter, but Black women's supposed lack of morality posed ideological threats to race progress and gendered notions of citizenship. Black women understood that the fight for citizenship was indeed a physical, moral, and civic struggle, and casting doubt on their virtue worked to question their prospects as worthy republican women.[26] Dominant portrayals of problematic sexuality and perceived immorality made Black women appear "unworthy of the benefits of first-class citizenship."[27] Even some middle-class Black people believed that certain Black women lacked the necessary qualities to contribute to civic betterment. African American reformers like Jane Edna Hunter essentially proposed that "dives and brothels," places where women with "questionable" virtue dwelled, compromised the "headway which the Negro had made toward the state of good citizenship."[28] But for self-described respectable Black women who argued for the integrity of Black womanhood, they nevertheless experienced a racial and political disadvantage vis-à-vis white women—even those white women who were considered "unvirtuous." Many Americans perceived virtue and political value to be mutually constitutive for women. Black women were presumed to have neither.

Still Unfit: A Racial and Gendered History of Physical Culture

While members of the press, insurance actuaries, political figures, and "noble men" who visited southern churches made the case against Black citizenship, others made the case against Black fitness by emphasizing the physical inferiority of Black people and arguing for an exclusively white physical culture. In 1899, President Theodore Roosevelt delivered a speech titled "The Strenuous Life" that encouraged Americans to adopt a life of hard labor, industry, and virility. Although he directed most of his remarks to men, he urged all Americans to lead "clean, vigorous, [and] healthy" lives.[29] Roosevelt instructed young boys to practice "manly exercises" and to invest in "rough sports" that required endurance and physical prowess.[30] In issuing this instruction, he admonished that anything other than the strenuous life would lead to the nation's decay. According to Roosevelt, the strenuous life was essential to American progress and a distinct national identity, especially as the United States began asserting itself as a world power after the Spanish-American War. As a skilled sportsman and hunter, he embodied the pinnacle of manhood and civilization, and he used the fitness of American men to gauge the vigor of the nation.[31] Roosevelt and his followers believed urbanization would weaken the American public and found physical culture helpful in protecting the country from failed health and instability.[32] Social and health reformers, journalists, politicians, and teachers agreed, openly discussing their anxieties about weakened middle-class manhood and, in turn, promoting physical fitness and exercise.[33]

While Roosevelt is not credited with inaugurating the physical culture movement, he represented one of its most politically significant adherents. Historians have analyzed the glaring gendered nature of Roosevelt's language and his construction of the so-called strenuous life, but Roosevelt's comments also indicate the racially fraught nature of physical culture.[34] The physical culture movement coincided with the era of the "negro problem" and eugenics, yet the story of how race influenced the development of the movement is still untold. From its advent, ideas about white supremacy and biological differences between genders undergirded the physical culture movement and shaped notions about who could be a fit citizen.

Writings of white progressive reformers reveal the anxieties they shared about physical weakness and white racial destiny. White bicycle enthusiast and temperance leader Frances Willard committed herself to a life of physical activity and, in doing so, elaborated on race, exercise, and health. Her remarks on physical culture in 1891 at the annual meeting of the Woman's Christian Temperance Union (WCTU) display the relationship between exercise and white racial advancement:

Physical culture is the question of the future for Americans. *All true progress is built upon physical lines.* Crude and modern as our bodies are to-day, they shall be as beautiful to-morrow as those of Diana and Hebe, of Mercury and Apollo. Once [we] let the girls and young women of the great public school system be regularly and systematically taught the delights of the modern style of gymnastics, its grace, its healthfulness, its happiness, [they] will not endure the constricting process so long shared by us with the women of barbaric tribes. *Only ours has been more harmful to the race*, because involving more vital interests and organs and visiting a sadder retribution upon posterity. [emphasis added][35]

As the president of the WCTU, Willard played a significant role in white women's reform and suffrage movements and likely left a profound impression upon her audience. From Willard's perspective, this audience understood that progress for women was not simply a mental or moral undertaking but a physical endeavor. Willard's proposal that "true progress" was built on "physical lines" operated as both a racially charged and a gendered affirmation.

Willard's beliefs about African Americans illuminate the ways in which ideas of racial difference likely factored into her statement on women's physicality. Just a year before her WCTU speech, Willard commented that Black people represented "dark faced mobs whose rallying cry is better whiskey, and more of it. . . . The grog shop is their center of power."[36] Although, at times, she expressed some sympathy for the plight of African Americans, her loyalties rested with the protection of white women, whom she believed Black men threatened. Willard drew ire from Ida B. Wells in particular for her comments concerning African Americans' inherent penchant for alcohol and destructive behavior. Wells explained in her autobiography that Willard "unhesitatingly slandered the entire Negro race in order to gain favor with those who are hanging, shooting and burning Negroes alive."[37] The supposed physical and corporal superiority of white women's bodies, indeed the "physical lines," served as a crucial component of Willard's ability to champion women's rights on the one hand and commit racial slander on the other. The growing physical culture movement was essential to this kind of thinking, as many perceived this health crusade as a means to ensure white physical fitness and dominance.

Willard also revealed her racial biases in her references to Diana, Hebe, Mercury, and Apollo. The invocation of Greek gods most likely concerned those who resembled these figures, which hardly included African Americans. Nineteenth- and twentieth-century white admirers of Greek mythical sculpture often weaponized them as evidence of white superiority, despite the fact that many sculptures of Greco-Roman figures were not originally white.[38] More to the point, white eugenicists of the late nineteenth and early twentieth centuries would reference figures like Mercury and Apollo to reminisce about a celebrated, if imagined, past of racial superiority.[39] If the progress of civilization was built on physicality—and, as Willard noted, specifically the physical grace of girls and young women—did Black women have a place in this civilization?

It is difficult to believe that the girls and young women whom Willard encouraged to master the modern style of gymnastics included girls and women of color, as she essentialized the health and beauty of women and girls as white. For Willard, progress and posterity depended on the physical composition of white women.[40] As the New Woman emerged from her Victorian confines in the late nineteenth century, her clothing, leisure activity, and consumer behavior reflected emerging ideas about comeliness, gender equality, and modernity. Wearing bloomers, riding bicycles, owning a gym suit, and being a card-carrying member of the YWCA signaled a modern white woman embracing the technologies of turn-of-the-century physical culture.

As exercise grew in popularity during the Progressive Era, white women continued to express concern for the health and beauty of the (white) race. Ella Adelia Fletcher, the author of the physical culture advice book *The Woman Beautiful*, highlighted this point in 1901:

> It is becoming a recognized principle in therapeutics that for incipient ails [sic] it is not so much pills and potions that are needed as *the regulation of diet and exercise*, and without attention to these all the medicines in the pharmacopeia are of no avail. *It will be a blessed thing for the beauty and health of the race* when this is generally known, for the crowning injury which the American people inflict upon their physical well-being is their indiscriminate consumption of patent medicines, the sale of which in this country alone exceeds that in all the other nations put together! [emphasis added][41]

Fletcher's language around exercise, health, beauty, and "the race" reveals a paradox. If the logic of white supremacy assumes inherent physical superiority, texts like *The Woman Beautiful* tacitly admit faulty logic by advocating exercise. In other words, if white people were indeed physically superior to all others, they would not need exercise to ensure "physical well-being." When Frances Willard proclaimed that idleness "harms" the race and Ella Fletcher wrote that diet and exercise "bless" the race, they implicitly challenged notions of intrinsic white racial superiority. Their words intimated uncertainty about white supremacy tied to the body, and they presented exercise as a strategy to protect a tenuous sense of racial superiority.

Dudley Allen Sargent, a preeminent physical educator in early twentieth-century Boston, also commented on the stakes of physical culture for white racial advancement. Sargent operated the Hemenway Gymnasium at Harvard University, and in 1881 he opened the independent Sargent Normal School of Physical Training, which became one of the most prestigious physical education training institutions in the country. Scores of Black women attended the school to specialize in physical education, including the head of Howard University's physical education department, Maryrose Reeves Allen. Around 1916, however, Sargent closed his doors to Black applicants as both de jure and de facto segregation hardened in the early twentieth century.[42]

In a contribution to a special issue of *Annals of the American Academy of Political and Social Science* titled "Race Improvement in the United States," Sargent explained how "a sound physique" contributed to white mental and moral development. He argued in 1909, "The leisure now gained through the great reduction in the hours of labor affords an admirable opportunity for physical and mental culture and recreation and for all-round personal improvement. To embrace this opportunity is the only way to counteract the narrowing and deadening influence of our highly specialized occupations, and to keep up the mental and physical vigor of the race."[43] "The race," in this context, did not refer to the human race, but to the white race. Sargent's concern with white vigor materialized in how he used the tools of physical culture. Relying on anthropometric measurements, physical examinations, and even nude photographs of student athletes, Sargent sought to safeguard white physical strength and dominance.[44] His comments, then, suggest an unease about the harm that industrialization caused to white bodies and minds. He wrote at a time when eugenic fears of white "race suicide," motivated by the rise of social Darwinism, informed approaches to physical development and improvement.[45] The notion that physical culture would help maintain white mental and physical vigor became a recurring theme by the first decade of the twentieth century. This nervousness about white vigor illuminates why gymnasiums, playgrounds, pools, and other institutions of fitness became heavily guarded white spaces. Recreational arenas were especially contentious in the Jim Crow era and represented a significant portion of the civil rights battles that African Americans waged over public accommodations later in the twentieth century.

White physical educators like Sargent must have recognized that allowing African American women unfettered access to these fitness spaces would compromise an agenda built on strengthening white bodies enervated by professional "desk" work and leisure culture. Fears of Black fitness likely served as one reason why Sargent eventually prohibited Black enrollment in his school. For segregationists, women like Maryrose Reeves Allen served as a cautionary example of what admitting just one Black woman into a physical education program could do, as she eventually used her training to teach PE to thousands of Black women college students across several Black institutions. Black women created their own campaign of physical fitness and Black racial advancement while contesting policies akin to Sargent's.

One year after Sargent championed physical culture for the strength of the white race, on the opposite side of the country, the *San Francisco Sunday Call* celebrated physical culture for producing Marguerite Edwards, "the most perfect girl in the world."[46] Marguerite's mother, Edith Edwards, taught her daughter the fundamentals of physical culture "before she could walk" (see fig. 1.1). The paper explained that Marguerite served as a paragon of beauty and health in the eyes of judges, artists, and her mother. Mrs. Edwards claimed that "every child can be made perfect even if nature is tardy" and that "tuberculosis or kindred diseases can find no foothold in the system of the properly trained child." Edwards's encouraging words on health might have resonated with African Americans who suffered and died disproportionately from tuberculosis in the 1910s. However, the means that Edwards used to achieve perfection in Marguerite were often unavailable to working-class Black mothers. Edwards spent hours a day exercising her daughter's limbs, managing her physical movements, supplying her with outdoor recreation, and studying the newest exercise techniques to ensure her physical development.

Yet even middle-class Black women, who may have had the time to devote to their children's physiques, would have taken issue with some of the values adopted by Mrs. Edwards. She noted that as a child, Marguerite stood nude, "rising on her toes, poising on her heels, forward and backward; then sitting on her heels, muscles tense . . . , rising and falling quickly and regularly." As she grew older, Mrs. Edwards beamed that Marguerite, a twelve-year-old girl, had a "body [that] is the envy of all the women who have seen her." She also allowed an artist, Count Geyza de Perhacs, to paint

Figure 1.1. "The Most Perfect Girl in the World" article by R. E. Wales, with exercise demonstrations. *San Francisco Sunday Call*, April 10, 1910, 5.

Marguerite, whom the paper noted the child was "visiting with." Marguerite was "frequently . . . seen climbing the hills with Joaquin Miller," a frontiersman in his seventies when the article was published. Many of these behaviors, even if they helped to produce physical perfection in young women, would have been repugnant if not verboten for middle-class Black women, who tended to protect their daughters from sexualized display. Even the clothing Marguerite donned in the article, or lack thereof, would be unacceptable to publish in the Black press.[47]

Although an explicit mention of race is not included in the article, Marguerite's status as a model of female perfection speaks volumes about race, gender, and the body in the early twentieth century. The notion that "every child can be made perfect" through physical culture may appear to be a race-neutral logic of health and environment, but it suggests that those who succumbed to illness such as tuberculosis lacked proper parentage and physical training. While this implication is not as overtly pernicious as that of Frederick Hoffman and others who claimed that the Black race would eventually perish from disease, it presents those who become sick as fully responsible for their illnesses and physical imperfections. The geographic context in which this article was published may also reveal its racialized undertones. San Francisco, one of the epicenters of eugenics in the early twentieth century, experienced rabid xenophobia, and many of its residents and medical professionals feared the epidemiological consequences of immigration.[48] The city even hosted a Race Betterment Exhibit at the Panama-Pacific International Exposition in 1915, the brainchild of John Harvey Kellogg, another prominent physical culturist who supported selective marriage pairings and the creation of a eugenics registry. Even without uttering a word, Marguerite Edwards represented a bodily ideal to which young white women aspired, and this ideal hinged on physical culture.

One of the most overt ways exercise enthusiasts promoted white racial advancement was by openly advertising physical culture's implications for eugenics. The above examples subtly suggest the racism inherent in dominant exercise discourse, but the father of physical culture, Bernarr Macfadden, was more forthright as he explained his fears about white racial deterioration within the eugenic zeitgeist of the early twentieth century. In *Macfadden's Encyclopedia of Physical Culture*, he stated unapologetically, "Eugenics is the name of the modern study of science which is concerned with racial improvement through the better breeding of human beings. . . . The consistent physical culturist, in the broad sense of the term as it applies to racial improvement, will therefore naturally concern himself with putting into practice the fundamental principles of this new science." Macfadden perceived eugenics and physical culture as common-sense, interconnected movements. He called eugenics a "big and splendid program" and added that physical culturists "will do more than any other force toward bringing about this great result."[49] This ideology sought to encourage exercise in those who held similar eugenic ideas but were not "consistent physical culturists." White women occupied a vital role in Macfadden's argument because they actually reproduced "better" human beings and could guarantee racial improvement.[50]

Segregation of gyms—arguably the most important space for improving physical fitness at this time—supported white supremacist discourses of physical culture by physically marginalizing Black women from exercise.[51] Urban fitness facilities in schools, colleges, and settlement houses provided robust exercise outlets for white women of various financial means. Rose Gyles, for instance, instructed women's and children's athletic programs using weights, drills, gymnastics, and games in Chicago at the Hull House Settlement in the late nineteenth and early twentieth centuries.[52] Settlement programs like Hull House catered to poor white immigrant women and facilitated group exercise for residents. On the other end of the class spectrum, women's athletic clubs in Chicago and New York furnished elite white clients with Turkish baths and expensive sports facilities for those who could afford the membership.[53] This individualized instruction provided an alternative for privileged white women who preferred not to exercise with working-class women at public gyms. Black women rarely received the opportunity to take part in the recreations of Hull House or enjoy exclusive, private outlets for exercise. The widespread segregation of fitness spaces and health facilities ensured that Black women would remain on the outskirts of the modern exercise movement. White fitness facilities came equipped with gymnasiums, apparatuses, and professionally trained teachers, while many Black branches struggled to gain a meager fraction of these resources.

Although African Americans struggled to secure suitable exercise facilities, they made the most of the physical activities in which they did participate and treasured the civic benefits of athletics. For example, the Afro-American Notes section of the *Pittsburgh Press* explained in 1918, "One of the many good results growing out of these annual inter-city athletic contests, whether tennis, baseball, field and track, football or basketball is the fraternization of young men in various places. The spirit of generous rivalry it cultivates, the home pride it engenders and the physical and mental fitness it builds up, as a natural consequence. Then too it is a positive deterrment [sic] to vice and loose living which is so incident to the idle youth."[54] The combined physical and mental benefits of these activities held immense meaning for African Americans vying to prove their fitness. But between 1890 and 1920, when exercise became a necessary regimen for health, beauty, and "race improvement," white women and men attempted to take full possession of physical culture. In the process of racializing exercise as exclusively white, they also determined who could claim fitness. Nevertheless, African Americans, particularly Black women, staked their own claims to exercise and notions of fit citizenship.

The Origins of Black Women's Physical Culture

As some white Americans advocated physical culture and racist eugenic logic, African American women used exercise to achieve overlapping corporal and civic goals. Physical culture tightened the relationship between physical fitness, gendered discourses of citizenship, and notions of racial advancement. Aspiring-class African American women in particular perceived a natural connection between physical culture and prevailing ideas of racial progress. The Progressive Era proved ripe for this relationship.

The simultaneous development of racial uplift campaigns and the physical culture movement allowed for the marriage of physical fitness and Black advancement. The era of racial uplift was characterized by a middle-class crusade to improve the social conditions and images of African Americans while boosting prospects for full-fledged citizenship. Uplift practices involved reforming Black conduct by encouraging health, education, prudent spending, sexual purity, and several other values many considered righteous and politically tactical. Although the physical culture movement was a primarily white campaign and did not share the same motives, it also supported seemingly productive, health-sustaining habits indicative of civic goodness.

Some Black health advocates believed that the principles of physical culture and racial uplift would enable African Americans to become better individuals, parents, community members, and citizens. Well-known African American "race men" and "race women," including W. E. B. Du Bois, Mary McLeod Bethune, Nannie Helen Burroughs, and Booker T. Washington, all advocated some form of physical culture for Black people.[55] For these Black reformers and others, striving for physical fitness became just as important as striving for other forms of fitness (such as intellectual, moral, or civic fitness). Racial uplift advocates believed they could not morally elevate the race without physically strengthening the Black female population through exercise.

In the nineteenth century, "race elevation" consisted of demonstrating morality, intelligence, and sobriety.[56] For the most part, these qualities still applied to racial uplift ideology in the early twentieth century. But African American demonstrations of physical capability and feats of corporal achievement also became vital to Progressive Era racial politics. Thinking critically about the intersection of race, gender, and self-presentation in the early twentieth century, Black women utilized exercise to present themselves as "fit" during the age of physical culture and racial uplift. From their perspective, moral fitness coincided with physical fitness, and both proved essential for racial and civic uplift. Beginning around 1890, their speeches, magazines, advice literature, and newspapers provided the intellectual and ideological scaffolding for twentieth-century Black exercise.

The history of Black women's exercise began with race women arguing for the health and physical development of Black girls and women in the late nineteenth century. Educator Olivia Davidson, for example, became an important advocate of young Black women's bodily care in the 1880s. She attended Hampton Institute, married Booker T. Washington, and served as vice principal of Tuskegee Institute—a résumé that granted her significant influence in Black female circles. But Davidson did not rest on her laurels. A close look at her personal life and pedagogical values uncovers the ways in which she struggled for Black women and girls' wellness, including her own.

Throughout her life, Davidson faced profound health challenges that undoubtedly shaped her views on Black women's bodies. Her hospital record and personal correspondence reveal that she suffered from weakness, constant pain, and tuberculosis, which probably caused her death at the age of thirty-four in 1889.[57] Booker T. Washington mentioned briefly in *Up from Slavery* that Davidson "literally wore herself out in her never ceasing efforts in behalf of the work she so dearly loved."[58] Davidson's unceasing efforts to get Tuskegee established were marked by bouts of illness and fatigue, and she regretted how these periods of affliction stalled the important race work she performed at Tuskegee.[59] At a time when tuberculosis posed a significant threat to Black life, many African American reformers' enthusiasm for physical culture indeed stemmed from their personal battles with illness in addition to social and political imperatives.

In 1886, Davidson addressed the Alabama State Teacher Association about African Americans' physical condition, particularly the condition of Black women's bodies. Although she made these remarks before the nationwide popularity of exercise, they foreshadow how Black women would later link the health and fortitude of Black women's bodies to the strength of the race. The title of the speech, "How Shall We Make the Women of Our Race Stronger?," pointed to both external and internal senses of strength.[60] Davidson commented on specific ways that Black women and girls could strengthen themselves, and eventually the race, in physical, moral, and mental capacities. She prioritized Black women's physicality in her talk by noting, "Let us consider how the physical development of one woman can be accomplished: James Freeman Clarke in his inimitable essay on the training and care of the body says, 'Good health is the basis of all physical, intellectual and moral development. We glorify God with our bodies by keeping them in good health.' Mainly because I believe this is true, I have put this part of my subject first."[61] She decried the prevalence of "nervous and organic diseases" that blocked "the highest avenues of usefulness" for Black women, and she placed the healthy Black female body at the heart of African American progress.[62]

Davidson's comments indicate a shift in the late nineteenth century in which Black leaders tied notions of progress to the material body in addition to less tangible characteristics of morality and intelligence. She condemned the damaging effects of tobacco, alcohol, and morphine, not because of their moral consequences but because of their "evil results upon our bodies." These results, she believed, could be inherited by future generations. Davidson explained to the teachers, "The drunken parent destroys or weakens not alone the body God gave him for the temple of his own soul, but transmits to the child a heritage of suffering, perhaps observable in general organic weaknesses or in fearful deformities or painful diseases."[63] Placing gender at the center of her analysis, she asserted that girls were more susceptible to "inherited weakness" due to their "delicate organizations," and for this reason it was imperative to invest in the health and physical development of Black girls.

Davidson believed that Black women teachers could have a meaningful influence on the physical habits of young Black people. She urged educators to teach "physiology and hygiene" to prevent the spread of disease and slow the physical deterioration of the youth.[64] At her own Tuskegee Institute, while a robust physical education program had not yet been formed, administrators by 1886 had incorporated "physiology and hygiene" into the curriculum.[65] Davidson also encouraged the teachers to show their female students "in every way possible how to care for their bodies." As someone who struggled with balancing her work at Tuskegee with managing her own illness, her invocation of bodily care may have stemmed from unfulfilled desires for herself. As she crafted her speech, Davidson may have pondered how she could transform her individual longing for vigor into a larger campaign for Black women's health.

In a prescient statement that resonated with Black women reformers in the twentieth century, Davidson reminded her audience that "the young women and girls are the hope for the race." For Davidson, the future of the race literally rested within the bodies of Black girls. She described Black women's bodies as "beautiful temples" that were "defiled" by improper diets, alcohol, snuff, and "sheer physical exhaustion." Her musings were not mere speculation. Davidson revealed that her insights were empirically based, as "several years of work in positions that brought me in close contact with many of the women and girls of the race have brought a deep conviction of the need for them of physical, mental, and moral development."[66] She used her lived experience both as an educator and as someone who suffered from physical impairment to argue for Black women and girls' moral and physical fitness.

It is easy to imagine that if Davidson had delivered this talk twenty years later, she would have mentioned specific exercises in her speech. For African Americans who struggled with a host of health problems, the specter of weakness, physical deformity, and debility was more than enough reason to encourage Black people to exercise. For Black women specifically, exercise helped to diminish the markers of internal and external weakness that compromised healthy Black womanhood. Davidson's beliefs about Black women's bodies as inherently valuable but in need of physical care set the stage for Black women's physical culture and ideas of fit Black womanhood in the twentieth century. Other Black women at the turn of the century and thereafter espoused Davidson's thinking about the natural beauty and glorification of Black women's bodies and integrated physical exercise into their discussion of healthy, beautiful, and morally sound corporality.

Almost a decade after Davidson's speech and five years before Bernarr Macfadden's first physical culture publication, Mary P. Evans, editor and writer of the Black women's magazine the *Woman's Era*, introduced exercise into the conversation on enhancing Black women's bodies. Evans's work with the *Woman's Era* preceded her other important activist work, including helping to establish the Boston branch of the NAACP, growing the organization's membership, forging an anti-lynching campaign, and challenging segregation in Washington, DC.[67] In 1894, she authored a three-part series titled "Health and Beauty from Exercise" that, like Davidson's speech, urged Black women to prioritize their physical development. Evans listed numerous benefits of exercise:

> Faithful, earnest and painstaking physical exercise, such as has been indicated under intelligent direction, rewards the girl who keeps it up with health, youth and beauty. It keeps the body in the best condition for throwing off disease. It enables you to keep in the best condition for work with the hands or with the brain. It is a wholesome and powerful preventive of morbid, sickly and injurious brooding and thinking. It helps you to see things, to know people, and to judge them in a broad instead of a narrow spirit. It prepares you to meet disappointment, sorrow, ill treatment and great suffering as the strong, courageous and splendid woman meets them. It is a great aid to clear, quick and right thinking.[68]

Evidently, exercise helped with disease resistance, made one a better worker, inspired positive and capacious thinking, and strengthened body, mind, and spirit. Evans averred that these qualities encouraged "right living and right acting" and, as mentioned above, "right thinking." Without stating the point explicitly, Evans linked "faithful, earnest and painstaking physical exercise" to desirable civic and moral qualities such as diligence, good judgment, and intelligence. Her arguments represented the foundational ideological and discursive work that Black women did to bind physical fitness to civic fitness.

Evans contended in a different paper that her female readers could not attain distinctly feminine qualities of beauty and grace without some form of physical activity. These qualities, combined with a cultured mind, made for the most "useful" young Black woman: "Fortunate indeed is the girl endowed with beauty, grace and mind. She is a power, an influential centre around which constantly revolve opportunities for usefulness. These three are mutually dependent. . . . And only by developing all does the well balanced, well proportioned and strong woman result. Very often the homeliest faced girl may obtain this proportion by regulated exercise and study. There is no royal road to a graceful, elegant body, as there is not to a cultured mind."[69] Here, Evans maintains that healthy and physically developed Black girls and women could be the most "useful" for the race (similar to Davidson, who spoke of "the highest avenues of usefulness"). According to aspiring-class Black women, the most useful girl was the one with interconnected qualities of "beauty, grace and mind," which young women could develop through exercise. Evans's comments challenge those made by William Cabell Bruce in 1891, who asserted that Black people lacked the qualities that constituted "useful citizens." Evans, Davidson, and others may have advocated for what Davidson termed "physical development" and what Evans called "regulated exercise" to counter ideas of Black people as useless citizens. As African Americans sought citizenship rights in the late nineteenth century, racial uplift by multiple means, including exercise, apparently helped produce a politically "useful" Black female figure for the twentieth century.[70]

It might appear unusual that Evans, in the tradition of racial uplift ideologues, would concentrate on beauty and cast aspersions on "the homeliest faced girl" instead of focusing singularly on education or moral character. The subject of beauty, however, corresponded directly with Black contestations over racial inferiority and the supposedly substandard Black body. Challenging racial denigration, even through affirmations of Black women's attractiveness, was vital to the political strategies African Americans devised during the Progressive Era and after. Historian Stephanie Camp asserted that late nineteenth- and early twentieth-century Black writers considered beauty to be "a taproot of black life, consciousness, and black politics."[71] Because beauty was intertwined with notions of race and gender, the subject naturally occupied the pages of a decidedly Black female publication like the *Woman's Era*. Beauty and strength are almost synonymous in the magazine, and a strong body served as the foundation of an active mind and moral character. As a progenitor of Black women's physical culture, Evans tethered beauty to exercise in ways that presaged how Black women in the twentieth century would make the two inseparable.

A series titled "Women at Home" featured in the same magazine focused more on Black women's health than on beauty. Columnist Elizabeth Johnson explained, "Few things are so beneficial to tired and nervous dispositions as a daily draught, one hour long, of pure air and sunshine; in other words, outdoor exercise is the spring necessity."[72] She added that spring was the ideal time to form "walking clubs" and advised that her female readers avoid "patent medicines" and embrace nature as a curative measure for weakness. Johnson's words offer a blueprint for Black women's physical culture. She provided sound advice to ward off tiredness, discouraged the use of potentially harmful drugs, and proposed group exercise through walking clubs. Johnson also ingeniously reclaimed the outdoors (and its pleasures, like fresh air, sunshine, and the joys of springtime) as ideal spaces for Black women's exercise. By doing so, she helped to revise the notion of the great outdoors as the exclusive territory of white men. These small, scattered pieces of advice in the 1890s served as the seeds of a more robust exercise culture in the twentieth century in which physical activity became necessary for Black women's health. Like Evans, Elizabeth Johnson foretold how Black women would use exercise to transform the Black female body.

In addition to magazines, advice literature provided African Americans with explicit exercise guidance consistent with racial uplift imperatives. Also referred to as "conduct literature," this media outlet literally instructed Black readers how to behave. Advice literature avoided contentious electoral politics and instead emphasized how individual behaviors could affect the destiny of the entire race.[73] Michele Mitchell notes that "the genre concocted idealized versions of womanhood and manhood for a people anxious to prove their fitness for national citizenship and the franchise."[74] In this way, advice literature served as behavioral guides on citizenship, and its writers conceived of citizenship as "desirable activity." Historians often credit advice literature with propagating respectability politics through directives in temperance, chastity, cleanliness, and other polite behaviors. But conduct literature also advocated exercise as beneficial to Black individuals, families, and racial futures.

In *College of Life or Practical Self-Educator: A Manual of Self-Improvement for the Colored Race*, published in 1895, the authors blended typical prescriptive advice with exercise instruction. As indicated in the title, the book claimed to provide methods of "self-improvement for the colored race" and highlighted "examples and achievements of successful men and women of the race as an incentive and inspiration to the rising generation."[75] The book served as an "educational emancipator and guide to success" dedicated to the "millions of sons and daughters who daily feel the need of education denied them in youth and are desirous of securing that self-culture which will aid them in obtaining success in life." Readers could presumably use this text to train themselves in matters of character, thrift, etiquette, courtship, and domestic life.[76]

The authors, Henry Davenport Northrop, Joseph R. Gay (both white), and Irvine Garland Penn (African American), included the topics of health and physical fitness in many chapters of the 656-page advice book. Penn, like Olivia Davidson, was a staunch advocate of Black education, and he particularly championed "self-development and self-evaluation."[77] By the time *College of Life* was published, Penn had edited a Black newspaper in Virginia, written a book about other Black journalists and editors, and had coauthored the influential pamphlet *The Reason Why the Colored American Is Not in the World's Columbian Exposition* with Ida B. Wells, F. L. Barnett, and Frederick Douglass.[78] He specifically authored the pamphlet section titled "The Progress of the Afro-American since Emancipation." Penn also helped organize the African American exhibits at the Atlanta Cotton States and International Exposition in 1895 and worked closely with Booker T. Washington on the exposition. Although it is difficult to distinguish the individual authors' voices, this biographical information suggests that Penn may have perceived his role in *College of Life* as part of his larger political imperative to display Black achievement, argue for African Americans' worthiness as citizens, and continue to struggle for Black self-determination. The book's focus on health and physical fitness likely served this imperative.

The authors argued for Black fitness in the plainly titled chapter "The Importance of Exercise." The chapter began by describing the "weak, dyspeptic, nerveless, draggy, pale, [and] puny" man as "a dismal failure from the start." Although the book noted the importance of cultivating a life of the mind and practicing diligent study, Northrop, Gay, and Penn recognized that "the 'perfectibility' of the human race depends much more on physical than mental culture, for intellect, energy of will, and strength of moral fibre are largely dependent on sound bodily health."[79] As Evans and Davidson had explained before, Black people benefited greatly from prioritizing physical and not just intellectual development. The authors acknowledged that in the United States, "physical culture is also beginning to be made part of the ordinary school curriculum," and the book heralded this trend to a specifically Black audience.[80]

In order to best argue for the "importance of exercise," Northrop, Gay, and Penn turned to experts in fitness, medicine, and physiology, including Dr. Morell Mackenzie, the personal physician to the English royal family. Citing Mackenzie, the *College of Life* authors agreed that "the British baby is from the first allowed an amount of liberty in the use of his limbs benefitting the future citizen of a free country" and believed that the Lings or Swedish system of exercise "would add immensely to the usefulness of board schools as nurseries of efficient citizens."[81] *College of Life*, through the perspective of Mackenzie, connected physical activity to the production of good citizens. The chapter informed readers about the kinds of exercises they should practice, recommended how often they should exercise, and offered the "healthful sports" in which they should participate. Northrop, Gay, and Penn gave readers illustrated, systematic instructions on how to use single and parallel bars to achieve a sound body.

The authors provided vivid visual examples of healthy, thriving Black individuals who functioned as race representatives in the book. Readers of *College of Life* and other advice literature did not have to imagine how Black people embodied racial success; they could easily see it. One of the most remarkable examples of this imagery is Mademoiselle Le Zetora, the "colored lady athlete" and "heavy weight act" featured on the final page of the "Exercise" chapter. The book does not elaborate on who she is, her profession, or precisely why the authors included her likeness. This photograph is the only mention of Le Zetora in the book and is presumably meant to speak for itself (see fig. 1.2).[82] The image, however, relays several messages about race, gender, and corporality. As Davidson and Evans argued, Le Zetora's image contends that beauty and strength can be complementary. The photograph separates daintiness from weakness, intimating that this is a body to which Black women should aspire. The image of Le Zetora lifting a seventy-pound weight also suggests that racial uplift might take the form of literal physical lifting.[83] As part of a book that claimed to show examples of Black success, Le Zetora's placement in this text and particularly in this chapter serves as a signifier of desirable Black female corporality achieved through physical exercise.

Physically developed Black men also received attention in *College of Life*. On the page opposite Le Zetora's photo, the authors included an image of Peter Jackson, the Caribbean-born late nineteenth-century heavyweight boxer whom the authors referred to as a "fine specimen of physical development" (see fig. 1.3). Authors featured Jackson in the chapter "How to Strengthen the Muscles," in which they warned readers about the dangers of inactivity and cautioned them not to rely on labor alone to provide adequate exercise. They explained, "The consequence of [exercise through labor] is that the more or less one-sided action belonging to most forms of daily occupation in the long run disturbs the harmony of the body, so that even working men often are greatly in need of systematic gymnastic exercises to counteract the one-sided influence to which their frame has been subjected in their occupation; how much more, then, persons leading a sedentary life, and having essentially mental occupations?"[84] By placing statements like this next to the image of Jackson's chiseled form, Northrop, Gay, and Penn helped to redefine ideas about the Black laboring body.

MLLE. Le ZETORA

COLORED LADY ATHLETE—HEAVY WEIGHT ACT

Figure 1.2. Mlle. Le Zetora as a literal and metaphorical example of racial uplift. Henry Davenport Northrop, Joseph R. Gay, and Irvine Garland Penn, *College of Life or Practical Self-Educator: A Manual of Self-Improvement for the Colored Race* (Chicago: Chicago Publication and Lithograph, 1895), 300. Schomburg Center for Research in Black Culture, Manuscripts, Archives and Rare Books Division, New York Public Library Digital Collections.

FINE SPECIMEN OF PHYSICAL DEVELOPMENT,
PETER JACKSON, ATHLETE.

Figure 1.3. Authors deemed Peter Jackson a "fine specimen of physical development."
Henry Davenport Northrop, Joseph R. Gay, and Irvine Garland Penn, *College of Life or
Practical Self-Educator: A Manual of Self-Improvement for the Colored Race* (Chicago:
Chicago Publication and Lithograph, 1895), 301. Schomburg Center for Research in
Black Culture, Manuscripts, Archives and Rare Books Division, New York Public Library
Digital Collections.

While the authors' enthusiasm for physical exercise did not necessarily align with the material realities of African American labor demands, especially during the era of its 1895 publication, at the very least, they *imagined* Black physicality as healthful, self-determined, and self-directed. Moreover, through these chapters on exercise and strength building, the book contested the idea that Black bodies were meant exclusively for low-wage, backbreaking work.

While *College of Life* welcomed Black women and men to join the mounting exercise movement, the authors acknowledged the unfairness women experienced with regard to physical activity. They also recognized how women's exercise and sports challenged Victorian ideas about acceptable female behavior. Addressing the unfair gender divide in exercise, they again cited Dr. Mackenzie: "I need not dwell on the necessity of exercise for women further than to say that competent authorities look upon it as the best safeguard against certain diseases peculiar to their sex, the enormous prevalence of which at the present day is no doubt in great measure due to the physical indolence which many of them have been taught to consider as a grace rather than a defect—I had almost said a vice."[85] Mackenzie's words disputed the beliefs that exercise compromised gracefulness and, more profoundly, that inactivity functioned as an admirable quality of womanhood. This text defied gender conventions by presenting exercise as wholly beneficial to Black women's health and bodies. It invited readers to shift their ideas of acceptable Black female physicality.

College of Life offered exercise as an ideal method of ridding the race, especially Black women, of the "vices" of indolence and disease. As African Americans pursued their citizenship entitlements at the dawn of the twentieth century, many feared that these vices would keep Black people from full participation in civic life, and the authors offered exercise as a remedy. While this genre of Black literature did not endorse direct political engagement, it provided, ostensibly, the information and tools for African Americans to better argue for their place in the body politic. Such writings show that Black people began creating their own culture of exercise in the late nineteenth century, before the widespread adoption of "physical culture" in the United States.

The term "physical culture" began to appear more often in Black advice literature after 1900, and authors tied it even more closely to notions of racial advancement in the twentieth century. In 1904, G. F. Richings, a white man who considered himself a friend of the race, published the eleventh edition of *Evidences of Progress among Colored People*. Richings had "for a number of years been collecting facts in relation to the Progress of the Race since Emancipation."[86] Benjamin Arnett, a Black bishop who wrote the introduction to the book, claimed that Richings "traveled East and West, North and South, with his eyes and ears open. For several years he has thrown these facts on the canvas to be seen and read in the New and Old World." Arnett made sure to convince readers of Richings's rigor, accuracy, and comprehensiveness. He continued, "The pages of this book will take the place of the canvas; the dim light of the lantern will be superseded by the clear light of reason, and the race that has been so long misrepresented will appear in a new light as the representative characters of this book pass through a thorough examination as to their capacity of self-culture, self-improvement, self-support and self-deference."[87] Richings sought to prove that emancipation and Reconstruction had not been failures and that African Americans had made considerable progress since slavery. He endeavored to disabuse his white audience of the idea that "unsavory" Black people they encountered represented the entire Black population. He provided an illustrative example: "The mistress of the household finds [a country girl from the South] ignorant and sometimes absolutely stupid, and instead of classing this girl where she belongs, as all races are divided into classes, she immediately arrives at the conclusion that because the girl hails from the South, she must be a fair specimen and a true representative of all the colored people in that section."[88] Part of Richings's objective served to highlight the most excellent African Americans to counteract the damage that "country girls" caused to the racial uplift project.

Accomplished race women, seemingly the diametric opposite of the "country girl," are featured prominently in *Evidences of Progress*. Richings uses several instructive examples of Black women's community work that proved critical to racial progress and ideas of noble womanhood. He highlighted, for instance, Black women who managed the Thayer Home for Colored Girls in Atlanta and explained some of the operations of the home: "Miss Flora Mitchell, who superintends this home, is in my opinion, one of the finest specimen [*sic*] of noble womanhood I have ever met. The work of the home is done by the occupants alternately, so as to give all practical knowledge of model housekeeping. Lectures are given on domestic science, food, dress, physical culture and social ethics. In short, the aim of the Home is to fit young ladies to conduct and adorn a model Christian home."[89] Indeed, the act of "fitting" young Black women held a double meaning. Through physical culture, the home enabled its residents to become physically fit, and the other lessons taught by Miss Mitchell instilled moral fitness. The lectures on physical culture are most remarkable, considering that "physical culture" as a modern, designated movement was still in its early stages. Evidently, physical culture did not merely serve a rhetorical function in Black elite circles but became part of the practice of racial uplift for apparently downtrodden young women. Black women integrated physical culture into practical lessons on homemaking and Christian stewardship for coming-of-age Black girls.

Conduct literature material similar to *College of Life* and *Evidences of Progress* permeated other print outlets like Black newspapers during the early years of the twentieth century. The Black press, in particular, mirrored advice books by offering specific instructions on women's exercise and tacking on the civic meaning of physical activity. Black physical culturists suggested various methods for Black women to attain fit bodies, minds, and temperaments through exercise. They recommended calisthenics, gymnastics, sports, and walking as the physical activities that would ensure physical fitness (in addition to conscious eating and abstention from drugs, tobacco, alcohol, and patent medicines). Although not always explicitly branded as "physical culture," the advice they published in the Black press constituted a corpus of Black physical culture literature that shaped the development of African American exercise literacy in the early twentieth century.

An article from the *Wisconsin Weekly Advocate* reflects the kind of short and direct exercise advice that often appeared in Black newspapers. Published in 1903, it stated, "A few simple gymnastic exercises after the bath, if only for a few minutes, help to stimulate the circulation and clear the brain, besides developing the figure."[90] Based on burgeoning exercise science, this was sound counsel that almost any health news outlet could have published. But "developing the figure" was laden with racial, political, and gendered meaning often mediated by the Black press. Bodily development for Black women served profoundly personal and public objectives. A healthy body, shaped by exercise, boded well in the public sphere and promoted the circulation of positive Black images. Contributors to the Black newspaper the *Washington Bee* understood that a physically fit body was politically important for young Black women who entered "the world"; as one writer for this newspaper proclaimed in 1912, "Just as it is believed that no woman is really educated without some knowledge of domestic life, so it is felt that no girl is ready to go out into the world without a well trained, graceful body."[91] According to the paper, an outdoor "regular course of gymnastics" was the best way to achieve a body that appeared ready and acceptable for the world to see.[92] For some African Americans, the ideal female body hinged on physical culture. This "exercised" body functioned as a stark contrast to typical depictions of Black matriarchs, domestics, and mammies—images that Black newspapers endeavored to challenge in the early twentieth century. These depictions were not the model of fit citizenship that the Black press and Black women more generally desired to portray.

The press's concern with exercise and the shape of Black women's bodies continued into the 1910s. In a 1913 edition of the *Chicago Defender*, a writer explained, "Most women, whether fleshy or thin, walk far too little. The woman who tends to be fleshy should walk for at least an hour every day and do it regularly and systematically."[93] The call for regular and systematic exercise was usually directed at Black women and primarily at "fleshy" Black women. Black fat disdain began before the turn of the century, and exercise factored significantly into how African Americans attempted to distance themselves from the liabilities of extra weight. However, the enthusiasm for exercise represented more than fat stigmatization—it signified a physical act that Black women were encouraged to do, whether they struggled with weight or not. Exercise helped to make *all* Black women's bodies fit.

In the 1920s, Black women continued to encourage exercise for its corporal benefits. Leola Lillard, an advice columnist for the *New York Amsterdam News*, wrote the "Key to Culture" column and authored articles on various middle-class topics, including "appropriate dress," "duties of the wife," "finger foods and the napkin," "church etiquette," and "street manners." Lillard conceived of these matters as "aesthetic contributions to society."[94] These aesthetic motivations led her to advocate physical culture for its assurance of a "graceful" body—a subject that the Black middle class seemed to endorse readily.

Lillard opined that women should walk purposefully to achieve "health and grace." She began by explaining, "Physical culture may be a 'fad,' but its aesthetic results are conceded. The graceful control of the body is the basis of a fine manner." Lillard recommended that women model their walking after "United States infantry men" who took "long strides" at "slow cadence." Most women, she claimed, took "short, quick, choppy steps" to a fault. Walking this way consumed "nerve-power," damaged blood circulation, and cramped the muscles. According to Lillard, exercise through proper walking techniques improved posture and overall appearance. She explained that if women were more conscious of their gait, they would make better "first impressions." Lillard reminded the reader that these impressions "are received through the eye before a word is spoken" and that a good walk portrayed good "character" and "breeding."[95]

Lillard's advice generates a critical question about Black physical culture: Whom did exercise serve? Her focus on health and grace suggests that some African Americans may have perceived physical culture as simultaneously beneficial to the individual and the race. Health may have served both individual and collective desires, while grace seemed to speak to larger Black middle-class imperatives of public bodily performance. Through their advocacy of physical culture, women like Lillard made strolling for health and walking for grace inextricable. Similar to Mary Evans, who wrote of the graceful woman as a powerful, "influential" figure, and the *Washington Bee*, which celebrated women with elegant bodies, Lillard presented the graceful Black woman as a figure that met visual, representational, and possibly political imperatives for the racial collective. In the age of physical culture, embodying grace signaled not only character but the actual body. But graceful bodies were not given, they were made, and exercise became unavoidable for upper-class Black women who sought enviable bodies and other "keys to culture" in the 1920s.

Lillard's suggestions on graceful walking draws attention to how some African Americans perceived citizenship as an act performed through the body. While she did not mention the issue of citizenship directly, her invocation of American military men, whom many considered the paragon of patriotism and upstanding citizenship, and her emphasis on making a "good impression" through walking urge us to consider how physical culture enabled new, implicit ways for Black women to perform citizenship. Physical culture, which reached its height during the 1920s, presented a prime opportunity for Black women to perform a version of physical fitness for citizenship that still complied with gendered concepts of gracefulness and a "fine manner." If Black female readers actually followed Lillard's advice, the act of walking, performed "properly," could function as a daily fitness practice and a quotidian performance of citizenship in action.

This particular brand of Black womanhood centered on fit bodies and citizenship carried implications for some African Americans' ideas of collective racial prosperity. In his weekly health column "Keeping Fit," Dr. Elliot Rawlings provided recommendations to *New York Amsterdam News* readers about the measures the race needed to take to become fit Black citizens. According to Rawlings, those who did not exercise devolved into a discredit to the race. The Black doctor exclaimed, "In the matter of health

and disease, the majority of Negroes are shiftless, unthoughtful, and ignorant. Sleep, diet, and exercise are never regulated according to individual
needs." He bemoaned, "The appetite for sex, food, and hilarity is that of
the unthoughtful and primitive man. There is no careful physical survey of
his body or nervous system. Most Negroes just live and soon die. How can
the race prosper if the majority of Negroes are indolent along the lines of
personal health, sanitation, and hygiene?"[96] In his diatribe, the health columnist affirmed that unregulated appetites and improper physical activity
were just a few of the markers of a race headed for failure. As a physician,
Rawlings likely spoke from a place of medical frustration in which most
of his patients suffered from easily preventable diseases. His frustration
also reveals emergent conflicts indicative of the simultaneous struggle for
Black health and citizenship.

Dr. Rawlings's vituperation represents one of the key tensions that
arose when African American health officials strategized the best way to
ensure Black well-being. Some adhered to a structural critique of American healthcare, while others, like Rawlings, zeroed in on personal responsibility and poor individual choices. Paradoxically, the good doctor used
his medical practice to treat Black patients in private while he reserved his
newspaper column to pathologize those same patients in public. Rawlings
likely vacillated between ambivalent feelings of dismay and disdain as
he attempted to ameliorate racial health disparities and juggle an overwhelming patient load. He seemed to desire race prosperity and longevity
but used counterproductive rhetoric to achieve it. Rawlings's commentary
is further compromised by the fact that his arguments about the inclinations of Black people were not accurate, nuanced, or gender-specific. He
omitted a critical detail by failing to acknowledge Black women's role in
keeping the race physically and morally fit. Unbeknownst to Rawlings (or
perhaps out of his willful ignorance), Black women had already begun
"surveying" their bodies and nervous systems in the late nineteenth century and had created a decidedly Black culture of fitness.

)(

African Americans entered into a fierce debate about their political worth
and deservingness of citizenship at the turn of the twentieth century.
These debates served as the ideological backdrop for Black physical culture. This chapter shows that Black people readied themselves to counter
ideas of "unfitness" in various ways. Physical culture functioned as a key,
albeit underappreciated, mode by which Black women argued for their

civic value. Because they actually reproduced the race, Black women had the formidable task of ensuring bodily progress and civic virtue for all African Americans.

It is not coincidental that physical culture and fit female bodies became increasingly indicative of racial progress between 1890 and the 1920s. Because exercise signified good "breeding," self-control, and positive civic behavior, Black women used it as a strategy to lay claim to citizenship. They understood that how Black women's bodies appeared and moved in public spaces carried political resonance. Through their early involvement with physical culture, Black women (re)shaped their bodies and, in effect, revamped outmoded notions of Black womanhood and Black debasement that stemmed from slavery. They created their own exercise movement and applied great figurative meaning to the pursuit of physical fitness. With these theoretical arguments for fitness firmly in place, as the following chapter shows, African American women used exercise to seek the concrete physical benefits of health and longevity.

CHAPTER 2

Healthy Bodies

BLACK WOMEN'S EXERCISE AND PUBLIC HEALTH IN THE EARLY TWENTIETH CENTURY

One January evening in 1923, a crowd of Black women entered a New York auditorium for a rare opportunity to hear the foremost fitness expert deliver a lecture on health. Members of the local Black YWCA filed into the auditorium to witness Bernarr Macfadden, a man whom one Black newspaper called "the world's greatest living marvel," speak on the virtues of wholesome eating and exercise. After asking "various questions on health, physical training, proper diet, and the general care of the body," the women left the talk "resolved to build up strong, healthy bodies."[1] Similar to these attendees, Black women around the country put the principles of physical culture to practice by teaching physical education, joining Black YWCAs, and organizing community health programs. Throughout the early twentieth century, African American women engaged with some of Macfadden's ideas in pursuit of "healthy bodies."[2] They used physical culture to devise a Black public health campaign of fitness.

Seeking the health benefits of exercise, African American women found creative ways to navigate racial, gender, and economic barriers to mainstream physical culture. Understanding that they would not be accepted in white fitness spaces, members of Black institutions, instead, invited Macfadden to speak at their churches (see fig. 2.1), printed summaries of *Physical Culture* in the Black press, and integrated exercise into their schools, clubs, and community health campaigns. Black women would sometimes negotiate with white institutions to ensure that Black girls obtained access to physical training and health education. At other times, they abandoned interracial cooperation altogether and formed their own fitness establishments. Whether they invited the father of physical culture to speak at their place of worship or persuaded white YWCA branches to allow Black girls to use their fitness facilities temporarily,

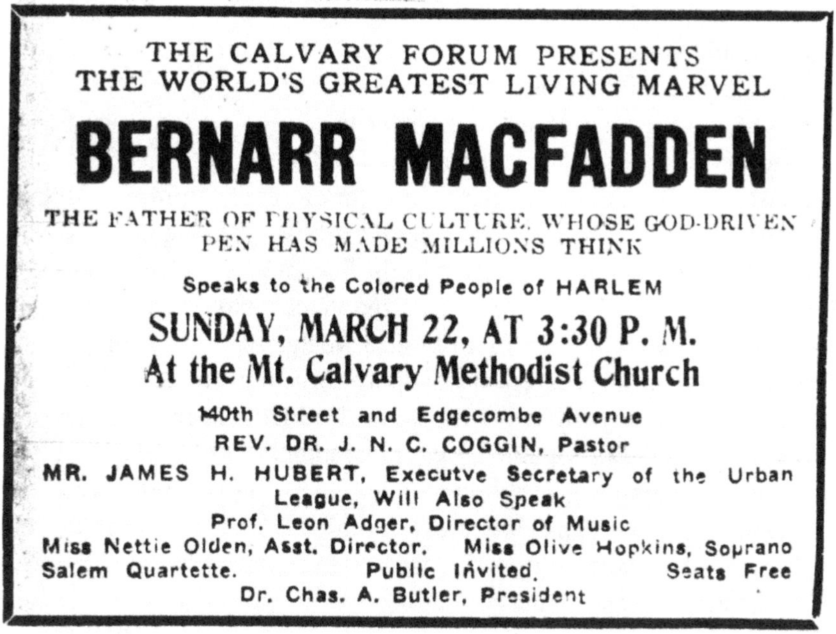

Figure 2.1. Advertisement for Bernarr Macfadden as the headliner for a health talk at a Black church in Harlem. *New York Amsterdam News*, March 18, 1925, 2.

Black women espoused the values of physical culture for the health and wellness of the race.

This chapter contends that despite profound structural barriers, Black women augmented their public health campaigns by integrating exercise into their health activism in the early twentieth century. In doing so, Black women created new meanings of Black health and citizenship that stood on ideals of bodily strength, vigor, and symmetry. The scholarship on the history of Black health has yet to uncover how African Americans used exercise as a health-seeking and life-sustaining measure. Research on Black public health in the Progressive Era has instead focused on responses to infectious and inflammatory diseases like tuberculosis, typhoid fever, malaria, and causes of infant mortality. These foci make sense as these illnesses affected African Americans disproportionately. Black women's health crusades, however, were expansive, and they did much more than resort to standard sanitation programs and vaccinations to address public health ills. Many Black women tied the most troublesome health issues to lack of exercise. An examination of physical culture reveals how African Americans practiced preventive healthcare through exercise in addition to how they reacted to the overwhelming health issues at hand.

Black exercise advocates promoted exercise not only as a public health good but also as a physical act that carried implications for real and imagined forms of survival, racial competition, and posterity. Eugenic notions of race survivability and anxieties about Black mortality informed African American exercise prescriptions. Black medical professionals asserted that high death rates prematurely stole the lives of Black citizens, compromised racial uplift efforts, and stigmatized Black people as an unhealthy race. They grew concerned that physical weakness, disease, and death prevented true racial progress and stalled citizenship-building efforts. Dr. Algernon B. Jackson, director of the public health department at Howard University, urged Black people, "We must increase our population, for population means power. . . . We cannot build with the untempered mortar of poor health and a high death rate."[3] He added that the responsibility fell on African Americans to "free [themselves] from the stigma of unhealthfulness."[4] Similar sentiments about longevity as "power" infused African American health rhetoric in the first few decades of the twentieth century. Before advising African Americans to "exercise every day in the open . . . in an hour when you can be in the sunshine," Dr. B. S. Herben of the New York Tuberculosis Association, who was likely white, asked imploringly in a 1923 edition of the Black nationalist newspaper *Negro World*, "Do you know that according to population, more colored people die in a year than white people? You are proud of your race and of the members of it who have done great things. You are proud of what it is going to accomplish for the good of the world. Did you ever do anything to make your race a stronger one? Did you ever stop to think that by keeping yourself and your family strong and healthy you will do a lot toward making your race a better one?"[5] According to these health professionals, a high Black mortality rate diminished not only Black lives but racial pride, strength, and advancement. They believed that lowering the death rate required Black individual and collective action and a wide range of behavior modifications. Exercise became just one of several interventions that Black health crusaders utilized in their quest to stem rising mortality rates and other health maladies.

African American medical professionals, health writers, community activists, and everyday Black people understood that high death rates and poor health statistics conveyed racial, social, and civic meaning. In the early twentieth century, a time of growing acceptance of the germ theory of disease, the debut of "Typhoid Mary," and anti-tuberculosis campaigns, mortality rates and vital statistics represented more than objective health data—they operated as biomedical indexes to assess who was a fit citizen.[6] Dr. Charles V. Roman, an influential Black physician, remarked on the racial implications of the putatively impartial field of medicine. He addressed the Philadelphia County Medical Society in 1916: "The race question has invaded our ranks and the truths of science are given an ethnic tinge. Vital statistics are interpreted in terms of ethnography, and mortality returns are taken as a measure of racial fitness; pathology has become the handmaid of prejudice and the laboratory a weapon of civic oppression."[7] Roman's position is supported by a history of racialized medicine in which "unbiased" health data reified pernicious ideas of racial difference.[8]

A corollary to Roman's thinking posits that winning public health battles functioned as a method for people of color to prove their racial fitness, overcome civic oppression, and affirm national belonging.[9] Although they were less likely than men to be physicians, Black women, who performed much of the intimate, health-related care work in Black communities, played a significant role in the intertwined public health and citizenship struggles of the early twentieth century. Securing public health achievements allowed Black women to position themselves as custodians of a vigorous, durable race fit for citizenship.

The following pages show how exercise became essential to achieving respiratory, cardiovascular, gastrointestinal, and reproductive health, as well as physical fitness, for Black people and especially African American women. The chapter first outlines barriers to Black health in order to situate the unfavorable milieu in which African American health seekers lived, worked, and strived. The subsequent section examines the specific ways in which Black women integrated exercise into existing public health arenas, particularly physical education, the YWCA, and community health programs. The chapter concludes by exploring the eugenic anxieties about Black girls' and women's bodies that accompanied the incorporation of exercise into public health campaigns. I interrogate this anxiety and explain why allegedly unfit, "round-shouldered girls" became a diagnostic and cautionary trope to encourage Black people to exercise.

Barriers to African American Health in the Early Twentieth Century

White theories of Black "unfitness" claimed that inherent racial inferiority, not environment, accounted for African Americans' health problems and high mortality rates. Inspired by social Darwinism and the likes of

Frederick L. Hoffman, white health pundits cast doubts on Black survivability and, by extension, racial fitness. In 1908, an unnamed writer for the
magazine *Health* wrote boldly:

> The Negro problem in the cities would very soon solve itself in the
> extermination of the race. . . . The Negro is essentially a "wild man." When
> he is brought to a large city, he thrives about as well as the Esquimo [*sic*]
> when he is brought from his icy country to the United States. I believe
> that as our country becomes more settled, as the Negro is brought into
> closer touch with civilization . . . he will die off, and thus solve the race
> problem.[10]

This writer's deduction about African American health and mortality,
although erroneous, served powerful rhetorical functions. It worked to
both discourage Black migration and reinforce notions of African Americans as uncivilized subjects who could not handle the modern, urban
landscape. The idea that Black city dwellers would eventually "die off" may
have also given white *Health* readers a false sense of ownership over urban
spaces and reassured them that those spaces would remain racially segregated. In the first few years of the twentieth century and before the Great
Migration in the 1910s, prognostications about Black survival, like the one
featured in *Health*, became crucial to debates on the "Negro problem,"
national progress, and the nation's future. African American health advocates, therefore, devised a two-pronged approach. They battled prevalent
diseases as well as the very idea that disease, urbanization, and civilization
would eliminate the race.

While vital statistics likely informed such racist mortality predictions,
they also provided important information for Black health crusaders to offer
health interventions. For example, in the "Health" section of the 1914–15
edition of the *Negro Year Book*, an annual encyclopedia of the "history and
progress of the race" published by Tuskegee Institute, writers explained,
"The death rate per 1,000 among Negroes [in] 1913: 24. By 1963 the rate can
be decreased to 12 per 1,000."[11] The report also claimed that "there is no iron
law of mortality" and that sanitation and preventive medicine provided the
best measures to increase Black life spans. Other important figures included
average life expectancy for Black people, the number of Black southerners
who fell ill each year, the earnings African Americans lost due to illness and
funeral costs, and predictions of future deaths from tuberculosis. Although
these numbers might indicate a justified fear of mortality, they also enabled

Black health writers to propose health possibilities. "A sufficiency of pure food, pure air, [and] pure water would add at once 10 years to the average of Negro lives," explained the *Year Book*.[12] Black institutions used life expectancy and disease statistics to imagine how small health interventions could lengthen and improve Black lives.

Despite the apparent simplicity of these interventions, securing sound medical care, in addition to healthy food, air, and water, represented a significant barrier to Black health. African Americans faced nearly insurmountable obstacles to health from the majority-white medical community. They experienced a paradoxical relationship with American healthcare and medicine. At times, Black people remained under exceptional medical scrutiny, serving as subjects of medical experimentation and scientific exploitation.[13] At other times, the medical community neglected them when their basic health needs required attention. This dichotomy of racialized medical practices continued throughout the twentieth century (and continues into the twenty-first) as the color line divided healthcare.

Historian Samuel Roberts states, "Segregation is inimical to good health."[14] Racial segregation characterized life for most Americans in the early twentieth century and inhibited fair and equal distribution of health services to African Americans. The best healthcare requires exchanging knowledge and resources within the medical establishment, and segregation obstructed interracial collaboration in medicine. As a prime example, in the first 100 years of its existence, the American Medical Association excluded African Americans from the organization.[15] For Black health and medical professionals, de jure and de facto segregation often prevented them from acquiring the newest technology, information, apparatuses, and training needed to tackle the most troublesome diseases within their communities.[16] Some scholars contend that Black people suffered disproportionately under segregated medicine, explaining, "African Americans have survived the worst health status, suffered the worst health outcomes, and been forced to utilize the worst health services of any other racial or ethnic group in the U.S. for nearly four centuries."[17] Separate healthcare arrangements for Black people largely account for this historical trend.

Segregation, in effect, created two disparate systems of disease prevention for Black and white Americans. Inequalities in housing operated as a primary culprit in the spread of tuberculosis, which became the most life-threatening illness African Americans faced in the first decades of the twentieth century. In Detroit, many Black families lived in "dark rooms" with poor ventilation that functioned as veritable breeding grounds for disease. In the 1920 survey *The Negro in Detroit*, researcher Forrester Washington discovered that "Negro families are forced to live in unsanitary, unsafe houses, some of which are a menace to the community and a reflection on the Board of Health. Yet, many of these people do not dare to complain for fear the landlord in retaliation may order them to move and they do not know where else they can lay their heads."[18] Black residents became locked into these living arrangements for years and lacked the ability to change their housing circumstances. Those who desired to expand their families had little recourse to raising their children in substandard housing.

Although Black families as a whole were negatively affected by unsanitary living conditions, members of the household seemed to experience the adverse effects differently. Washington explained that women and children were especially disadvantaged because they usually remained indoors while their male counterparts worked outside of the home:

> The colored women and children who do not work stay indoors most of the time and hence there is more sickness among them than among the men. While there are many colored women still doing "days-work"— nevertheless, the number has greatly decreased as men's wages have gone up. . . . The women are enabled to stay at home and care for their children. But remaining in-doors all day long, in overcrowded, improperly ventilated houses and improperly clothed, the colored women (and children also) have become a greater prey for pulmonary disease than the men.[19]

Apparently, women's "place" in the home put them in precarious positions and endangered their respiratory health. The report also mentioned that these homes lacked general cleanliness, not because the residents were inherently unkempt, but because the tenement owners kept the apartments in such disrepair that families (most likely women) received little incentive to keep their rented homes in good order.[20] Structural issues like these were common for poor people and help explain the high rates of illness in Black communities, particularly for women.[21]

Infectious diseases, many of which were poverty-induced, constituted the majority of Black physical health difficulties. Accordingly, local health agencies documented the problem of viral and bacterial illnesses in African

American populations. In Philadelphia, Black communities suffered disproportionately from tuberculosis, pneumonia, diarrhea, enteritis (intestinal inflammation), and nephritis (kidney inflammation).[22] In Atlanta, neighborhood clinics designed to serve poor African Americans reported that many Black patients suffered from inflammatory diseases. Tonsillitis, adenoiditis (inflammation of the adenoids—lymph tissue above the mouth's roof), and swollen cervical glands (lymph nodes) represented just a few of the reported ailments.[23] "Swollen glands" is a general diagnosis but may have indicated illnesses as serious as tuberculosis or syphilis or as minor as the common cold. These maladies, even the minor ones, added insult to the injury of housing inequity, food insecurity, employment discrimination, and other affronts to Black life.

Some African Americans lived with the daily reality of persistent illnesses. In his days as a struggling college student at Tuskegee Institute, novelist Ralph Ellison often wrote home about his seemingly never-ending bouts of head colds and dyspepsia. He penned in one letter to his mother, "Quite a number of us [Tuskegee students] are suffering from colds and this one I have is extremely unpleasant."[24] A few days later, he wrote to his hometown girlfriend, "My stomach is still bad and has me eating first one meal in just one day when [I'd] like so much to digest three (smile)."[25] His next letter to his mother noted, "I suffer with those colds in the head again, and I think I will have to start using a spray if they don't stop soon."[26] Ellison's correspondence sheds light on the everyday nature of African American health afflictions. His letters serve as a reminder that Black people often lived with feelings of malaise in addition to chronic infectious diseases. Nevertheless, Black people, whether they were ordinary citizens or promising writers, continued to study, work, and care for others through health problems, both big and small.

Sufferers of persistent illnesses sometimes turned to local city health bureaucracies for aid—many of which made only modest attempts to alleviate Black public health issues. They increased their efforts as Black southerners migrated west and north in the 1910s. In 1920, the Detroit Board of Health employed three Black nurses to split their time between house-to-house visits and clinical work. The board also opened a clinic exclusively for Black infants.[27] Likewise, the New York City Department of Health canvassed Black neighborhoods to locate residents who needed healthcare and made recommendations on where they could receive medical attention.[28] Their suggestions often pointed to existing Black institutions like churches, settlement houses, and schools. Essentially, these health agencies did not ignore Black people, but their efforts proved insufficient, considering the massive influx of southern migrants who needed medical services. They often reinforced segregation and maintained health disparities by directing African Americans to Black institutions that struggled to find the time, money, space, and human resources to accommodate pressing medical needs.

Despite their lack of material resources, Black institutions strove to provide medical care and fitness facilities. A shortage of public welfare programs and the segregation of public recreational facilities resulted in many Black and poor people's failure to meet a broad set of health aspirations.[29] Historians rarely frame the lack of fitness programs as a public health threat during this period; nonetheless, Black women described the dearth of gyms, pools, and parks as crises that posed hazards to individual and community health. With the proliferation of gyms, bicycles, and exercise equipment in the twentieth century, African Americans began to see these apparatuses as essential to their well-being. They understood that access to well-equipped facilities enabled one to develop bodily strength, improve flexibility, and enhance muscular and immune systems. Restrictions to these modes of physical fitness indeed jeopardized total, holistic health.

Black newspapers documented African Americans' unsuccessful efforts to exercise, secure equipment and facilities, and even teach physical education. The *Chicago Defender* noted on its front page that a white YWCA displayed "race hatred" in 1924 by prohibiting an African American woman from enrolling in the Y's Central School of Hygiene and Physical Education in New York.[30] While the rejection from the Y may have operated as "business as usual" for extant segregated institutions, these individual denials resulted in severe consequences for Black communities and the collective struggle for health. The unnamed Black woman whom the Y barred from the program had serious intentions of becoming a physical education teacher.[31] Other Black women may have read this account and become discouraged from pursuing similar career paths. If Black women could not enjoy the same facilities as white people, it was imperative that they at least retained the opportunity to learn the profession to instruct classes within their communities.

Mattie Pearl Adams met the same fate when she tried to enroll in the Dudley Sargent School of Physical Education in Boston. The school had been known to admit African American women candidates, but administrators stated that they "thought it best to discontinue that policy and would not hereafter accept pupils other than white."[32] The Dudley Sargent

School served as the preeminent institution to study the science of physical education.[33] The new policy relayed a clear message that African Americans, especially Black women who attended these institutions in larger numbers than men, were unworthy of acquiring the best physical culture training. During this time of severe racial exclusion, a quality education in calisthenics and gymnastics could greatly improve Black women's health and career prospects. Policies like that of the Dudley Sargent School attempted to reify racial difference and keep Black women in their conscribed places. This practice, of course, remained unsurprising to Black readers, and it may have even inspired some Black women to develop their own spaces of health and healing. But by and large, these restrictive policies had a profoundly negative effect on prospective students who planned to specialize in and disseminate the virtues of exercise.

White-only fitness facilities represented one of the most intractable forms of health discrimination. The aforementioned incidents in New York and Boston were not isolated; rather, they serve as touchstones of the many ways in which institutional racism inhibited the health and physical fitness opportunities of African Americans, even in the ostensibly progressive northern United States. Gymnasiums, swimming pools, and summer camps, for example, functioned as the three most controversial and inaccessible spaces in early twentieth-century discussions of YWCA integration. They were also ideal facilities for women's calisthenics, gymnastics, and sports.[34] Exercise and recreational spaces, which often required interracial touching and physical exchange, remained off-limits and hindered Black women's opportunity for physical culture. Although by 1920, fifty-nine Black YWCA branches or centers existed, many of them lacked gymnasiums or pools.[35] After the legitimization of the germ theory of disease, the spread of tuberculosis, and the subsequent racialization of infectious illnesses, municipal pools became especially contested terrain for desegregation. Innumerable episodes of fitness discrimination proliferated in the segregated landscape of early twentieth-century America and greatly reduced African Americans' participation in physical culture.

Economic disparities also limited Black people's exercise options, as many poor and working-class Black women simply lacked the financial means to participate in mainstream physical culture.[36] Even if they could gain access to the Y Central School of Hygiene or the Dudley Sargent School, most working-class African Americans could not afford the tuition. White women like Gwyneth King Roe opened their own private gyms in Washington, DC, and New York. She catered to high-end white patrons, charging $1 per class session and $5 for private sessions (approximately $28 and $140, respectively, in 2022 dollars). Roe also required clients to purchase gym suits and proper shoes.[37] Such requirements proved unfeasible for most Black women.

White physical culturists advertised the benefits of at-home exercise machinery, but again, the cost of many of these consumer goods remained prohibitive for working-class people. Bicycles, which gained prominence in the 1890s and offered benefits of fresh air, mobility, and exercise, ranged from $60 to $100.[38] *Physical Culture* often featured advertisements for fitness machines, like Bernarr Macfadden's "Electric Massage Exerciser" that promised to cure disease and restore "vigorous, pulsating" health. The Exerciser ranged from $1.50 to $2.50 in 1900, equivalent to around $42 to $70 in 2022.[39] Bodybuilder Eugen Sandow's "Developer," a home exercise and strength-training machine, was even more expensive. He priced the Developer at $5 in 1900.[40]

Several other consumer exercise products posed cost challenges. In 1920, Wallace Rogerson introduced "Wallace Reducing Records"—the first in-home instructional exercise and weight loss records. Rogerson sold the records by mail and advertised them in women's magazines. Traditionally, the mail-order business functioned as a way for African Americans to circumvent segregated spaces of shopping. These records, however, required an expensive subscription for the entire set. The sheer cost of these alternatives made them impractical, considering many Black families' material realities. The exercise technology that inspired a commitment to physical fitness in white Americans was simply out of reach for most Black people. The monetary cost of conventional physical culture could be exorbitant and represents just one of the many barriers to Black health and fitness.

Black Women's Exercise and Public Health Work

In the early twentieth century, African Americans began to institutionalize public health through schools, the YWCA and YMCA, and community health programs. These three institutions served as spaces for both public health advocacy and exercise promotion. Black women supported exercise imperatives as physical education teachers and students, YWCA leaders and devotees, nurses, health workers, and founders of community health initiatives. Taken together, schools, Ys, and community programs demonstrate the ways in which African American women indexed physical fitness as a Black public health imperative. In turn, they became authorities on exercise, the body, and physical training.

Physical Education

Formal education became a significant moral and political imperative for Black people after the official end of slavery in the United States. Achieving literacy, mastering basic math skills, and acquiring agricultural and domestic training represented important pillars of African American freedom and citizenship.[41] Education enabled newly emancipated people to attain a measure of independence and self-efficacy. The hopes for formal education seemed to atrophy, however, after federal troops abandoned the South and the Freedmen's Bureau, including its schools, was dismantled. Southern African Americans soon realized they would have to depend on their own mutual aid societies and other forms of self-help to seek schooling. When envisioning education in the post-Reconstruction period, a bifurcated model of either industrial or liberal arts education often comes to mind. But African Americans made physical education important to notions of Black edification and integrated the subject into Black industrial, agricultural, and liberal arts instruction.

Physical education functioned as a form of citizenship training for all young people across the color line. PE inculcated notions of personal and social responsibility, reinforced ideals of democracy, and provided practical training for military service, all of which supported the ethics of American citizenship.[42] These civic ambitions applied to Black pupils too, but physical education served more immediate aims for African American children. In his 1906 study, *The Health and Physique of the Negro American*, W. E. B. Du Bois asserted that "improper [physical] education" contributed to the high "death rate and sickness" of African Americans.[43] He expounded, "The children get a great deal of so-called mental and a little moral, and often a smattering of industrial, but the fundamentals of physical education in order to develop the bodies of the children, is criminally neglected at least among Philadelphia's poorest Negroes."[44] A writer for the *Atlanta Independent* commented similarly on the long-term effects of deficient physical education for Black schoolchildren: "When the little Negro 'tot' finishes the public school he is in worse physical condition than he was when he entered, for the reason that he has been packed in an unsanitary room in a delapidated [*sic*] schoolhouse for ten years, where he had neither fresh air, room nor facilities for physical culture, by which to develop a healthful body and a vigorous mind. The little fellow comes from school a physical wreck."[45] In addition to civic and ideological objectives, physical education programs served a critical public health mission for Black children. African American elementary, secondary, and higher education institutions designed these programs with this high-stakes mission in mind.

Black learning institutions understood that the life of the mind was not removed from knowledge of the body. The Kansas Industrial and Educational Institute, the second oldest Black college in the state, affirmed that "a strong body is the foundation for a strong mind" in its advertisement of physical education classes.[46] Using the original Latin phrase, promoters of Wiley College in Marshall, Texas, proclaimed, "Mens sana in corpora sano—a sound mind in a sound body—is the torch of idealism that has guided the destiny of Wiley College since the memorable year of 1873. . . . A sound mind in a sound body for the Negro youth of the Southwest."[47] The college supported this statement by highlighting the athletic and recreational programs it offered to prospective college students. Likewise, Black schools like Spelman and Hampton served as both safe spaces for physical activity and hedges against white-led efforts to keep African Americans out of gyms, white YWCAs and YMCAs, and playgrounds.

Physical education proved especially critical for the kinesthetic training of African American women and girls. From the turn of the century until around World War I, Black higher education institutions mandated physical education for Black female students, requiring them to participate in gymnastics, calisthenics, games, and hygiene lessons. But these same institutions assigned different physical activities, like athletics and military drills, to male students.[48] Compared with their male counterparts, Black women and girls became adept at the art and science of movement, physical activity, and health. Even Angelina Weld Grimké and Alice Dunbar-Nelson—learned Black women who are not usually associated with rigorous physical endeavors—received degrees in and taught physical education. Black women occupied essential roles in mastering, instructing, and spreading the pleasures and pains of mandated physical activity.

Physical education became intertwined with citizenship instruction, public health, and a host of gendered racial uplift objectives for Black women and girls. Many African Americans considered physical education a respectable profession, and it granted Black women physical educators praise and admiration in their communities. This admiration stemmed from the expectation that physical education would empower young people to care for themselves in a variety of ways. Teaching "physical culture" was not relegated just to sports, games, and other physical activities but included other health-sustaining lessons on food and dress.[49] S. L. Grant, a

Black teacher from Tennessee, studied cooking, dressmaking, and "physical culture" at Fisk University and used her training to teach girls physical education. In 1901, she volunteered to teach courses on "hygienic cooking," "healthful clothing," and physical education at the State Agricultural and Mechanical College for Negroes in Normal, Alabama. The Black newspaper the Indianapolis *Freeman* recognized her as a leader and "race woman" for her selflessness and commitment to educating young women.[50] The paper considered her a worker for "the elevation of the Negro race," a "competent woman to lead her people" with the ability to "ennoble and lift up all with whom she came in contact."[51]

It is difficult to imagine that Grant would have received such adulation had she not adhered to gendered prescriptions for Black girls and women. Providing young women lessons in bodily care, nutrition, and light physical activity functioned as a gendered form of racial uplift endorsed largely by aspiring-class community members. At the turn of the century, Black women offered lessons in sanitation, "medicalized domesticity," and hygienic homemaking as some of the many contributions to racial advancement.[52] These lessons often flowed into girls' physical education to the great appreciation of other race women and men. Grant's students and colleagues enthusiastically welcomed these lessons, as "the teachers and students of Normal are unstinted in their expressions and gratitude for the great services which she has rendered them."[53] Grant garnered this enthusiasm by merging her physical education lessons with gendered norms of domesticity. While they sought to uplift young people through physical education, Black women teachers remained dedicated to traditional expectations of respectable womanhood.

A more recognizable race woman, reformer Nannie Helen Burroughs, also believed firmly in the gendered advantages of physical education for young Black women. Born in 1879 in Virginia and the daughter of formerly enslaved parents, Burroughs represented the postbellum generation of African Americans who used education, including physical education, as a primary tool for Black social advancement. Producing "fit" students, she believed, constituted a key objective for Black educational institutions. Burroughs once averred that if Black college students "go forward morally clean, spiritually developed, and physically fit," they would "make a place" for themselves in the world.[54] At her own National Training School for Women and Girls in Washington, DC, she assured that the school would inculcate "character" and "personality" in its female students through domestic science and physical culture courses.[55]

Burroughs is usually acknowledged for her staunch advocacy of industrial work and professional domestic labor.[56] An overlooked aspect of Burroughs's legacy, however, is how she linked the physical development of the Black female student body with preparation for the labor market. Burroughs championed traditional notions of womanhood in which women were uniquely suited to make the home and all of its attendant duties—childcare, thrift, and cleanliness—paramount. In her effort to raise young women to what she called "glorified womanhood," Burroughs believed that Black women should be physically prepared for their domestic roles, and physical education, along with "domestic science and the arts," proved vital to this preparation.[57] For some African American women, the domestic body and "glorified" Black womanhood required physical culture.

Black institutions of higher learning endeavored to provide robust fitness programs and exercise spaces for their students. Elite schools, in particular, made sure to create these healthy spaces and advertise their efforts as a selling point and recruitment tool. The all-girls Spelman Seminary in Atlanta (now Spelman College) promoted its commitment to physical culture and public health by describing its dorm rooms. The 1885–86 catalog stated, "Rooms are large, airy, *well heated and ventilated*, and neatly furnished. Grounds are extensive for recreation, and there are delightful walks in every direction" (emphasis in original).[58] Spelman portrayed its institution as a bastion of health with promises of climate control, air circulation, and space for physical activity like walking. At the time, with 600 students enrolled, only privileged women could afford to attend the school.[59] Nevertheless, Black learning institutions often made health and safety fundamental to explaining the quality of education that students would receive. In addition to the ventilated rooms, in the late nineteenth century Spelman began to establish a physical education program and made clear the benefits of exercise. While the school did not house a gymnasium at the time, it partitioned space for female students to exercise and take the "delightful walks" Spelman so proudly described. Spelman's early history of physical education highlights the clear divide in the health prospects for African Americans who could enjoy the salubrious surroundings of an elite college and those who were forced to live in the aforementioned "dark rooms."

When it came to gaining health through physical education programs, financial resources undoubtedly broadened options for exercise. Women of means could afford to enroll in schools that instituted daily physical activity. A well-to-do Black family from the early twentieth century, the

Chisholms, is an apt case in point. Helen James was born in 1876, married Frank Chisholm in 1910, and had a daughter, Helen Emily Chisholm (named after her mother), in 1911. Helen James and Frank Chisholm attended Hampton Normal and Agricultural Institute and Tuskegee Institute, respectively, and Frank Chisholm also spent time at Harvard University. As an educator and freelance writer, Helen James Chisholm served as a pillar of the various places in which she taught and wrote, including Honolulu, St. Helena Island, and Connecticut. Through their education, careers, and social standing, the Chisholms reaped the physical benefits of a decidedly middle-class existence.

Female members of the Chisholm family often partook in physical education, athletics, and more informal leisurely walks, seemingly without much financial trouble. In 1897, Helen James Chisholm wrote down some of the supplies she needed for her courses at Hampton in her student account book. Next to such items as "dictionary" and "board," she listed the cost of a "gym suit."[60] She paid two dollars for the suit, which would total around sixty dollars today. Surely, such purchases would have posed difficulties for struggling Black families at the time, especially during the depression of the 1890s. Hampton developed a physical education program in the 1890s, and if Chisholm participated regularly, she most likely experienced immense health benefits (see fig. 2.2). After her days as a student ended, she decided to partake in less structured forms of physical culture. Her diary notes that she took leisurely walks almost daily when the weather permitted, and at times she played tennis.[61] Her daughter Helen Emily Chisholm played on her school's basketball team and attended practice nearly every weekday. Like her mother, she also played tennis, took long walks, and experienced the advantage of exercising in a school gymnasium.

African American higher education institutions became especially concerned with physical culture for its potential to ensure physical health and to properly "shape" young Black women's bodies and habits.[62] Despite lacking the modern equipment they desired, Black schools placed a premium on physical education for its ability to institutionalize values of bodily control and self-discipline. Critical to the imperative of bodily discipline was the oft-dreaded physical examination. Also called "physical efficiency" exams, these fitness tests included assessments of students' ability to run, jump, and throw, in addition to poise and weight appraisals and medical and hygiene evaluations.[63] At Hampton Institute, Black women physical educators made exercise and physical exams central to

Figure 2.2. An example of the type of physical education Helen James Chisholm most likely enjoyed. "Indian and black girls exercising with medicine ball," Hampton Institute, 1899 or 1900. Frances Benjamin Johnston Collection, Prints and Photographs Division, Library of Congress, LC-USZ62-26789.

molding Black girls' health, bodies, and behaviors. One 1921 report read, "The physical examination also gives the director an opportunity to study the needs of the individual girl and to interest her in reaching a higher level of health by controlling her own habits of exercise, eating, sleep, study, and recreation."[64] Hampton's "higher level of health" imperative shows how some Black physical education programs went beyond defining health as the absence of disease. These PE programs embraced a more holistic view of bodily health and sought to "control" Black girls' behaviors in service of this view.

Physical education allowed Black women to secure notions of "fit" Black womanhood through the aforementioned physical examinations. At Howard University, teachers performed physicals as a way to ensure the general health and fitness of the school's female students. The *Howard University Record* noted in 1923, "One of the many fine things that Dean Slowe was instrumental in bringing about is a physical examination for the young women before registration and incidentally for the whole student body. This formed a very long, trying ordeal, but it will be one more sure telling part of this structure of a womanhood, [that is] physically, mentally, and spiritually fit."[65] "Dean Slowe" referred to Lucy Diggs Slowe, dean of women at Howard and a steadfast advocate of physical assessments as a first step in securing student health. She was, at times, uncompromising about instituting the examinations and mandating exercise for Howard women. She noted that "frequent complaints have been made by students that their work in physical education is too strenuous," but despite their grievances, she retorted adamantly, "Students have to take it."[66] Howard's female students, as well as thousands of other women around the country, "took" physical education to shore up healthy Black female bodies.

YWCA

Like schools, the YWCA served as a critical space for Black women and girls' collective exercise, health education and activism, and expansive conceptualizations of Black health. Black YWCAs proved especially valuable in the first few years after World War I, when African American membership grew exponentially.[67] Black Y leaders used the increased membership and interest in the organization to mold Black girls into their image of health. But Black girls and their elder advocates often struggled to secure the facilities, equipment, and space to materialize their vision of fit Black womanhood.

Fitness facilities operated as one of the most valuable and sought-after tools that reformers used to further their public health goals for Black girls and young women. Black female adolescents, however, found themselves in a web of recreational neglect rationalized by their race, gender, and age. Irene McCoy Gaines, secretary of the Industrial Department of the YWCA in Chicago, expressed great frustration about this neglect: "One may find in the territory known as the 'Black belt' more than 10,000 young women (colored) and girls without adequate recreational facilities (except the most degrading sort—vicious cabarets, cheap dance halls, dingy, ill-ventilated movie houses). The community does not afford her a single swimming pool or gymnasium."[68] Black women like Gaines consistently framed health-sustaining swimming pools and gymnasiums as the diametric opposite of improper leisure venues. The moral and public health repercussions of such outlets concerned African American Y leaders.

Gyms and especially pools proved difficult for Black female patrons to access, while white Ys rarely experienced trouble securing these highly coveted facilities. Historian Martha Verbrugge notes, "If a main YW had first-rate resources, then a separate property for blacks looked more like deliberate discrimination than a goodwill gesture."[69] While white YWCAs sometimes capitulated on racially integrated cooperation, certain kinds of Black-white activities remained verboten. White organizers heavily segregated activities that required the most physical exertion like swimming, basketball, gymnastics, and calisthenics, while sedentary activities like Bible study remained acceptable integrated activities. White YWCA officials believed that physically active Black female bodies posed biological threats to white women.[70] Their consternation reflected dominant public health concerns about the dissemination of "Black" diseases and the putative contamination of white spaces. Venues that fostered close proximity of sweating, heavily breathing, and scantily clad Black and white women became unsettling to the racist status quo.

Occasionally, white Y locations allowed Black women to use their gyms—as long as white women did not occupy the space at the same time. Against their true desires for their own facilities, Black Y leaders sometimes took advantage of this show of "beneficence" from white Ys. In 1916, the *Philadelphia Tribune* announced that the "Central Association [white branch] at 18th and Arch Streets, has opened its gymnasium to the South West [sic] Branch [Black branch] for physical training. It is hoped that our girls and women will take advantage of the opportunity, as a temporary means for physical development, until the Southwest Branch has its own equipped building. Girls' clubs are asked to apply for basketball, indoor tennis, and other forms of physical culture."[71] If the Southwest Branch ever received its gym equipment, it probably took several years for residents to raise the money or to convince the Central Association to allocate funds to the Black branch. Despite the inherent inequality of separate workout facilities, this Black YWCA served as just one of many spaces that afforded Black women the advantage of bettering their health outcomes, bodies, and "physical development" through exercise. This particular Y also highlights the state of Black health at the time. Opportunities to exercise in a state-of-the-art facility were indeed temporary. Black women rarely received consistent, high-quality access to health and fitness outlets like that of the Central Association gymnasium. Instead, they carved out exercise spaces wherever and whenever they could—even for a short time in a segregated gym.

Activist, suffragist, and Black YWCA secretary Addie Waites Hunton of New York also believed in the value of exercise, but she wanted Black women to have their own facilities. Born in 1866 in Virginia, she represents another example of the post-slavery generation of women who actively transformed Black women's health by advocating for physical culture.

Described as a "well known clubwoman and worker for uplift," Hunton in 1912 petitioned to have the Lexington branch of a Black Brooklyn YWCA build a gymnasium in the New York neighborhood. She was inspired by the "scores" of young African American women in the borough who expressed interest in "opportunities for physical culture."[72]

The petition began with a committee meeting in which an interracial group of officers deliberated on making a formal request for gymnasium funds. The guest speaker at the meeting, white physician and women's health advocate Dr. Eliza Mosher, claimed that "shape and symmetry of the body, self-expression, intellect quickened through action, pleasure and recreation and benefits to motherhood" were some of the advantages that the Black Y members could expect with "gymnastic exercises." Mosher added that gymnastic exercise "improves nutrition, destroys the old tissues and gives new life to the body. It helps to carry off the waste, and with it are carried many diseases and ailments common to the human family. It also increases muscle thereby giving strength to the body."[73] The detailed ways in which Mosher discussed the value of exercise captured the national discourse about physical culture circulating in the early twentieth century. African American women were in conversation with some of the leading white health experts and used those conversations to create a Black culture of health and fitness.

The benefits that Mosher highlighted include several aspects of health, including digestive, intestinal, cellular, musculoskeletal, and reproductive. These health benefits, as Mosher mentioned, applied to the "human family," but as head of this Black Y branch, Addie Waites Hunton was well aware of racial and gender discrimination and most likely directed the conversation toward promoting Black women's health. Hunton was especially invested in the welfare of Black girls and defending Black womanhood. She once asserted that "the Negro woman has been the motive power in whatever has been accomplished by the race."[74] At another time, she traveled around the country and delivered lectures to around 2,300 young Black women.[75] Hunton recognized that although segregated, the Y allowed for a safe space for African American women and girls to develop their physical attributes and better their health prospects.

Community Health Programs:
The National Negro Health Week and the Neighborhood Union

Community health programs provided Black women another critical opportunity to use exercise to improve health prospects by lowering the

African American death rate. Tuskegee's clinic, for instance, merged public health, physical culture, and infant and maternal mortality prevention with its National Negro Health Week (NNHW). This health campaign began in 1915, shortly after Booker T. Washington's death, and lasted until 1951.[76] With the exception of hospitals and clinics built exclusively for African Americans, the NNHW was arguably the most successful Black public health initiative of the first half of the twentieth century. The NNHW evolved into a large-scale undertaking that involved dozens of Black healthcare professionals and reached thousands of African Americans. In 1936, thirty states participated in the campaign—health experts delivered 3,832 lectures, 68,700 people attended clinics, and volunteers distributed 160,310 pieces of literature. The list of activities included health pageants, vaccinations, physicals, and dental care services.[77] The 1925 Health Week held a similar program and marketed its platform on a basic "5 Points in Good Health Keeping" agenda, which involved "fresh air, good light, pure water, good food, [and] exercise."[78] Healthcare workers openly promoted exercise as a public health measure during the Health Week.

Nurses held especially insightful viewpoints on the integration of exercise into the NNHW. In a 1929 interview, registered nurse Mary E. Williams spoke with a visitor about her work at a rural health center as part of that year's NNHW campaign. Doctors and nurses associated with the clinic traveled from school to school to perform physicals and administer vaccines for smallpox, malaria, typhoid fever, and diphtheria. The clinic also held club meetings to encourage preventive health care among women. When asked about the obstetric issues health professionals tackled, Williams explained, "Our main object is 1) to decrease the death rate of mothers and babies and 2) to lead the mothers to appreciate the fact that the Doctor is their best friend. We put special emphasis on urinalysis for the protection against kidney trouble. Diet, exercise and air are emphasized. We tell them that pregnancy is normal. God never intended a woman to die in child birth."[79] As told by Williams, diet, clean air, and exercise, all key elements of physical culture, were behaviors that nurses stressed in the women's health portion of the 1929 Health Week. The exact number of women whom Nurse Williams and her colleagues reached that year is unknown, but if the aforementioned figures are valid, the number of poor women who received this kind of health counseling may have amounted to hundreds, if not thousands, of patients. Black women public health crusaders connected mortality, reproduction, and physical fitness in deliberate ways that addressed women's health and Black premature death.

Figure 2.3. A makeshift playground provided by the Neighborhood Union. Foundry Street Playground, 1912, Neighborhood Union Collection, Atlanta University Center Robert W. Woodruff Library.

Like the NNHW, the Neighborhood Union (NU) made significant health inroads in early twentieth-century Georgia. Founded in 1908 through the concerted efforts of Black women, the organization sought to improve the west side neighborhood of Atlanta by offering civic and social services, including public works, health and recreational facilities, and neighborhood beautification.[80] Once the founders realized that municipalities would not meet the health needs of Black Atlantans, they resorted to traditional strategies of self-help and mutual cooperation. One of the NU's primary aims was to "provide playgrounds, clubs, good literature, and Neighborhood centers for the moral, physical, and intellectual development of the young."[81] The Black female leaders of the NU believed "physical development" was so vital to community health that in addition to building clinics and securing trained nurses, they purchased a settlement house, offered "sport and games for the young of the community,"[82] and assembled a playground through a large-scale community fundraising and equipment donation effort (see fig. 2.3).[83] Black women of the NU volunteered to "supervise the play and protect the property" of the first playground in Atlanta for Black children.[84] As they worked to create spaces of physical development, they also broadened notions of Black public health.

Surveying Black Atlanta through house-to-house visits and other means of community assessment proved critical to the NU's public health measures. From the advent of the organization, Black women prioritized community health by conducting home visits to discuss tuberculosis prevention, hygiene, and sanitation. Black nurses from Spelman Seminary and Grady Hospital led home-care demonstrations that eventually expanded to health work in NU-established clinics.[85] Physical examinations, naturally, constituted an essential feature of in-home and in-clinic work and helped to gauge the need for physical culture and other community health interventions.

Although community health assessors assumed their roles with good intentions, some of these bodily examinations contained explicit, class-based medical objectives for both the examiners and the examined. In 1927, a small group of Black Atlanta women associated with the Neighborhood Union "weighed, measured, and examined" 518 poverty-stricken patients to chart health disparities in their community.[86] Their reports represented more than mere compendiums of health deficiencies; they also included concerns about Black brain development, physical strength, and deportment. Within their field notes, Black women surveyors offered solutions to these "defects" that often included, in part or in whole, physical culture. This group of surveyors were typically middle-class African American women. When they traveled to poor families' homes, they came with measurement apparatuses in hand—scales, measuring tape, charts, tongue depressors, and notepaper. These items served as tools that middle-class Black women used to interpret both physical and racial health.

Poor and working-class Black women usually bore the brunt of both middle-class Black and white-led health crusades. Poor Black women became the source of public health angst and surveillance in the early twentieth century. Because so many African American women worked as domestics at this time and carried age-old stigmas about questionable morality, hygiene, and chastity, they came under exceptional scrutiny about their place in the white home. In Atlanta, concerned white citizens proposed that Black domestic workers undergo tuberculosis exams, reifying TB as "the Negro servant's disease."[87] In New York, middle-class white women reformers supported various health tests and regulations for the Black women who entered their residences to work.[88]

While middle-class Black women who performed health assessments were not necessarily concerned with the safety of white homes, they sought to lecture, enlighten, and correct the putatively misguided ways of working-class and poor women. The founders of the Neighborhood Union, for example, were described as "a group of refined and cultured Negro women on the West Side" who served neighborhood women who rarely, if ever, received similar descriptions.[89] In the absence of neighborhood women's voices, it is important to imagine how poor Black women on the receiving end of public health and physical culture programs may have felt when they saw their middle-class counterparts approaching their homes, children, and bodies for inspection. It would be idealistic to assume that all Black women were always receptive to the efforts of Black health activists, even those advocates who performed critical, life-sustaining work in their communities. Middle-class Black women health workers, indeed, yearned for Black people's ultimate health and physical development. Nevertheless, this yearning became conflated with desires for Black propriety, racial fitness, and racial destiny.

Exercise, Eugenics, and the "Round-Shouldered Girl" Trope

Bernarr Macfadden believed that for health to be "known," it must be "seen."[90] "Seeing" health also proved paramount for African American physical culturists, health advocates, and concerned citizens, many of whom expressed dismay about a disturbing trend they observed in Black girls and young women. They took special note of the "round-shouldered girl" who suffered from ailing health, low energy, bodily asymmetry, and a lethargic demeanor. Exercise and other bodily practices became key interventions in the health and physique of supposedly unfit, round-shouldered girls. These interventions would enable young Black women to alter their postures and project physical and more notional forms of fitness.

Physical educators served as important agents in surveilling, diagnosing, and correcting round-shouldered girls. They did not provide photographic examples of this figure, but their descriptions proved illustrative. A. W. Ellis, assistant director of health and physical education at the historically Black West Virginia State College, described the severe need for physical education programs for these "deformed" young Black women. He concluded from his study of thousands of African American female students from fifty-two Black colleges and universities that revamped physical education programs "would help the round shouldered girl and the excessively fat girl to develop a symmetrical figure; the girl with the weak heart to engage in harmless activities and perhaps help her gain physical strength. With proper supervision many deformities may be corrected by some treatment in the department. It is the writer's sincere opinion that careful attention should be given to methods of developing strong, well-formed bodies."[91] Physical educators like Ellis would not tolerate the paunchy, weak, or round-shouldered girl. Ellis worried that Black higher education institutions focused too much on "acquiring academic training" and neglected women's physical training. While male students were offered "competitive athletics," young women's "physical activities," to Ellis's dismay, were given "little attention."[92] His remarks represent the disparate treatment that women and men received. Weight reduction did not function as a central concern for male physical education as it did for young women. Other matters of poise, posture, and symmetry also demarcated how physical educators approached PE for African American girls and boys, highlighting the added corporal burdens that young Black women carried.

Ellis's report is representative of the gendered conclusions that many health surveyors drew after they performed their assessments. Ellis and his contemporaries framed their female subjects as "deformed" and, in essence, created a diagnostic trope of a debilitated round-shouldered girl—a shorthand reference for young women they believed desperately needed physical culture. Educators and health professionals needed to "see" the health of these young people to ensure that they were indeed well. The physical proof lay in healthy, strong, and capable Black female bodies. While this is clear in Ellis's study, others helped create this trope and worried about what was at stake for these girls, their figures, and their futures.

Black journalists referred to women's "rounded" shoulders as an aesthetic shortcoming with potential medical consequences and character flaws. One African American woman writer cautioned that rounded shoulders "piles on additional years thickly," framing the condition as a menace to both youth and slenderness.[93] Another columnist, Madame Qui Vive, admonished of round shoulders, "Time will produce a permanent hump on the shoulders. The lung box will be so contracted that breathing will not be free and natural."[94] Apparently, round shoulders triggered serious consequences of the internal organs. Qui Vive, however, was not only concerned with medical ramifications. She also noted, "Throw the shoulders forward, let the back be rounded, and you'll assume the pose of discouragement and defeat. Lazy girls look like that, too. Too inert to

carry their bones about. Very bad!"[95] African Americans had worked especially hard throughout the nineteenth and twentieth centuries to counter
assumptions about Black indolence, and "rounded shoulders" seemed to
reinforce such pernicious notions. It is no wonder that "round-shouldered
girls" captured the imagination of Black health advocates. Their bodies
seemed to consolidate fears of visual debility, health adversity, and racial
stigma.

Historians Ava Baron and Eileen Boris contend that when studying
"the body," one must examine how the body functioned as a marker of
social difference.[96] Certain physical characteristics like round shoulders
did not merely indicate poor posture but also served as signals of morality, class, and fitness for citizenship. African Americans used physical
markers to delineate those who needed physical development and those
whose developed bodies could serve political purposes for the race.
Middle-class Black political and social agendas often rested upon Black
women's fit physiques—bodies that presented as vigorous, healthy, and
symmetrical.

Black women, consequently, bore the burden of reducing markers of
social difference and embodying "good" citizenship by producing healthy
progeny. As the first line of defense, Black women were expected to keep
themselves "strong and healthy" so that their children would inherit these
same qualities. For instance, at the 1894 Arkansas conference of Black
Baptist mothers, organizers asked, "How will the improvement of mothers,
mentally, morally, and physically, benefit their children?" The mothers
divided the answers by the three categories listed in the question. The
"physical" category espoused a eugenic, biologically determinant stance:
"According to Nature. If a mother is strong and healthy, her children as a
general thing will be healthy, or if the mother is weakly and in poor health
her children, with few exceptions, will grow up having a weak constitution.
. . . So let us as mothers try to improve all things good, since we know that
the improvement of our children depends greatly upon our own improvement."[97] Similar sentiments concerning the transmissibility of health continued into the twentieth century. In a more explicit explanation of the
mother-child connection, the National Association of Colored Women
stated in the 1930s that an "informed and careful motherhood" would
enable Black women "to produce a virile race."[98] The reproductive pressure for Black women to produce a "virile race" certainly inspired a desire
for physical fitness, enthusiasm for exercise, and a robust public health
campaign. This pressure was especially severe for young Black women on

the precipice of their reproductive years and in danger of morphing into "round-shouldered girls."

Eugenic anxieties about the physical and reproductive fitness of Black girls and the future of the race crystallized in spaces of physical culture. Ruth Arnett, a Black YWCA secretary, felt strongly about unfit young Black women and their future offspring. Out of frustration with Black girls who were too weak to complete their gymnasium exercises, she complained, "It is amazing to find large numbers of teen-age girls in the high schools who have been excused from gym for some trivial excuse. She can't run, she can't hike, she can't play tennis. . . . If this round-shouldered, flat-chested girl is to be our mother of tomorrow, what will the children be?"[99] African Americans used the "round-shouldered girl" as a cautionary trope to warn of a dismal future of unfit Black people and placed responsibility on Black women to reverse the trend. The gym served as the ideal place to correct these inadequacies and a space to reduce the concerns of women like Arnett, for whom these problems seemed dire. African American women advocated physical culture so that young Black girls could cultivate the next generation of a viable and robust Black population (see fig. 2.4).

The eugenic investment in Black girls' health, exercise, and athletics was also informed by anticipations of racial competition. In 1917, the *Norfolk New Journal and Guide* featured Miss Phyllis Waters on the front page with the heading "Colored Girl Makes Good." The paper stated boldly, "Again, a daughter of the race, in competition with the best stock of the favored people of the land has proven that blood will tell." Apparently, "the favored people" functioned as a shorthand for "white," but Waters did not compete with ordinary white people but with the "best stock" of whites. That was irrelevant, however, when Waters's pedigree, ancestry, and "sound mind in a sound body" proved no match for her white contemporaries. The *New Journal* described Waters's many accomplishments, which are impressive by today's standards, and was undoubtedly remarkable in the 1910s. She graduated with honors from the University of Michigan and was a star athlete, becoming skilled at gymnastics and serving as the basketball team captain. Waters was "ardently devoted" to "physical culture" and planned to pursue a career as a physical education teacher.[100]

Black girls who "made good" present a discursive case in point in which ideas of health, fitness, and racial competition converged under the banners of physical culture, and in these cases, Black girls embodied these ideas. One can imagine that the article's author, readers of the newspaper,

Figure 2.4. This image represents the kinds of physical training A. W. Ellis and Ruth Arnett had in mind. These exercises, they believed, would correct round-shouldered girls by making their bodies stronger, fitter, and "well-formed." Here, members of the Black Girl Reserves of the YWCA exhibit balance, coordination, agility, and preparedness through military demonstrations. Jane Olcott, *The Work of Colored Women* (New York: Colored Work Committee War Work Council, 1919), 95. Schomburg Center for Research in Black Culture, Jean Blackwell Hutson Research and Reference Division, New York Public Library Digital Collections.

and physical educators would interpret Waters as the diametric opposite of the round-shouldered girl. Indeed, some Black people adopted a eugenic approach toward notions of racial advancement, and physical culture informed this approach.

Anxieties about Black "round-shouldered girls" expose the fraught nature of exercise-infused public health work. "Fixing" the round-shouldered girl served as a method for Black people to distance themselves from both the stigma of poor health and the present and impending dangers of physical "deformity." Avoiding stigma, addressing real health concerns, and thinking of posterity became intertwined in the eugenic public health landscape of the early twentieth century. It is difficult to disentangle the ways in which public health programs allowed African Americans to both materially improve Black health and dream of positive racial destiny. Their public health work vacillated between a problematic, elitist venture and a campaign that allowed Black people to imagine a different future for themselves. The complex, health-informed struggle for citizenship created these entanglements of good intentions, negative implications, material benefits, and hopes for a better future.

)(

Motivated by public health imperatives, Black women engaged in exercise to improve, strengthen, and ensure the longevity of the race. Focusing on their physical culture allows us to see how African American women invested in the entire body—their reproductive systems, respiratory and cardiac functioning, and even mental health. Black women resorted to exercise to expand tangible health outcomes. In more conceptual ways, exercise culture provided a forum for Black women to compete for racial advancement. Some African Americans promoted physical culture as a hedge against Black girls' physical "defects" and exploited the movement for eugenic purposes. Using body measurements and other tools, middle-class Black women exerted their class privilege by marking deficiencies in poor Black populations. Regardless of their motivations, African American women found ways to circumvent numerous barriers to fitness.

The history of Black exercise provides a unique perspective of African American women's health and their multifaceted roles in public health programs. Black women represented the vanguard of Black physical culture in two ways. First, by choice, they actively sought employment and volunteer opportunities that would allow them to disseminate information on health and exercise as well as challenge segregated spaces of fitness. Second, by force—as "reproducers"—they carried the burden of demonstrating fitness in order to bear the next generation. Fit, healthy bodies held special meaning for Black women seeking to remake themselves and their futures, and exercise proved vital in their efforts. Beauty attained through exercise, as shown in the following chapter, also bore significant implications for how African American women reimagined themselves in the twentieth century.

CHAPTER 3

Plenty of Good Exercise

BEAUTY, FATNESS, AND THE FIT BLACK FEMALE BODY IN THE INTERWAR YEARS

In 1927, Madame Sara Washington, a Black beauty columnist for the *New York Amsterdam News*, wrote an article titled "Beauty Secrets: Fight Fat." The mere title alerted readers to the incongruous nature of fatness and beauty. Washington explained that exercise was fundamental to warding off "excess fat" and obtaining a beautiful body. She stated, "There is positively nothing that will aid beauty more than plenty of good exercise in the open." With a thriving cosmetics industry in the late 1920s, it may appear unusual that Washington did not recommend makeup, hair products, or the latest beauty trend on the market. More curiously, this advice seems atypical, as the scholarship on Black women's beauty culture is virtually silent about exercise. Washington, however, was among several beauty experts who recommended exercise to improve one's appearance. These women did not relegate Black beauty culture to just the face, skin, and hair—they used physical culture to conceptualize beauty as it applied to the entire body.

Washington described exercise as a "beauty secret" feasible for Black women of all ages and economic circumstances. Understanding that Black women faced significant economic barriers to exercise, fitness enthusiasts like Washington thought of ways to make exercise accessible. Anticipating excuses from her readers, Madame Washington explained, "If you complain that you can't 'go in' for sports, have no swimming pools, can't dance without music, can't afford to join the 'Y' or clubs where tennis, golf, basketball, hockey and bowling are supplied, haven't friends to join with you in winter or summer sports, or have reached years where your dignity will not permit you to be too youthful in your tastes, still and always, while you have your legs, you can WALK."[1] Washington enumerated every objection she could muster to underscore that Black women could, at the very least, walk for the sake of health and beauty.

In reality, Washington's advice was not a beauty secret and was not as accessible as she imagined. Scores of other Black women held similar beliefs about using exercise to attain beautiful and healthy physiques. Some Black women married beauty culture with physical culture and made exercise instrumental to notions of respectable Black womanhood and the civilized body. Women like Howard University physical educator Maryrose Reeves Allen believed that "everything in the health service and physical education points to the glorification of fine womanhood."[2] The "fine womanhood" to which Allen referred contained deep-seated class dimensions. Middle-class Black women, including beauty columnists, writers, teachers, college students, and clubwomen, used physical culture to advance their models of the fit and beautiful Black body.[3] Women with similar perspectives as Washington and Allen spoke to literate, newspaper-reading, college-educated women about the virtues of physical culture. They also advocated exercise as a weight loss method, which certainly represented a middle-class imperative. These women expressed discomfort about obesity and drew a relationship between smaller body sizes and attractiveness.

A focus on well-to-do Black women and their ideas of beauty may appear to be a narrowly defined study about elitism. But as previous chapters show, even middle-class Black women lacked full access to mainstream white exercise culture. In light of this exclusion, this chapter reveals how some middle-class African Americans created a fuller and more complex picture of Black women as modern, attractive, and fit. They understood the barriers to fitness and, at times, attempted to make physical culture more accessible to a larger population of Black women. Middle-class women used exercise to offer their contemporaries an alternative to problematic images of Black women as overweight servants who confined their mobility to domestic work. Although the field of African American history has produced many accounts of Black elites, the scholarship has yet to fully account for how middle-class Black people thought about the full physical and symbolic power of their bodies.[4] Exploring their beauty standards through physical culture is one way to understand this vital yet underexplored aspect of Black women's history.

With issues of class in mind, this chapter examines the nexus between ideas of fatness, beauty, and Black womanhood between the 1910s and 1940. It argues that middle-class Black women used exercise to promote their ideals of beauty, slimness, and the respectable Black body during the interwar years. From the turn of the twentieth century and particularly after World War I, Americans began to associate slimness with patriotism, good citizenship, attractiveness, and many other positive qualities. Not coincidentally, elite African Americans began to stigmatize fatness and encourage Black women to slim down, beautify, and improve their bodies through exercise. By identifying explicit historical examples of Black anti-fat bias, this chapter uses physical culture to expand how we think about beauty, Black women, and their bodies.

This study of Black beauty and physical culture illuminates how the body functioned as an important political space for African American women. Middle-class Black people understood that productive, fit, and responsible bodies fulfilled the desires of the state. Fat bodies, in contrast, projected dishonor and defied dominant medical and political treatises of the time. During this era of emerging fat denigration, mainstream physical culture publications represented white women's bodies as beautiful, graceful, and healthy—qualities that Black women ostensibly lacked. In response to this presumption, Black women used physical culture to offer replacement images of themselves as slim, desirable, and in good health against dominant portrayals of Black women as sick, overweight, and unattractive. This chapter, then, is not concerned with the actual weight and size of Black women or the physical ramifications of adipose tissue. Rather, it is interested in how Black women responded to the notion that they were excessively overweight and the role of physical culture in challenging that notion.

The following pages explore the relationship between health and beauty in the larger physical culture movement and propose new ways to conceptualize the history of Black beauty culture. The chapter continues with an examination of Black women's capacious definitions of beauty that did not always champion thinness and then transitions to a more robust discussion of Black women who strived for the fit, thin, and respectable body. I show that through their participation in the fitness zeitgeist, Black women sought to shed themselves of the liabilities of fatness and challenge assumptions about African American aesthetic values.

Health and Beauty in Mainstream Physical Culture

Advocates of women's exercise grounded physical culture in a belief that the healthy body amounted to the beautiful body and vice versa. White purveyors of health and exercise, however, did not apply this maxim to African Americans. Exercise books, magazines, pamphlets, and consumer products depicted white women as beautiful and civilized while excluding non-white groups from their pages. In exercise print culture, white women's bodies served as sites to measure the health and progress of the nation, ideal motherhood, and modern concepts of beauty.[5]

Physical culturists inundated the market with exercise equipment, health aids, and print material that they assured would help women realize their healthy and beautiful selves. White women authored texts like *The Body Beautiful* (1902), *Health and Beauty Hints* (1910), *Lydia E. Pinkham's Private Text-Book* (1910), and *The Art of Feminine Beauty* (1930) that not only provided advice on hair, skin, and cosmetics but also on how exercise could improve one's overall appearance.[6] Many of these texts captured the broad meaning of physical culture by including information on nutrition, proper breathing techniques, bathing, digestion, and calisthenics. They attracted female readers by highlighting the beauty benefits of these health regimens, particularly after World War I, when more women became consumers of cosmetics.[7] But physical culturists commented on health and beauty before the cosmetics boom. Nannette Magruder Pratt, the author of *The Body Beautiful*, stated confidently, "Some women want to be well, some want to be strong; all want to be beautiful. My opinion is that unless a woman is well and strong she is not beautiful."[8] According to Pratt and her contemporaries, exercise helped women maintain strong, healthy, and beautiful bodies. They not only linked strength to beauty but also noted the importance of these qualities for the early twentieth-century "New Woman."[9]

White men also authored texts on women's health and urged readers to exercise. In his 1904 manual on women's jujitsu, writer H. Irving Hancock claimed, "The day has gone by when women prize weakness as a dainty attribute of their sex, and the science of jujitsu points out the path for the new physical woman to pursue. Be Strong! There is neither grace nor beauty in weakness."[10] Authors of prominent physical culture books repeatedly associated exercise with beauty and strength. Hancock and his colleagues remarked that the New Woman left Victorian ideas about bodily propriety behind and embraced strength as a veritable marker of modern womanhood. Also commenting on physicality and womanhood, Bernarr Macfadden asserted around the same time that "womanhood might be termed a physical attribute" and affirmed that a "powerful physique," muscular development, and athleticism constituted the "feminine gender."[11]

Rhetoric that linked strength, athleticism, and womanhood permeated the physical culture movement. The best way to achieve these qualities, according to physical culturists, was through calisthenics, gymnastics, and sports like tennis and basketball. Through his *Physical Culture* magazine, Macfadden demonstrated the specific exercises that would ensure female beauty. He conducted the demonstrations himself or solicited the help of his family members or models. Readers could perform these exercises without equipment or maximize their results with globe weights and "exercisers" advertised in the magazines. Macfadden enticed women further into the movement through the magazine *Woman's Physical Development*. The first issue introduced American women to the burgeoning exercise print world precisely at the turn of the century. White subscribers to the magazine sought experts' suggestions on what they could do to become modern, healthy, and attractive women.

Exercise print culture also fomented interest in physical culture through its vivid portrayals of white female bodily perfection. In addition to articles on child-rearing and female athletes, the inaugural issue of *Woman's Physical Development* provided several images of the perfect woman's body. The feature article, written by Macfadden, titled "The Development of Womanly Beauty," instructed readers on the exercises they could perform to improve their busts through chest-expanding movements.[12] Macfadden directed readers to focus on two images: the first of a clothed woman draped in a white gown and the second of a bare-breasted white woman portraying the paragon of beauty (see figs. 3.1A and 3.1B).[13]

These images and the accompanying article concerned "the woeful ignorance of the average woman" who lacked the body, skill, or knowledge that the modern physical woman possessed.[14] The issue clearly targeted middle-class white women with lofty aspirations of voluptuous breasts. Editorials like this illuminate the potentially salacious nature of physical culture in which sex undergirded Macfadden's enterprise. Subsequent pages of the article featured instructional photographs of another white woman performing chest movements in body-hugging clothing—stretching, bending, and thrusting to achieve the perfect bosom. Macfadden engaged in controversial debates about sex and nudity and was often subject to obscenity laws because of his insistence on displaying women's bodies in such suggestive ways.[15] He even sought a presidential pardon from Howard Taft for his indiscretions in 1909.[16] Physical culture allowed white women to challenge ideas of propriety through provocative displays of their bodies, apparently in the name of health.[17] This component of physical culture, unsurprisingly, did not appeal to most respectability-bound Black women, and they, therefore, had to carve out their own less risqué fitness campaigns.[18]

Woman's Physical Development

FROM THE PAINTING "SAPPHO" BY PERRAULT

The Development of Womanly Beauty
By Bernarr Macfadden

How the Chest and Bust may be Developed and Beautified and Unsightly Hollows filled in

HE woeful ignorance of the average woman in reference to the proper care and thorough development of her body is deplorable. If her chest is flat, and angular outlines have appeared where there should be rounded curves she grieves in secret, and searches for some tonic or other means of "getting fat." Some even go so far as to imagine that all defects will be remedied if they can only be fat. Fat does not give shape to the body any more than paint gives shape to a wall. Fat simply covers over and fills in the hollows of the form made by the muscular and boney framework.

Therefore, if the body is angular or ill-shaped the first object should always be the development of the muscles that a proper and symmetrical

FROM THE PAINTING "STUDY," BY C. VOIL, 1892 SALON

Figure 3.1A. Illustration of Sappho in the article "The Development of Womanly Beauty." *Woman's Physical Development*, October 1900, 14.

Figure 3.1B. Illustration of O. Voil's *Study* in the article "The Development of Womanly Beauty." *Woman's Physical Development*, October 1900, 15.

Popular exercise literature exalted middle-class white women as the ideal and universal woman into the 1920s. Dr. John Hewins Kern's 1925 book on women's bodies and health, *Glorious Womanhood*, featured depictions of healthy, angelic, and ethereal-looking white women. Kern claimed that "there is no excuse for a woman to have an ugly body" and that physical culture was the "Aladdin's lamp" by which women could "remake" themselves.[19] The book also advertised the "minute exerciser" that Kern promised would reduce unsightly flabbiness and secure women's "abundant health." Helen Macfadden, Bernarr Macfadden's daughter, served as the model for the exerciser. As an ebullient example of physical culture's benefits, Helen Macfadden seemingly embodied the perfect combination of fitness and beauty.

In addition to using exercise to become healthier, American women sought thinner physiques through physical culture, as demonstrated in print media. Throughout the late nineteenth and early twentieth centuries, Americans increasingly regarded fatness pejoratively, and women became primary targets of these changing ideas about the body. The golden age of anthropometrics, changes in fashion and clothing manufacturing, the association between fatness and political corruption, and middle-class anxieties about slimness and self-restraint all deemed thin bodies ideal.[20] World War I amplified fat stigmatization due to the focus on food scarcity, physical fitness for war, and overall support for the war effort. Dr. Lulu Hunt Peters, nutrition expert and former Public Health Committee chair of the California Federation of Women's Clubs, asserted amid the conflict, "Now fat individuals have always been considered a joke, but you are a joke no longer. Instead of being looked upon with friendly tolerance and amusement, you are now viewed with distrust, suspicion, and even aversion." She admonished, "How dare you hoard fat when our nation needs it?" in her best-selling 1918 book, *Diet and Health with Key to the Calories*.[21] Peters's perspective represented a mounting sentiment among ordinary Americans that fatness indicated not only a personal failing but also a defeat for the state. Early twentieth-century health writers like Peters made unequivocal connections between slimness, patriotism, and citizenship.

As dedicated physical culture literature tended to embrace lean bodies, so did women's magazines. Popular women's periodicals like *Cosmopolitan* and *Good Housekeeping* advertised before and after photographs of white women who lost weight by dancing to aerobic "reducing" records, capturing the quest for thinness in the 1920s.[22] Using "Mrs. Derby" as a success story, *Cosmopolitan* explained to readers that Derby had shed a "mountainous burden of flesh," 103 pounds to be exact, through Wallace Reducing Records. The magazine mentioned that Derby, though "fat beyond hope" at first, later slimmed down to a normal size after four months of exercising to music (see fig. 3.2). Advertisers reified white bodies as healthy and beautiful, and if those bodies did not reflect said qualities, at the very least they could transform through products that promised to purge and reduce.

Sources on white women's physical culture are plentiful, but they tell only a partial story about the full range of women's beauty and fitness pursuits. Mainstream books and magazines suggest that only white women cared to beautify their bodies through exercise. But African American women also sought the beauty rewards that exercise offered, although with some social and economic adjustments. Black women had much at stake when it came to self-presentation, and, in turn, they created their own version of a combined physical and beauty culture.

Black Beauty Culture

The phenomenon of Black women's intertwined beauty and physical culture is less obvious because of historians' focus on the economic and entrepreneurial implications of the Black beauty industry. They describe, for example, the oppressive aspects of the business that used Eurocentric images to market Black beauty products, as well as how beauty culturists improved the economic standing of their communities through their work in the beauty industry.[23] While white physical culturists regarded exercise as a potential entrepreneurial venture, by and large, Black participants of the physical culture movement did not. Examining Black beauty culture as strictly entrepreneurial works to overlook the beauty practices (such as exercise) that did not have much business potential for African Americans.

Aside from the emphasis on industry, physical culture eludes the literature because discussions of hair and facial cosmetics dominate in the scholarship on African American beauty practices, with little reference to how body shape and fitness also influenced Black beauty culture. We know from the extant scholarship, for instance, that a rail-thin flapper aesthetic appealed to white women in the 1920s, but it is unknown whether Black women adopted similar ideas. As explained, diet and exercise helped the "modern" white woman achieve popular concepts of a slim and beautiful body. Evidence shows that Black women also valued these notions from the start of the modern exercise movement. They perceived beauty from the perspective of the entire body and used exercise to achieve a comely, middle-class physique.

At the same time that white physical culturists linked health to beauty, Black women expressed that they too could not detach notions of attractiveness from physical health.[24] Physical educator Maryrose Reeves Allen's academic work provides critical insights on this health-beauty tandem. Allen taught physical education at Hampton Institute and headed the women's Department of Physical Education at Howard University until the 1960s. Her thesis, written in fulfillment of her physical training degree,

Losing 103 lbs. to Music!

Wallace Makes New Record Reducing Mrs. Derby in Less than 4 Months

BEFORE   **AFTER**

ASTONISHING CHANGE BROUGHT ABOUT BY ONLY FOUR MONTHS' USE OF THE FAMOUS WALLACE REDUCING RECORDS

By William R. Durgin

QUINCY, ILLS.—In a happy little community of homes which fringe Vine street, I discovered Quincy's happiest woman. All because she accepted an invitation to try a novel way of getting rid of a mountainous burden of flesh. Only last January, she was fat beyond hope. By May, her weight was normal!

To readers who are overweight—a few pounds, or many —I shall offer Mrs. Derby's amazing experience, just as it was related to me:

"When the postman brought the phonograph record with a free reducing lesson, I never dreamed Mr. Wallace could make me weigh what I should. The best I had hoped for was a little relief—for I could scarcely get around, I was so heavy.

"The first few days of the course showed nothing, except I guess I felt better. After a time I began to lose. One day at market I stepped on the scales, and saw I had lost twenty pounds. Needless to say, I kept on with the records. Each week showed a little more reduction, until before long the neighbors all noticed the difference. I kept on losing right along, and I finally was down to the size my last picture shows."

Now, one might think 103 lbs. reduction in only four months required the most strenuous efforts. But Mrs. Derby did nothing extraordinary; she followed the regular instruction that Wallace gives anybody. It was no harder to reduce her than those but ten, twelve,

or twenty pounds overweight—it merely required more time.

To get thin to music is really a "lark" compared to any other method of reducing. In fact, Mr. Harry Derby told me his household was frankly skeptical of real results when his wife started the Wallace course, just because it all looked and sounded too good to be true. There is nothing to "take," you don't have to starve; just a few movements with a thrill to each—that seem all too short because they are set to music. I guess it's the sheer fun of *doing* it that starts so many men and women on the melody method of reducing. But it's the sudden, certain *results*—the fat that's played away to the tune of a pound a day—that keeps them enthusiastically at it, and telling others about it.

Mr. Newman, Quincy photographer (notice his signature to statement above), took two photos of Mrs. Harry Derby which are reproduced here. This is an indisputable evidence of Mrs. Derby's improvement—just as the camera saw it. I only wish you could see the lady herself! Not a sign of flabbiness, nor a wrinkle to show where the excess flesh had been. I am almost willing to believe her assertion: "I can now do anything a 15-year-old girl can do!"

I have met scores who restored normal weight and measurements by Wallace's novel, and so enjoyable method. My sister reduced by it, so did a brother; and two aunts of mine swear by it. Forty or fifty lbs. reduction through use of these remarkable records is fairly common. But Mrs. Derby's

achievement—103 pounds in a few days less than four months—sets a new record.

Are *you* overweight? And if you are, why remain so? *A normal figure is possible to anyone who has a phonograph, and will* *give Wallace's music method of reducing a chance.* The above should be sufficient proof of this, but Wallace still offers free proof in your own case.

Your simple request on the handy form below brings the full first lesson free of any charge whatever. A regular-sized, and double-face phonograph record, and photographic chart with complete instructions. Pay nothing; promise nothing, except to *try* it. Results will cause you to send for the rest of his course in a hurry!

Don't ponder another day as to whether Wallace can reduce *you*. Tear out this coupon, and let him prove he *can*.

WALLACE,
    630 S. Wabash Ave., Chicago:

Please send record for the first reducing lesson; free and prepaid. I will either enroll, or mail back your record at the end of a five-day trial.

Name... (715)

St. and No..

P.O. .... State...............
    Canadian Address: 62 Albert St., Winnipeg

Figure 3.2. Advertisement for weight loss records featuring Mrs. Derby. "Losing 103 lbs. to Music!," *Cosmopolitan*, December 1922, 145.

demonstrated the inextricable connection between health and beauty. She understood beauty to be twofold, consisting of a "physical" component, which included proper form, proportion, symmetry, posture, and poise, and a "physiological" component, comprising expression, charm, coordination, temperament, and color. For Allen, many of these beauty qualities required health and, most importantly, exercise.[25] To earn her degree, Allen created scales for measuring levels of women's beauty. Using college women as her sample, she explained in one of her assessments that "the results of these tests plus all others are to be used in a composite score for the entire body." Considering Allen's training, it is unsurprising that she considered the whole body in her ideas of health and pulchritude. Women like Allen thought of beauty as a corporal and physical quality, not merely a facial one.

Even those who did not receive formal training in physical education advised Black women to consider the relationship between middle-class ideas of beauty, exercise, and modern womanhood. In fact, the preoccupation with the beauty component of physical culture began early for African Americans. A 1902 article in the *Baltimore Afro-American* titled "Exercise Promotes Beauty in Women" stated that if the "modern woman" wanted to be "fascinating, brilliant, and beautiful," she would have to do so through athletics and exercise.[26] Even earlier, in his essay on Black amusement, W. E. B. Du Bois, arguably the foremost Black intellectual of the time, drew a parallel between women's athleticism and attractiveness. He proposed, "Here again athletic sports must in the future play a larger part in the normal and mission schools of the South, and we must rapidly come to the place where . . . the young woman who cannot walk a couple of good country miles will have few proposals of marriage."[27] While not commenting directly on beauty, Du Bois's statement presented a correlation between physical ability, fitness, and desirability.

Purveyors of Black beauty products also endorsed exercise as a path to comeliness. In an unconventional publication, which included the history of African-descended people, cosmetic ads, and horoscopes, the Black beauty entrepreneur Anthony Overton encouraged Black women's exercise in his 1921 *Encyclopedia of Colored People*. The book presented physical culture, in the form of athletics, as an ideal way to achieve beauty. As a successful owner of the High Brown cosmetics company, Overton cornered a considerable portion of the Black beauty market. Speaking specifically to Black women, the *Encyclopedia* stated, "Tennis, golf, and other outdoor games are pleasing methods of obtaining both exercise and recreation necessary to the woman who desires to become beautiful."[28] High Brown created a strong relationship between Black beauty culture and exercise, which is profound considering Overton's investment in a cosmetics industry that favored consumer products over more "natural" beauty solutions. More explicitly, the *Encyclopedia* noted, "As the foundation of a structure is of the utmost importance, just so the foundation of all beauty, health is of primary importance. Skin foods and hair growers can only begin where Nature leaves off and as cleanliness is the basis of all external treatment, cleanliness is also the basis of all internal treatment. To keep the blood pure is an essential of good health. This may be done by the means of proper exercise and dieting."[29] Consumer goods, indeed, could not meet all aspects of women's beauty needs. Overton admitted that these beauty aids—his stock-in-trade—could go only so far in securing the true source of beauty. He classified exercise as a beauty ritual, which signaled the various ways in which Black women could improve their images.

Literature on Black physical culture in the form of theses, newspaper articles, and encyclopedias provide verbal testimony of the beauty benefits of exercise, but photography presents rich visual evidence of Black women's exercise habits. Visual imagery is especially illustrative of the confluence of beauty, exercise, and sport. In the early twentieth century, portraiture constituted the most popular form of photography, which makes it difficult to locate sport-related "action" photos. However, the action photography that exists provides fruitful terrain for analyses on Black women's combined physical and beauty culture. In a series of images that tennis player Amanda Falker took for the *Chicago Daily News* in 1909, the paper presented the optical combination of beauty and sport in motion (see figs. 3.3A and 3.3B). In these photographs, Falker moves across the court, seemingly unrestricted in her dress, swinging her racket in return of a serve. With her hair coiffed perfectly and her dress in compliance with the strength and agility required of tennis, Falker impressed dexterity, poise, and beauty upon her viewers. Falker's choice of hairstyle, dress, posture, and movement represents what visual culture theorist Tina Campt terms "records of intentions"—images that evidence the subject's aspirations, articulations, and self-imaginings. Amanda Falker's photographs are not merely a record of what happened one day in 1909 but are "personal and social statements that express how ordinary individuals envisioned their sense of self, subjectivity, and their social status."[30] This kind of Black photography presented the marriage of fitness and beauty and is among the tradition of visual activism and

Figure 3.3A. "Amanda Falker Swings Racket." SDN-008067,
Chicago Daily News collection, Chicago History Museum.

Figure 3.3B. "Amanda Falker Holds Racket." SDN-008066,
Chicago Daily News collection, Chicago History Museum.

BELLES OF THE BALL
Basket Ball Team, Normal School, No. 2, Washington, D. C.

Figure 3.4. Portrait of "Belles of the Ball." Schomburg Center for Research in Black Culture, Jean Blackwell Hutson Research and Reference Division, New York Public Library Digital Collections.

photographic staging that African Americans created in the early twentieth century.[31]

Although less action-based, portraiture is also useful in examining the visual aspects of Black women's physical culture. Images like the 1917 "Belles of the Ball," a girls' basketball team of "Normal School, No. 2," in Washington, DC, have much to convey about Black physical and beauty culture (see fig. 3.4). Through portraiture, the photographer and the team created an image of fitness, beauty, and respectability. The girls' self-chosen appellation of "belles of the ball" bounded Black female aesthetic and athletic abilities within the nation's capital. Although the image does not document the team's physical skill, the girls' uniforms and sports paraphernalia serve as "authentic" articles of their physicality. In presenting themselves as "belles" of the "ball" (both as a dance and as an athletic apparatus), the team members affirmed their beauty while simultaneously asserting their mastery of a physically intense sport. Images like this and of Falker worked to dispel old myths of the masculine, physically unattractive athlete and instead rooted Black beauty in fit bodies and physical activity.[32]

One Size Fits All?

Within this history of beauty and physical culture, it is important to acknowledge that not all Black women espoused a thin body ideal, and exercise was not the path they chose to become beautiful. Mostly self-described "respectable" middle-class women adopted ideas about slimness and beauty. Other Black women embraced more diverse approaches to beauty that emanated from an artistic tradition. Blues women like Ma Rainey, Bessie Smith, and Ernestine "Tiny" Davis did not abide by popular conventions in their careers or personal lives.[33] Their music, bodies, sexuality, and concepts of Black womanhood challenged dominant ideas held by the Black elite. Blues singer and pianist Gladys Bentley, for instance, defied propriety. She was a heavyset, free-spirited entertainer who dressed in men's clothing and sang eyebrow-raising, double entendre–laden lyrics.[34] Bessie Smith sang "Easy Come, Easy Go Blues" and explained to her listeners,

> Don't want to be no skinny vamp or nothin' like that
> Daddy always knows just where his sweet mama's at
> I'm overflowing with those easy come, easy go blues.[35]

Some women did not care to be a "skinny vamp" and refused to exercise to become thin. Instead of calorie counting, Smith sang in one of her popular numbers, "Gimmie a pigfoot and a bottle of beer,"[36] and other Black female entertainers focused on failed romances, the hardships of life, and physically demanding work as opposed to beauty rituals. Dan Burley, a Black musician and journalist, wrote about fat Black entertainers:

> The slim, trim figure desired by women has been so exemplified as the keynote of beauty and success, that it is not uncommon for females to glance around in holy horror, and ill-concealed amusement at their buxom, well-fed sisters who pass them on the street. . . . But weight is not a barrier to fame and fortune. Instead, weight has brought international attention and riches to hundreds whose talents were and are accentuated by hefty torsos. Take for instance, our most famous of blues singer[s]: Mamie Smith, Bessie Smith, Trixie Smith, Edith Wilson and Ma Rainey: People flocked to hear them, bought their records, [and] hung their pictures in their homes. People loved them for their ability, made all the more remarkable because of their extra poundage.[37]

By Burley's account, while fatness compromised women's attractiveness "on the street," it did not imperil the achievements of blues women. He proposed that extra weight may have, in fact, garnered them added success and fame. Blues entertainers seemed to live by a different set of beauty rules.

Many of these Black female musicians did not adopt the thin ideal that middle-class people, popular culture, and show business often glamorized. Their music targeted working-class women who thought about beauty more broadly and in ways that did not confine comeliness to thinness. Scholar Andrea Elizabeth Shaw proposes that historically, Black women's fatness functioned as a political statement and a form of rebellion against white oppression and unrealistic Western beauty standards.[38] While the aesthetics of blues women demonstrably challenged white beauty norms, they may have also sought to resist beauty standards imposed by Black physical culture. Black women's beauty history in the first few decades of the twentieth century contained a wide range of ideas of comeliness.

In 1914, the *New York Age* held a beauty contest with sundry models of attractiveness in mind. One of the ads for the contest featured photos of six women of "various types from which the ideal American-Negro beauty may be evolved." As seen in figure 3.5, the women represented different shapes and body sizes. Some, like the three in the top row, appear to be more voluptuous, and the three in the bottom row seem thinner. Notably, all entrants were eligible for this competition that sought to "standardize" Black female beauty. The contest was one of self-selection—women submitted their own pictures to nominate themselves, indicating that Black women of different body types probably thought of themselves as attractive enough to enter a competitive beauty contest.[39]

In reality, most Black women did not have the luxury of holding narrow ideas of a beautiful body. The size and shape of Black women's bodies ebbed and flowed with times of feast and famine, work, illness, and personal preference. A predilection for slender figures, nonetheless, is also part of a larger story about Black women's beauty culture. Middle-class African American women often preferred a lean physique and engaged in physical culture to achieve their fitness goals.

The Fit, Respectable, and Beautiful Black Female Body

While some Black women adopted generous definitions of a beautiful body, others engaged in exercise as a direct route to beauty. Discussions of Black women's exercise and beauty often dovetailed with issues of weight. Assumptions that Black women had little interest in losing weight often overshadow this history. Historian Peter Stearns claims that throughout the twentieth century, apart from isolated cases, "the preoccupation with weight and dieting did not catch on among African American women."[40] He suggests that an African culture that embraced bigger bodies and a matriarchal structure that encouraged Black women to "create their own beauty standards" allowed increased fat tolerance in the Black community.

In novelist Alice Randall's 2012 *New York Times* article titled "Black Women and Fat," she notes that Black women's preference for rotund figures explains their tendency to be disproportionately overweight. Using Lucille Clifton's 1987 poem on Black women's voluptuous hips, a popular 1967 song decrying women with "skinny legs," and "curvy" Jazz Age dancer Josephine Baker as supporting examples, Randall cited the historical underpinnings of Black culture's celebration of fatness and concluded that "many black women are fat because we want to be."[41] Several scholars challenged Randall's general conclusions, but her historical claims remain uncontested.[42] Black women did not always embrace fatness as some imagine. Since the turn of the twentieth century, some Black women understood the social consequences of extra weight and exercised to offset obesity.[43]

Figure 3.5. Six of several "beauties" entered in the *Age*'s beauty contest. "Beauties Entered in the Age's Beauty Contest." *New York Age*, August 20, 1914, 1.

Historical records present an early, unexplored history of Black women's physical culture that challenges presumptions about Black women's level of fat acceptance and their relationship to weight. For some, beauty conflicted with the fat body, and exercise served as the remedy. Newspapers display an incipient fat-consciousness for African Americans in the nineteenth century. In 1864, a writer for the Philadelphia-based Black newspaper the *Christian Recorder* stated, "A fat person, however rubicund and jolly, is never well."[44] Two decades later, this sentiment intensified. In

1878, the same press featured an advertisement for "Allan's Anti-Fat" with the heading "Are Fat People Healthy?" The ad asserted that fat people "are the easy prey of acute and epidemic diseases, and they are the frequent victims of gout, heart disease and apoplexy." Seeking to target overweight people, the manufacturer asked, "Why are fat people always complaining? Asks some one who entertains the popular though erroneous notion that health is synonymous with Fat. Fat people complain because they are diseased." In addition to addressing the relationship between fatness and illness, the ad also commented on the physical and psychological drawbacks of carrying excess weight: "Obesity is an abnormal condition. . . . Excessively fat people are never strong, and seldom distinguished for mental powers or activity."[45] This commentary illustrates the beginning of a national shift in the late nineteenth century when fatness implied sloth, aberrance, and weakness. Americans no longer associated corpulence with robustness; rather, it became a stigma of ill health precipitated by irresponsibility and lack of self-discipline.[46] These advertisements indicate an early preoccupation and anxiety about body size for African Americans. They presaged how Black writers would use fat-shaming tactics to influence Black beauty culture.

Denigrations of fatness abound in the Black press. Journalists and health experts used various terms to describe fat women in Black newspapers: lazy, deranged, sluggish, mammy, out of style, abnormal, ugly, and a menace to good health.[47] From this short list alone, it appears that African Americans, or perhaps Black newspaper editors, did not think highly of Black women whom they perceived as overweight. Middle-class African Americans did not loosely attach these terms to fatness; they made them fundamentally and categorically constitutive of the fat body. Black women could not afford to be interpreted as more shiftless, mentally unstable, deviant, and unattractive than the American public already assumed them to be. White women were also targets of fat stigma, but they did not carry the extra burdens that "fat" Black women did. Overweight white women were not considered "mammies" and did not receive the concomitant defamations that accompanied one's perceived role as a fat and happy servant. From the late nineteenth century and especially after World War I, fatness became an added liability for Black women during this time of expanding beauty markets, preoccupation with the New Woman, and a war-produced emphasis on patriotism tied to the thin and fit body.

As Black female consumers were fully aware of fat stigma, they were unsettled by images of overweight Black women in the advertising industry. In a 1932 study on Black consumerism, Fisk University economics professor Paul K. Edwards presented southern urban African Americans, both male and female, with advertisements featuring stereotypical depictions of Black women as mammies. Respondents viewed ads for pancake and soap companies of smiling overweight Black women who donned handkerchiefs on their heads. Most Black women across class and occupational levels disliked the advertisements, but the "professional" Black women commented explicitly that they "do not like [the] big, fat colored woman" featured.[48] The women surveyed added that for this reason, they would be less likely to purchase products that presented Black women in such uncomplimentary ways. Other participants explained that they did not appreciate seeing Black women in servant roles or African Americans generally performing menial labor. But the "big" and "fat" Black woman elicited a visceral rejection from professional Black women who, as noted, cultivated a particular interest in fitness, recognized the social costs of carrying extra weight, advocated for physical culture, and understood keenly the power of representation.[49] Aware of all the other harmful assumptions about Black people, middle-class African American women attempted to avoid the pejorative qualities linked to fatness and made exercise a key component of their campaigns to improve their images.

Black women crafted many of these campaigns within the early twentieth-century club movement. Historiographical accounts of Black women's clubs usually center on society women who discussed current events, classic literature, and, for the more political branches, fundraising, racial uplift, and social reform.[50] Some of these organizations, however, prioritized not only book clubs and sewing circles but also exercise. Within these clubs, weight consciousness became a concern for Black women, and they resorted to various fitness regimens in order to shed pounds. One of the most peculiar—yet apparently effective—ways to lose weight was through "rolling clubs." In 1910, the *Savannah Tribune* reported on a fourteen-member Black women's club in Oklahoma that gathered to "roll off" their excess weight. According to the article, "Society matrons and buds who are inclined to obesity have organized a 'Roller Club' here. They are getting so thin their relatives and friends are alarmed. . . . Everything fat and feminine here is on the roll."[51] Members of this club convened weekly to roll on hard surfaces in a desperate attempt to slim down.

In a prescient statement, the founder of the roller club asserted, "It is the style to be hipless now, and one might as well be dead as to be out of style." Through her claim to contemporary "style," the founder tied Black women to modern concepts of beauty and thinness. Demonstrating that Black women were not immune to the negative qualities associated with extra weight, these women used group exercise to become thinner and achieve "ideal" body types. Indicating distaste for overweight women and espousing disparaging beliefs about fatness, the author of the article referred to the clubwomen as "the fat women" and informed readers that the founder was "one of the stoutest creatures west of the Mississippi." At the time the article appeared in print, many considered fatness a derogatory trait, and the author used these references to shame corpulent women.[52]

Some exercise enthusiasts did not need an organized club to inspire a collective of women to come together in the pursuit of thinness. In 1923, a group of Black women from the South Side of Chicago did what many women do when they want to lose weight—they joined a gym. In the era of segregation, however, they lacked access to first-rate white YWCA facilities, pools, parks, and other fitness spaces. The women, instead, turned to their neighborhood church, where members opened the Greater Bethel gymnasium.[53] The *Chicago Defender*, the most prominent Black newspaper of the time, reported that "overweight" church members, nurses, stenographers, clubwomen, and the Girl Reserves of the Black YWCA in Chicago got fit through classes in "German and Swedish gymnastics" and "light apparatus work." The article's author remarked on the stakes of this exercise initiative, stating, "The realization of the exercise habit is latent in the women of Chicago, as evidenced in the large percentage of women overweight." The article noted not only that these overweight women tarnished the reputation of their South Side community but also that the "physically unfit" held the country back from being a "really great nation." The paper explained that obesity accounted for the large percentage of people with "physical subnormality" that compromised the country's ability to compete globally, particularly during World War I.[54] For Black women with aspirations of full citizenship, obesity became a pressing issue to tackle in their personal and civic lives.

Class mattered greatly in how Black women evaluated themselves and each other in terms of body weight. An especially intimate foray into the class dimensions of Black women's weight and bodies appears in the records of writer, teacher, and socialite Alice Dunbar-Nelson. Dunbar-Nelson often expressed anxieties about her weight and wrote about how physical culture influenced her day-to-day existence. In her troubled relationship with her husband—famed poet Paul Laurence Dunbar—it became evident that exercise affected Dunbar-Nelson's romantic life and vice versa. In one letter to her husband, she mentioned how their relationship infringed upon her ability to exercise. After recovering from a beating Dunbar meted out in 1897, Dunbar-Nelson admitted, "I went over to the 'gym' tonight for the first time since the night we—well. The result was disastrous. I was not as strong as I supposed and fainted in a minute."[55] Her abrupt pause refers to the night her husband physically abused her. For Dunbar-Nelson, the gym and her inability to exercise provided the opportunity to reference the gravity of the injuries she endured. The abuse, already deplorable on its own, also prevented her from exercising.[56] Intimate partner violence took its toll on their marriage, but Dunbar-Nelson seemed equally concerned about the damage it took on her exercise habits and corporal sense of self. Being incapable of going to "the gym" was difficult for Dunbar-Nelson, as she considered it a space of health, healing, and bodily improvement.[57]

Physical culture contained opportunities for recovery and self-care, but its connection to beauty presented Black women with new methods of self-surveillance and bodily appraisal. Dunbar-Nelson exercised and meditated regularly for general health, but negative perceptions about her body also motivated her exercise behaviors. In her October 3, 1921, entry, for example, she reflected on the physique of her companions during a trip to Pennsylvania: "Carrie and I are so big, and prosperous and white looking; she a rosy plumpness of 165-1/2, I a made-up face, tall, broad-shouldered Juno of 167."[58] Additional entries display her weight-consciousness and apprehension about her size. Even more telling is her April 1, 1927, entry in which she admitted she would "start some drastic reducing dieting on 1200 calories per day."[59] Dunbar-Nelson's recording of her weight and caloric intake suggests that she used her diary as a device to document, quantify, and regiment her body into a desired size. Her efforts sometimes proved successful, as she exclaimed, "Found I lost eight pounds. Whoopee!"[60] But more often, she commented on her inability to discipline her body, stating, for example, "Nothing will do me any good until I learn to control this body of mine."[61] Dunbar-Nelson and other Black women likely engaged in physical culture to gain some modicum of control over their bodies.

Although she did not mention it in her diary, her admission of "drastic reducing dieting" suggests that Dunbar-Nelson and other Black women possibly sought weight-loss aids to achieve the control they desired. Black women who wanted to lose weight through emerging exercise products and dieting relied upon the Black press for relevant information. The advertisement sections of Black newspapers are especially revelatory of the variety of "reducing" technology offered to Black women. While these ads do not indicate Black women's actual patronage of weight-loss products, they display key components of Black women's fat denigration—including the commercial availability of slimming products for African American women, the explicit linkages between feminine beauty and thinness, and the intra-racial stigmatization of fat people.[62] The *New York Age*, for example, often advertised "Fat Fade," a thirty-day treatment that promised to "make superfluous flesh just fade away" for the cost of one dollar.[63] The advertisement appeared exclusively among other beauty ads for hair pomades, wigs, straightening combs, and skin lightening creams. Vowing to enhance women's natural beauty, Beecham's Pills aspired to attract Black female clientele in the *Cleveland Gazette*. In the newspaper's advertisement section with the heading "My Lady Beautiful," Beecham's Pills informed its readers that "health is true beauty. . . . Reasonable care in diet, regular exercise, and due amount of sleep with an occasional dose of Beecham's Pills will keep most women in health."[64] The Beecham's Pills ad was subtle—later in the decade, the advertisements became more explicit in their vilification of fatness.[65] In 1918, the *Chicago Defender* ran ads for weight-loss pills like one for "Tabasco tablets," whose manufacturers asserted "too much flesh is undesirable as most quite stout people will readily admit and it detracts from one's good appearance."[66] The paper followed in the 1920s with "Silph," a weight-loss chewing gum that would remove "several pounds a week" for those who suffered from "excess fat." Interested buyers could purchase Silph for fifty cents for a week's worth of supplies.[67]

Black newspaper editors included these ads in their presses because Black women consulted the burgeoning "reducing" market to find new ways to shed pounds and improve their appearances. This market became so robust in the 1920s that some consumers, overwhelmed by the number of available products, sought expert advice on the best slimming methods. In 1926, a woman named Cora wrote to the *Pittsburgh Courier* column "Beauty Chats" seeking information from beauty specialist Madame Creditt-Ole on the most effective way to lose weight. The columnist, who had also held positions as a beauty shop owner and a traveling teacher for the Madam C. J. Walker Manufacturing Company, responded, "Cora—If you are overweight, count your calories; balance meals; avoid all fat forming foods; walk early in the mornings and after meals; exercise. . . . Use Wallace reducing records, they have proven useful to some."[68] As noted, Wallace Reducing Records made their debut six years earlier, and advertisements for the albums featured Mrs. Derby's dramatic weight loss in white women's magazines. In addition to the traditional advice on exercise that Black women had advocated for years, Creditt-Ole suggested new ways to eliminate extra fat with exercise records and calorie counting. As a mediator between ordinary women and their beauty goals, Creditt-Ole's role as a leader in beauty culture informed her weight-reduction advice.

Outside of the weight loss aid market, Black journalists promoted thinness and beauty by advising various gendered physical activities and moderate eating. A columnist for the *Baltimore Afro-American* urged women in 1905 to avoid corsets and instead use walking or "simple calisthenics" to achieve a thin, feminine body that would allow them to look "beautiful" in their "gowns."[69] The *Savannah Tribune* explained in 1910 that gardening was a practical way to exercise—a method that would simultaneously beautify oneself and one's yard. The article stated, "Working in the garden and picking flowers make gentle exercise that tends to improve the figure." It also explained that if a woman worked earnestly in her garden, she would use the same muscles as she would in a gymnasium.[70] Between 1926 and 1927, the *New York Amsterdam News* ran a health advice column that provided diet and nutrition information. The writer for this column cautioned expectant Black women, "The pregnant woman must not overeat with the idea that she must eat for two. To eat for two would be all right, but she sometimes eats for four."[71] Black newspapers functioned as a primary outlet to discourage overeating and to endorse physical activity to combat fat, which writers admonished compromised both good health and attractiveness.

The aforementioned articles' invocation of evening gowns, flower gardens, and a presumed control over one's appetite indicates a middle-class fixation with beauty and body size. Body weight, among other qualities, served as a metric to judge African Americans' attractiveness and character. The fat and idle Black female body represented pernicious racial and gendered ideas that many (particularly elite) African Americans disdained. In the early twentieth century and interwar periods, the image of the overweight, unattractive, and putatively asexual "mammy" dominated media images. Artists used these depictions to sell food, services, cleaning products, sheet music, dolls, postcards, and comedy show tickets.[72]

Editors at the *New York Age* knew what was at stake with the proliferation of these images and expressed their concern in their advertisement for the previously mentioned Black beauty contest. They declared, "To show the world at large the development of physical and spiritual comeliness is an undertaking of considerable magnitude, but the results to be attained make the effort well worth the while. It will counteract the world's conception of the American Negro woman based on the caricatures and exaggerations published in the comic weeklies."[73] These contests operated as political projects amid the torrent of disgraceful images of African Americans that circulated in the growing consumer economy.[74] They served as opportunities to display Black women's bodies in ways that challenged typical representations of Black women as "mammies." Physical culture allowed Black women to distance themselves from this popular and damaging trope in two ways. Optically, African American women who exercised projected slenderness and fitness—in contradistinction to the overweight domestic servant. Physically, the Black exerciser served herself, whereas the "mammy" constantly served others. In these ways, the Black woman physical culturist presented a viable counterimage to the mammy figure. As a real person and symbol, she demonstrated that health, fitness, and beauty did not remain the exclusive domain of white women.

Black women may have also wanted to avoid fatness for its moral consequences. Scholars have hinted at a relationship between weight and propriety in Black women's history, but these tacit references merit further examination. In *I've Got to Make My Livin': Black Women's Sex Work in Turn-of-the-Century Chicago*, historian Cynthia Blair documents how anti-vice crusaders described Black prostitutes in their police reports as "obese wenches," "big," "gigantic Negresses," and "Amazonian," as tall as six feet and weighing 220 pounds.[75] These references appear at a crossroad of race, gender, fat bias, illicit sex, and criminality. Although Blair frames this language as an exoticization of these women, the consistent portrayal of "disreputable" Black women as "obese" indicates that fatness may have also functioned as a form of public denigration and violation of respectability. In other words, Black prostitutes were putative blights on society not only because of their line of work but also because they were overweight, which at the time signified a host of unsavory qualities. It is unclear if these depictions reflected the "actual" size of the sex workers, but their descriptions suggest how fatness acted as a discursive tool to demonize and criminalize Black women and further marginalize them from the category of lawful citizenship.[76]

The physical body, indeed, informed classifications of both deviance and respectability. Physical culture's leader Bernarr Macfadden likened body fat, ugliness, and indolence to a form of social criminality and sin.[77] Nineteenth- and early twentieth-century physiognomists and pseudoscientists mapped criminality onto the Black body.[78] Likewise, the African American aspiring class understood respectability to come not only from educational pursuits, church membership, decent homes, and good marriages but also from the dress, comportment, and physicality of the body. For some Black women, fatness appeared to reinforce deviance and violate decorum.

Women served as specific targets in the Black community's surveillance of fat bodies. Overweight men received some attention for their seemingly rotund figures, but they did not attract the same kind of ire as women. In 1928, Black writer Salem Tutt Whitney explained the urgency for stout women to lose weight in his "Timely Topics" column. He expressed distaste for fat women in show business and suggested they engage in different forms of physical culture: "Exercise and proper diet will keep one's weight normal; it is difficult for an audience to take a fat woman seriously. Fat is generally the result of laziness, lack of exercise, and an abnormal appetite. . . . Leave the decision to any audience and the fat women in the show business would all be in the side shows."[79] Fat women, according to Whitney, embodied an aberrant corporality befitting a sideshow act, and their fatness was utterly self-induced.

As a counterexample, around the same time, a different newspaper praised Black female performers who kept slim waistlines and a male performer who did not. In a review of *Bare Facts*, a Black musical that premiered in Harlem, a reviewer observed, "The medal for grace, however, had to be shared between Troy Brown, who reminds me of [a] huge fluffy cotton ball in spite of his approximately 2 or 3 hundred pounds, and . . . a couple of tall slender brown-skin chorus girls who know their calories."[80] These chorus girls represented the direct opposite of the overweight sideshow performers Whitney described. The review suggests, moreover, that a man in entertainment could be *graceful* at over 200 pounds, while grace could be awarded only to thin women who monitored their caloric intake. This commentary regarding female bodies in show business reveals how some African Americans perceived fat and thin Black women in the public sphere.

Fat Black men, especially those considered successful, seemed to be judged on a different value system than Black women. The *Baltimore Afro-American* reported on William C. Matthews, noted early African American baseball player and, later in his life, lawyer and politician. The headline "Matthews Too Fat in Hospital" suggests that Black men shared some of the burdens of fat stigma, but a closer examination of the article indicates otherwise. The paper explained that Matthews had been "undergoing treatment in a hospital recently for a threat [*sic*] affliction with which he has suffered for some time, and a measure of overweight." The reason provided for his "affliction," however, was that he had been too busy with important work: "In recent years, Matthews has been so active in matters of state, that he has virtually neglected his personal health." The article continued to sing Matthews's praises by disclosing that he had been presented with a "magnificent Tiffany Swiss watch" for his great work.[81]

Matthews may not serve as a perfect example to examine why African Americans excused male fatness—he was a pillar of his community, accomplished, and hospitalized, which elicits sympathy. This sympathy, nevertheless, cannot be divorced from his male status that protected him from certain types of bodily scrutiny. Earlier articles in the *Baltimore Afro-American* further illuminate the allowances men received when their body weight was judged. In 1910, the same paper claimed, "The fat man is usually good-natured, has strong resistance to disease and is a good citizen, as is generally proved by his large circle of friends."[82] Although the reasons provided for the "fat man" serving as a good citizen were dubious, the basic premise supposed that overweight men could be acceptable, even commendable members of Black society. Black men like Father Divine, the Depression-era leader of the utopian spiritual group the Peace Mission, gained members and popularity as he gained weight.[83] Fat Black women did not always receive such generosity from the Black public. They contended with a Black physical and beauty culture that endeavored to limit their caloric intake, regulate their physical activity, and shame their bodies.

)(

Thin Americans seemed to receive several intertwined benefits—assumed beauty, social acceptance, and presumptions of good, patriotic citizenship. Black women were aware of these benefits. Although beauty appears to be a vain motivation for physical culture, a broader examination of beauty culture helps uncover the personal and political ramifications of Black women's exercise. The exercise culture that Black women created allowed them to gain control over their bodies, appearances, and images—an undertaking both flawed and redeeming. Black women and men sometimes engaged in fat-shaming when imparting the virtues of a comely and healthy body. They placed, in effect, value on certain bodies over others and created problematic hierarchies of beauty. At other times, Black women appreciated the opportunity to exercise outside of burdensome and exhausting labor and enjoyed the simultaneous health and beauty benefits of intentional physical activity.

Black physical culture provides an alternative way to understand Black women's manifold concepts of beauty, their civic participation, and how they interacted with popular culture in the twentieth century. Black women created a vision of a counterintuitively fit, slender, and decidedly beautiful female body in real and imagined ways. By adding this account to the literature on Black beauty culture, this study does not suggest that all Black women aspired to be thin or that thinness should be glorified in the context of Black women's history. It posits, instead, that Black women's bodily aesthetics, as articulated through physical culture, add nuance to historiographical accounts of what African Americans deemed beautiful and desirable. This history also shows that African Americans did not necessarily equate slimness to whiteness. Black women did not emulate a white standard of beauty; instead, they created their own Black middle-class aesthetic and staked their own specific political claims to thinness. Physical culture served as the mode through which middle-class Black women expressed fat hostility, and this hostility shaped how they defined corporal beauty. Some Black women sought to draw attention away from the laboring and exploited Black female body, and they presented their bodies as sites of attractiveness and fitness. As the next chapter demonstrates, Black women's motivations for exercise shifted away from beauty in the 1920s to accommodate the economic exigencies of the Great Depression in the 1930s.

103

CHAPTER 4

Never Idle

BLACK WOMEN'S ACTIVE
RECREATION DURING THE
GREAT DEPRESSION

In 1939, a year that marked the tenth anniversary of the worst economic crisis in U.S. history, reformer Janie Porter Barrett helped young Black women weather the devastation of the Great Depression with the least likely fiscal consolations: games and sports. Through the Virginia Industrial School for Girls, Barrett sought to rehabilitate wayward African American girls and stem the evils of Depression-era indolence through recreation.[1] Under the heading "Never Idle," a newspaper reporter in 1939 observed that at the Industrial School, "the girls work hard and constantly but not too hard. They are not permitted to be idle."[2] Apart from the work the young women performed on the 147-acre farm, including planting crops, canning goods, and laundering clothes, they kept idleness at bay by playing tennis, volleyball, croquet, and baseball. Barrett organized each of the girls' dorms by baseball teams and kept "rivalry at a high pitch" through regular inter-dormitory competitions.[3] While Barrett had instituted this kind of friendly rivalry and recreational programming in earlier years, the Great Depression deepened anxieties about Black inactivity. With special attention to these increased anxieties, this chapter argues that Black women reformers, teachers, and activists developed active recreation programs to provide wholesome diversions that would combat the dangers of "free time." Women like Janie Porter Barrett ensured that Black children and adults were "never idle" and that they continued to pursue the virtues of fit citizenship even in their leisure hours.

Kinesiologists and recreation advocates define "active recreation" as leisure activities that require endurance, strength, and agility.[4] The term is a historical one that appeared in African American print outlets as early as the mid-nineteenth century. In 1851, a woman author writing for the *Liberator* stated, "Woman was made for running, climbing, dancing, and all other feats of active recreation and healthful exercise."[5] Black women in the twentieth century thought along the same lines, but they also considered how active recreation could enhance their citizenship efforts.[6] Reformers reasoned that when African Americans made deliberate decisions to spend their leisure time in ways that exhibited morality, physical acumen, and bodily productivity, as historian Marcia Chatelain claims, they "signal[ed] their right to full citizenship."[7] Active recreation provided Black women with a forum to express national belonging through leisure behaviors that exemplified American values of physical fitness, industriousness, and wholesomeness. These qualities ran counter to prevalent ideas of African Americans as feeble and ill-equipped to contribute to American progress. Black women considered active recreation a vehicle for Black citizenship and not merely frivolous physical activity.

African Americans created a clear relationship between recreation and citizenship. Active recreation, in particular, appeared civically advantageous because it did not invite the kinds of white voyeuristic "slumming" that other forms of Black amusement did, like black-and-tan clubs, saloons, and various nightlife venues.[8] Avoiding these sites of so-called iniquity mattered deeply to reformers who classified these kinds of amusements as civically harmful. The *Baltimore Afro-American*, for example, reported on this specific issue in 1905 and framed the popular recreational activity of "excursions" as detrimental to Black citizenship efforts: "There is one question which is supreme and vital to us, and that is the matter of franchise, and [in] banishing entirely the matter of 'excursions,' . . . we should seriously address ourselves to this one supreme question of defeating the measure which has for its object the undoing of Negroes as citizens."[9] By placing excursions on what the paper termed the "black list," one of the most widely read Black presses made explicit the role of wholesome recreation in the struggle for enfranchisement. Later in the twentieth century, reformers rationalized that active recreation proved useful because it instilled moral codes that allowed young African Americans to demonstrate their fitness for citizenship. Charles Williams, physical education director at Hampton Institute, stated plainly in 1917 that his main objective was to use recreation to "produce clean, strong citizens of our young people."[10] For Williams, wholesome recreation played a crucial role in contributing to "domestic peace" and "national prosperity," and African Americans needed to be part of this undertaking.[11]

Black women helped to strengthen the link between citizenship and recreation during the Depression by overseeing more physical sorts of leisure, believing that supervised recreation would keep Black bodies active and out of the "devil's workshop." They perceived active recreation as oppositional to commercialized amusements, which did not meet their standard for respectable leisure activity. Active recreation may have also diverted some Black women from the sexual pleasures they sought during the Depression by allowing reformers to recast pleasure in a more non-sexual, "wholesome" way.[12] Active leisure, in essence, became appealing because of its symbolic meaning. African American women hoped that it would challenge popular notions about Black primitivism, and as this chapter shows, active recreation proved vital to contesting centuries-old depictions of African Americans as crude and indolent.

This study is not the first scholarly work to chronicle "the problems of leisure" during the Great Depression.[13] In *The March of Spare Time*, historian Susan Currell outlines the debates about leisure during the crisis. She charts how white experts, reformers, and New Deal workers made the distinction between redeeming pastimes and unwholesome recreation during a moment of heightened sensitivity about "free time" and the moral core of the nation. Currell makes an important intervention by demonstrating how and why Americans perceived recreation as a salve for the country's economic woes, with policy makers and social scientists believing that "the skills learned in leisure would produce a mentally and physically fit workforce, and leisure could revitalize a sick and ailing economy."[14] Agreeing that a newfound and intense national anxiety about recreation emerged in the 1930s, I explore the following questions in this chapter, with race at the center of my analysis: How did African Americans address the problems of Depression-era leisure without allocated recreational facilities (such as playgrounds and parks that were built exclusively for white communities)? What did leisure mean to Black people in the 1930s who did not believe that recreation would address their economic problems? In other words, what social and political significance did recreation have for African Americans during the Great Depression, a demographic that already felt economically disadvantaged before the 1929 stock market crash and held less hope than their white counterparts for economic resolve? As this chapter demonstrates, the continued struggle for citizenship, or at least the perception of fit citizenship, inspired Black Depression-era leisure culture.

While the study of Black recreation reveals the civic virtue of specific kinds of leisure activity, it also opens new possibilities for understanding how African Americans gained respite from lives marked by the brutality of segregation, the horror of racial violence, and the difficulty of earning livable wages. Historian Robin D. G. Kelley reminds scholars of the Black past that "for members of a class whose long workdays were spent in back-breaking, low-paid wage work in settings pervaded by racism, the places where [Black people] played were more than relatively free spaces in which to articulate grievances and dreams. They were places that enabled African Americans to take back their bodies, to recuperate, to be together."[15] Historian Stephanie Camp similarly demonstrates that it is possible to position Black women's bodies, even under bondage, as sites of pleasure and not merely suffering.[16] The writings and images of Black people who participated in active recreation reveal that joy often undergirded their leisure-time activities. Although this study primarily concerns the relationship between leisure and citizenship, it also recognizes that citizenship seeking and pleasure seeking sometimes overlapped for Black people.

This chapter begins with a study of race and recreation that details how leisure became intertwined with notions of racial difference and citizenship in the decades preceding the Great Depression. This discussion explores how reformers, writers, teachers, and social scientists ascribed political significance to leisure activity in the early twentieth century and provides critical historical context for understanding the recreational anxieties of the 1930s. The chapter ends with an examination of how physically intense modes of recreation informed ideas of good Black citizenship during the Depression. This final discussion reveals that the pursuit of "fitness" continued to meet the real and representational exigencies of the time and that Black fitness advocates continued to conceive of exercise and citizenship as inextricable political categories.

Race and Recreation before the Depression

While preceding chapters examine how Black women embodied citizenship through the pursuit of health and beauty, this chapter's focus on recreation allows for a fuller understanding of citizenship as a "desirable" activity. Recreation, or how people choose to spend their leisure time, operated as one of many ways that white individuals and institutions racialized Black people as weak, dangerous, immoral, and perpetually childlike. In the aggregate, these qualities not only framed Black people as racially inferior but also positioned African Americans as unfit citizens who made poor decisions with their free time. This framing materialized in American print culture, settlement houses, and, for young people, schools.

In the late nineteenth and early twentieth centuries, African American children experienced the joy of recreation through their school's physical education periods and recess hours. While Black youth reveled in these times of leisure, white women who supervised Black children's physical education used this opportunity to observe and criticize Black physicality. Sometime between 1895 and 1897, Jessie Coope, a white woman PE teacher at the historically Black Hampton Institute, wrote to the school's president about her Black female charges' "dire" physical state. She bemoaned, "I have been surprised to find how weak the girls are physically" and thought her students and Black girls generally "showed little interest in outdoor recreation." She expressed to the president that Hampton girls needed to "take more exercise out of doors."[17] Coope's comments represented more than mere frustration about her students' enervation—they indicated misgivings about Black fitness for American civic life. The language of physical weakness and assumptions about African Americans' apathy for the great outdoors worked to exclude Black people from an American collective identity and dismiss them from nation-building projects.[18] Coope's rhetoric contributed to popular notions about African Americans' inability to be worthwhile citizens. Her sentiments echoed those of some white YWCA officers who claimed that Black girls and women showed little interest in physical activity and active forms of recreation.[19] She wrote at a time when active recreation began to epitomize "good" recreation, and Black girls, apparently, struggled to live up to the physical and civic demands of these new leisure trends. Coope's private correspondence reflected larger public attitudes about race and recreation that gained credence in the twentieth century.

White media outlets often disseminated the idea that African Americans gravitated toward unsophisticated, retrograde forms of leisure. Recreational print media portrayed Black people as simpleminded, unrefined, and primitive rapscallions. *Outing* magazine serves as a prime case in point. The periodical ran from the 1880s to the 1920s and featured editorials on sport, recreation, and "travel and adventure." In its April 1900 edition, a writer for the magazine represented Black leisure precisely in the abovementioned ways. At a time when basketball, bicycling, and football became increasingly popular at the end of the nineteenth century, *Outing* disregarded the fact that African Americans participated in these sports and instead confined Black recreation to "'possum huntin.'" Writer F. A. Olds explained,

There is no sport which possesses a tenth of the fascination for the negro, certainly for the North Carolina negro, that "'possum huntin'" does. The 'possum is something which brings to the surface all the unctuousness of the darkey, and the darkey does not live who can stop a smile at the sight of one of these queer animals. The prerequisite for the hunt is a negro, an elderly one preferred, a couple of dogs, kept up during the day so as to be "sharp" for the hunt, a light, an ax, and a sack.[20]

Seemingly, hunting for possums was so embedded in Black culture that the activity could not be conducted appropriately without an elderly Black man.

While white discourse confined Black adult leisure to crude recreations, it also made deeper commentaries on African Americans' character, intelligence, and failure as modern citizens. *Outing* magazine simply reflected extant white attitudes about African American civic virtue. Anthropologist Hortense Powdermaker addressed some of these attitudes in her ethnographic study of Mississippi. Her research revealed prevalent white notions about African Americans, including, "Negroes are like children, incapable of self-discipline and forethought, living only in the moment" and "The Negro smiles, laughs, and enjoys himself no matter what straits he is in," in addition to general sentiments about Black laziness.[21] These attitudes were not confined to the American South. Influential figures like Dr. Shirley W. Wynne, the statistical research chief at the New York City Department of Health, believed that the Black man "has the physique of a man and the mentality and morality of a child. Therefore, if we do not supply him with wholesome amusement, he is bound to fall the victim of the 'rascal' who will supply him [with] unwholesome amusement."[22] Racist ideology about the recreational lives of African Americans informed these perspectives. Leisure functioned as one of many front lines for Black people to contest pernicious depictions of themselves.

Representations of degraded Black leisure added insult to the injury of everyday recreational segregation. Racial segregation of amenities profoundly shaped discussions about leisure in the early twentieth century. Separate and inherently unequal facilities accounted for the most significant barrier to Black leisure, as racial doctrine influenced virtually every aspect of American social and political life. In addition to segregation's role in preventing Black people from enjoying certain kinds of entertainment, immigration played a part in how white reformers established recreation programs within the existing milieu of racial exclusion. In the northern and midwestern states, white reformers participated in de facto segregation by concentrating their energies on specific immigrant groups, excluding African Americans, who were also in dire need of public accommodations. Organizations like the Illinois Athletic Club welcomed European immigrants; its handbook stated that "any person, not a citizen of the United States attached or assigned to the Consulate of a foreign country[,] may be admitted to the Club as a Foreign Consulate member" as long as that person paid the club fees.[23] Similarly, the Gads Hill Social Settlement, chartered by the State of Illinois, displayed a specific investment in using recreation to stimulate "better American citizenship" in its primarily immigrant contingent. The settlement opened in 1898, and only ten years later it developed impressive active recreation facilities, including a basketball court and gymnasium equipment consisting of a vaulting horse, a punching bag, rings, and a turning bar.[24] White organizations like Gads Hill and the Illinois Athletic Club failed to invite African Americans into their facilities, and at times whites aggressively discouraged Black people from trespassing on European immigrant recreational spaces.[25] Recreational segregation served as a prominent reminder of African Americans' second-class citizenship.

White reformers grew concerned about the recreational opportunities of immigrants for several reasons. Eastern and southern Europeans began immigrating to the United States in large numbers from the mid-nineteenth century with an upsurge in the 1890s, and from a population standpoint, they outnumbered African Americans in northern cities. White Progressive Era reformers focused on this growing and potentially "threatening" population to curb anarchy, extremism, and crime.[26] Reformers reasoned that active recreation and certain forms of play would sublimate immigrants, help them acculturate to the American ethos, and provide citizenship instruction. Victor von Borosini, an affiliate of Hull House, the most famous settlement house at the turn of the twentieth century, explained the benefits of recreation for immigrants in his study "Our Recreation Facilities and the Immigrant." According to his report, "Recreation in any form provided by public agencies in the United States does not tend to counteract the good influence and teachings of home and church, as many seem to think; on the contrary, it emphasizes them. A certain amount of discipline is necessarily maintained at the playgrounds; selfishness cannot be indulged in, for everyone must have a chance. Bad habits, such as uncleanliness of mind and body, will disappear, for fear of public exposure and scorn."[27] Apparently, proper recreation imparted lessons in morality, promoted high character, and even curtailed poor hygiene. Put simply, recreation served as a multipurpose tool for Americanization.

Opened in 1889, Hull House in Chicago served as a prime example of wholesome recreation targeted at immigrants. Hull House operated as a large-scale settlement furnished with a state-of-the-art gymnasium, physical education teachers, and robust sports programs. The founder, Jane Addams, proved to be the quintessential reformer. She rejected her elite upbringing and committed herself to policy reform in child labor, workplace safety, education, and a host of other social welfare issues. As stated, the programs of Hull House catered to immigrants, so African Americans represented only a small portion of its residents. This disregard became a point of tension for some Black women, especially since African Americans began making their way to major cities at the turn of the twentieth century.

Fannie Barrier Williams, a prominent Black reformer, writer, and activist in the Chicago African American community, addressed the trouble with these targeted programs in an essay about settlement houses:

> It is these people of foreign tongue and foreign customs who are seeking to adjust themselves to the freer and more responsible life of democracy in America that have the helpful agencies of Hull House and the Chicago Commons. What this class of newly made citizens need in the way of protection, guidance and sympathy is needed even in a greater degree by the throngs of native-born colored people who are swarming into our larger cities. The possibilities of good from such work is quite beyond estimation. But the poor colored people who come to these cities of the North are the only people for whom no directing agencies to save and protect have been arranged.[28]

Williams framed the social programs of Hull House as a vital safety net for vulnerable populations, especially since these programs helped to transform immigrants into American citizens. Implicit in Williams's statement, however, was the irony of institutions like Hull House that sympathized with immigrants seeking to become citizens while overlooking "native-born" African Americans who, oddly enough, needed the same courtesy.[29] Williams's words suggest that the white reformers of Hull House did not merely treat Black migrants with benign neglect but rather actively excluded African Americans from an ideological and spatial citizenship-building project. As Saidiya Hartman has noted, "[White] progressive reformers and settlement workers were the architects and planners of racial segregation in northern cities."[30]

Writing specifically on the problems of recreation for Black city dwellers, later in the essay Williams provided a fictionalized account of a young Black waiter who lived in the city and encountered formidable barriers to wholesome leisure. She explained that he had essentially nowhere to go for amusement, including the nearby white-only YMCA. His meager options included a saloon and other iniquitous, crime-laden venues. Williams posited that the dearth of healthful recreational spaces for young African Americans prevented them from fully developing their bodies, minds, and talents for the betterment of the individual and the race. She decried that society "is doing everything that heart and brain can devise to save white young men and white young women, while practically nothing is being done for the colored young men and women, except to prosecute and punish them for crimes for which society itself is largely responsible."[31] Like other Black women reformers, Williams perceived recreational inequality as a serious issue with grave social and legal consequences. Writing at the turn of the century, she foreshadowed Black women's increasing proclivity to attach amusement to matters of "native-born" citizenship and racial uplift during the Progressive Era and beyond.

Also commenting on the intersection of recreation and national identity, historian Kathy Peiss contends that under industrial capitalism, "leisure has come to be perceived as a realm of autonomy and choice." However, this was not the case for the young working-class immigrant women chronicled in her early twentieth-century study. "Patriarchal relations," she writes, created a "sexual division of leisure" that compromised recreational autonomy for young immigrant women.[32] Peiss is correct, and when Black females are inserted into her argument, it becomes clear that society's ideas of race, gender, and class further limited Black women and girls' leisure choices. Speaking to this issue, Fannie Barrier Williams suggested that Black girls needed extra attention from reformers when she explained that "because of this tyranny of race prejudice that the colored girl is called upon to endure," she must "overcome more difficulties than confront any other women in our country."[33] This argument inspired some Black women to develop Black girl–centered recreational programs.

Fears of racial "mixing" during children's recess hours supported both a racial and a gendered division of leisure. Dance operated as a popular but highly controversial form of active recreation. Although dance served as a fun and healthy way to exercise, it could breach social codes depending on the type of dance and the dancers' identities. In 1911, an innocent dance exercise between a Black boy and a white girl in a physical education class proved so scandalous that it ended in litigation. The following example from the *New York Times* highlights how interracial and especially active recreation presented an issue in the North, even in one of the most "liberal" parts of the country. With a heading of "Compelled to Dance with Negro, She Says," the article explained that at a Flushing Civic Association meeting, the father of a white girl filed a legal complaint against the girl's teacher at Grammar School 23.[34] During the "physical culture exercises," the instructor paired Beatrice Chapman with the "negro boy" Charles David, which drew the ire of Chapman's father and other members of the association. Despite the fact that "considerable latitude is allowed [to] the teachers in arranging the exercises in the physical culture period," the teacher apparently went too far in having a Black boy dance in close proximity to a white girl.[35] The association found in its investigation that the teacher's pairing was especially disturbing since the class contained two pairs of African American boys and girls who could have been matched together. The mere image of mobile and active Black and white bodies together, even in the case of children, proved too dangerous. Black boys were not immune from the trope of the terrorizing and depraved African American male who sought to pervert white girlhood. Having Beatrice and Charles dance so closely, even in the context of physical education class, was more than enough to generate outrage in white communities. Active recreation brought these issues of gender, racism, and leisure to a head.

Black people understood that if they wanted access to racially uncontroversial active recreation, they would have to develop these programs in their own communities. The desire for robust recreation options became even more pertinent as Jim Crow policies hardened in the South and excluded African Americans from active leisure spaces. This exclusion was often tied to missed opportunities for civic development for African American youth. Secretary-treasurer at Howard University and Black recreation proponent Emmett J. Scott explained in 1925, "The negro child must have facilities for recreation to the same degree as the white child, if he is to develop into the healthy and right-thinking citizen that the country needs and the nation requires. In the interest of the community and the nation, as well as the negro child himself, there is urgent demand that greater facilities than are present[ly] available be provided for wholesome recreation during leisure hours."[36] Scott's comments revealed two key points that many recreation advocates echoed. First, Black reformers made leisure vital to their citizenship agendas and ideas of national belonging. As Scott declared, recreation facilities helped produce a "right-thinking" Black citizenry. Second, recreation presented a nearly irreconcilable paradox for reformers. Proper recreation could aid in citizenship efforts, but African Americans could not chart their course toward citizenship because they lacked full access to the necessary facilities.

Playgrounds and parks provided a great civic benefit to all communities, but they often reflected deep-seated racial inequalities that prevailed in the 1920s. White reformers created organizations like the Playground and Recreation Association of America to introduce organized, urban play to mostly white children as European immigrants and industrial workers populated American cities. It was not until 1919 that the Playground and Recreation Association began to address the needs of African Americans with decidedly separate field secretaries, activities, and facilities. Historian Jeffrey Pilz, who has written about African Americans' interaction with the association, posits that the organization's playground movement simply "kept blacks in their place—the ghetto."[37] African Americans experienced profound discrepancies in outdoor leisure spaces in cities around the country (see table 4.1, which displays figures in Houston as an example). Because access to outdoor space held great civic meaning for African Americans, and the denial of this access represented one of the many assaults on citizenship, reformers tackled this kind of recreational segregation intensely.

Whether active recreation took place in the great outdoors or enclosed spaces, Black women could not deny its personal and social benefits for young people. Active recreation garnered the attention of Black women who thought that the ways in which adolescents spent their leisure hours represented a political choice with either severe costs or socially desirable gains. Lucy Diggs Slowe, dean of women at Howard University and an avid tennis player, made pointed comments on the importance of recreation for young women and men. In 1921, she asked a series of rhetorical questions to the 400 students of the all-Black M Street Junior High School located in Washington, DC. Evidently, she grounded her queries in a critique of passive recreation:

How many leisure hours do you have in the course of the day? If you stop to count them, you will find that you have many free hours at your disposal. What use do you make of these hours? Do you stand around on the [corner] of the street looking aimlessly up and down

Table 4.1. Recreation Figures in Houston, Texas, 1929

	Whites	Negroes
Population	220,000	70,000
Number of parks	27	1
Number of acres in parks	2,473	10
Number [of] square feet per person	468	6
Annual cost of operation	200,000	5,000
Annual appropriation for parks, including additional equipment and maintenance	205,000	[no figure provided]
Number [of] people employed in park system year round	92 to 100	1
Number employed during summer	130	1
Number of wading pools	6	6
Number of tennis courts	20	2
Number of golf links	1	0
Number of baseball diamonds	8	0
Number of athletic fields	1	0
Number of parks having additional equipment	15	0

Source: Jesse O. Thomas, *A Study of the Social Welfare Status of the Negroes in Houston, Texas* (Houston: Webster-Richardson Publishing, 1929), 94, box 2.325/F64.3, folder Jesse Thomas: A Study of Social Welfare, Black Texas Women Collection, the Dolph Briscoe Center for American History, University of Texas at Austin.

---

the thoroughfare? Do you sit in neighbors' houses indulging in "small talk"? Do you gaze in a half-dazed fashion out of your window, having absolutely nothing to do? If you have been spending your free hours in any one of the above mentioned ways, you have been wasting valuable time. It is possible to spend your leisure in such a way as to get rest from toil and profitable recreation at the same time.[38]

Slowe added that if the students did not have a hobby, they ought to "cultivate one." Some of the hobbies she believed that students should develop included gardening, "tramp[ing] in the woods," and playing sports with the larger goal of getting "acquainted with the great outdoors." Slowe's concept of constructive leisure did not seem to accommodate activities like daydreaming, observing neighborhood life, or simply resting—pastimes that could also qualify as productive, useful, or restorative. Instead, she invoked the image of students merely looking, sitting, and gazing to arouse unease about Black indolence. Avoiding laziness and keeping Black children active countered stereotypes of African Americans as shiftless while also responding to active recreation's emphasis on bodily movement and the "profitable" uses of leisure.

Forrester B. Washington, director of the Atlanta School of Social Work, served as one of the most thorough researchers of Black recreation in the 1920s and agreed with Slowe's premise. In 1928, Washington conducted an extensive study on African American recreational inequality, focusing on Black migrants' leisure activities. He stated, "There has been much talk about housing, health, crime, family disorganization, and the like, and very little about recreation. Yet recreation is at the same time at the root of the migration of the Negro and much of the social pathology which has grown out of it."[39] Many of Washington's assessments stemmed from his previous 1920 survey of Detroit residents' leisure behaviors.[40] In that study, he questioned 1,000 Black heads of household on the kinds of recreation they engaged in before moving to the city. Out of the eighteen different responses he received, the five most cited consisted of mildly active hobbies (in order from most popular to least): fishing, hunting, hunting and fishing, sitting down, and attending church. The only response out of all eighteen that involved continuous physical movement was "working around [the] house." Several of the categories in the study entailed little to no kinetic expenditure, such as "lying around," "drinking liquor," "sitting down," "talking," and "doing nothing."[41] Washington contended that migration to the cities had not improved the situation. Rather, migration worsened it by replacing a few recreational activities for African Americans with more but harmful kinds. He cautioned the reader that wholesome recreation remained inaccessible while commercial vice had "welcomed [African Americans] with open arms."[42]

Washington's 1928 study surveyed fifty-seven cities and examined Black recreational facilities and leisure activities. The results were dismal. The amount of land, if any, allotted for Black-only recreation was significantly disproportionate to the Black population. African Americans received few opportunities to enjoy public playgrounds, parks, swimming pools, and beaches, and unsurprisingly, whites fought vigorously to keep their leisure spaces racially segregated.[43] In some cases, Black residents paid taxes for segregated public facilities that they could not use, such as a stadium in Charleston, South Carolina, for which there was "a special item on their tax bills," but Black Charlestonians could not step foot in the facility.[44]

A profound observation came at the end of Washington's report in which he addressed the issue of white public opinion as a barrier to Black recreation. He claimed that these opinions mattered for understanding the kinds of recreation outlets offered to African Americans. The problem manifested in how whites perceived Black people as naturally drawn to immoral leisure activities and, in effect, naturalized Black interests as fundamentally deviant and wanton. He explained, "A large section of the American white public seems to believe that the Negro does not desire wholesome recreation—that his taste is sordid in this regard. This attitude tends not only to exclude him from wholesome leisure time facilities but also tends to super-impose upon him improper and undesirable leisure time activities." The report went on to mention that employers did not present their Black workers with healthful recreation, like company sports leagues, but instead offered them gambling clubs and "immoral" race records "so obscene that the companies have not the courage to advertise them in their regular catalogues, but issue special booklets for Negroes."[45] Advocates of racial uplift recoiled at these practices, not only because they deemed these records distasteful but also because they understood that white public opinion shaped the types of leisure allocated for Black migrants. According to Washington, lack of wholesome recreation led Black people into lives of idleness and eventually crime. Black women reformers sought to combat this trend, as they believed inactivity reinforced notions of Black recidivism and was the reverse path to citizenship.

In the few years before the stock market crash of 1929, Black people organized to correct some of the recreational injustices outlined by Washington. The idea that active recreation proved advantageous for the race and the nation preceded Depression-era recreational work and inspired leisure programming in the 1920s. In 1923, the *Norfolk New Journal and Guide* reported that "wholesome and abundant play" could make "one of the strongest contributions to Negro progress" as well as to "healthful citizenship."[46] The following year, the paper reported that supervised, active recreation "is training colored children and young people" in "team work," "good citizenship," and "character."[47] The *Pittsburgh Courier* expressed similar ideals for a Black Girl Scout troop organized by Urban League representative Virginia Woodson of Allegany County in 1928. According to the paper, Woodson called for "drills, hikes, active recreation and constructive training for use in [the Girl Scout's] leisure periods."[48] This training helped the girls to develop "leadership skills" that undergirded their roles as burgeoning Black citizens. As a troop leader and member of one of the most influential racial uplift organizations of the early twentieth century,

Woodson thought it sensible to use active recreation to reinforce the Girl Scout attributes of preparedness, honor, and duty—qualities that the Urban League deemed indicative of good citizenship.

Undeniably, region influenced who could access "good citizenship," as many rural Black people experienced critical shortages of recreational programs. Nevertheless, Black women offered rural children active recreation through self-help organizations, like the Gulfside Association. A Methodist Episcopal Church bishop instituted Gulfside in the 1920s to deliver educational, religious, and recreational programs to poor African Americans in Waveland, Mississippi. Located on the Gulf of Mexico, the program drew the interest of hopeful Black women reformers in Texas, Louisiana, and Mississippi. Capturing this optimism, the *Sea Coast Echo* newspaper (Hancock County, Mississippi) reported that "Gulfside was first of all to reach negro leadership and through them reach the large negro population adjacent to Waveland in the interest of better homes, better schools, better churches and better citizenship."[49] In an attempt to meet these objectives, Black women missionaries, extension agents, sorority members, and Sunday school teachers spent several summers in the late 1920s creating Camp Fire Girls groups and other recreational clubs for Waveland residents, particularly children.

Reformers made wholesome and active recreation central to the aims of the program. A memo from a bishop who worked on the project stated that Gulfside was to place "an emphasis on health and sane recreation."[50] A letter to the founder of Gulfside described the necessity for such a goal: "In these days when commercialized sports and amusements are bidding on every hand for the time and money of our people and the crying need of trained leadership is constantly before us, we need nothing so much as a place like Gulfside where our people may go and where our leadership may be trained."[51] The letter explained that the indulgences of commercialized leisure fell outside the realm of possibilities for Waveland residents, but the association's female members supplied plenty of alternatives. Additional correspondence describes the activities residents enjoyed, including swimming, tennis, volleyball, basketball, croquet, and hiking. These activities were to be provided "by and for Negroes."[52]

Like they often did, Black women worked together to improve the lives of young people and were effective in bringing active recreation to rural communities. While they supplied Black Mississippi residents with active leisure, reformers emphasized the importance of physical fitness, self-determination, and cooperation—skills that one religious leader claimed would result in "the production of prepared negro boys and girls."[53] Another member of the association averred that Gulfside was well suited for the "recreational, religious, educational, and social advancement of the race."[54] More explicitly, the New Orleans paper *Southwestern Christian Advocate* stated in 1927 that because of Gulfside, "here recreation will be given its rightful place in the scheme of racial uplift."[55] This kind of recreational uplift enabled rural families to occasionally escape their harsh living and working conditions by combining exercise, leisure, and pleasure. Programs like Gulfside had good reason to continue into the foreseeable future, but they were ill-prepared for the severe economic challenges that awaited them just a few years later.

Black Active Recreation during the Depression

The 1930s were marked by abject poverty, disillusionment, and mass unemployment. Around 14 million Americans were out of work, and 9 million lost their savings. African Americans suffered immensely and experienced a 50 percent unemployment rate, compared with 25 percent nationally, by 1932.[56] Dr. Milton S. J. Wright, a Black economist, explained in reference to the crisis, "Whites, in their frantic efforts to survive[,] took from the Negro, not only many of the newly acquired jobs, but even of the so-called traditional Negro jobs. This left the Negro almost entirely upon the mercy of charity."[57] But African Americans had experienced close encounters with financial straits and job discrimination in previous decades, and as Richard Wright put it, "The simple, sad fact was that they had less to lose [during the Depression]."[58] It is unsurprising, then, that Black people who had been disappointed with previous presidential policies would look upon the new Roosevelt administration with cautious optimism.

Immediately after his inauguration in 1933, President Franklin D. Roosevelt's first order of business was to propose new ways to repair the economy. Rejecting the laissez-faire approach of his predecessors, Roosevelt offered Americans a "new deal" with an unprecedented measure of government intervention. Shortly after his inauguration, though, the *Pittsburgh Courier* admonished, "We say to the [Roosevelt] Administration Good Luck. Hundreds of thousands of Negro voters helped to roll up the immense majority that has placed you in power. . . . You can be sure of our good wishes, loyalty, and support. But we want action."[59] African Americans and other groups feared the New Deal might operate as more of a rhetorical endeavor than a practical one, and those concerns proved partially valid. Acts from the first and second New Deal, like the Agricultural Adjustment Act and the Social Security Act, actively excluded sharecroppers, domestic workers, and day laborers—jobs that African Americans occupied disproportionately. In effect, tens of thousands of Black women and men were virtually ineligible for government relief programs.

Despite these deprivations and even with diminished faith in the administration, some African Americans attempted to work within the government to supply recreation to poor, rural Black youth or, at the very least, make leisure a point of conversation. Black state official John Larkins asserted that "a depression with federally sponsored recreation programs by WPA [Works Progress Administration] and NYA [National Youth Alliance] helped to make North Carolina recreation conscious."[60] Mary McLeod Bethune, a member of Roosevelt's "Black Cabinet," contributed to this consciousness through her work with African American youth. As part of her appointment in the Division of Negro Affairs, Bethune headed the National Conference on the Problems of the Negro and Negro Youth in 1937 and likely raised the issue of government-sponsored recreation for Black children. Other Black women participated in recreation reform through New Deal programs. As a representative of the National Council of Negro Women, Lucy Diggs Slowe joined the New Deal's Committee on Education and Recreation in 1937. She explained that the committee "provided an opportunity for careful and studied consideration of the problems confronting the Negro by persons whose training made it possible for them to consider these problems intelligently and scientifically."[61] Supplying recreation became so crucial in the 1930s that Black women tackled the issue with scientific precision and careful study.[62]

Members of various African American organizations and other individuals reasoned that recreation required not only intensive study but also agenda setting and institutional investment. Between 1930 and 1933, the National Association of Colored Women qualified "[Black] children without proper recreation" as an urgent problem.[63] The association firmly held that "deficiencies" began in childhood and therefore sought to "[overcome] the handicaps which burden the race by trying to create a better environment for every Negro child."[64] Using recreation to correct "handicaps" and "deficiencies" became a common strategy among Black national organizations like the National Association of Colored Women, whose members believed that improper environments produced inadequacies in Black youth. Wholesome recreation constituted one way that African American organizations addressed Black childhood development and larger racial "burdens" during the Depression.

Most of the direct study and implementation of active recreation, however, happened not in national institutions but on the ground through grassroots community organizations. During the Great Depression, Black women community workers framed exercise, gained through leisure activity, as vital to subsistence and basic human needs. The Black women who organized the Atlanta Community Chest described physical activity as essential to human life during the economic crisis. The Community Chest operated a social service agency that oversaw sixteen African American organizations, including the Legal Aid Society and the Neighborhood Union. Its 1933 brochure listed various human needs: "Bread? Yes. Clothing? Yes. Shelter? Yes. Bare subsistence? Yes. But oh, much more, much more than these! Man does not live by these alone. He has other insistent needs. He dies unless these other necessities are also supplied. More slowly but none the less more sure." The other important aspects of life included "friendship," "relaxing entertainment," and "bodily activities."[65]

According to the organizers of the Community Chest, "bodily activities" proved critical to maintaining one's well-being. Even during an era of abject poverty and material deprivations, African Americans conceived of physical activity as an "insistent need" and not a trivial pastime. The Community Chest endorsed exercise both ideologically and practically by instituting several athletic and playground initiatives for Atlanta residents. In 1933, the organization provided recreational opportunities to 10,340 children and "social relaxation and recreation" to 9,851 adults.[66] As leaders of the Community Chest and its related organizations, Black women framed physical activity as a serious matter for Black people who found themselves with unprecedented amounts of free time. They acknowledged that exercise would help African Americans avoid the "slow but sure" death that came with furnishing only the bare provisions of food, clothing, and shelter.

The Community Chest provided Atlantans with relatively consistent active recreation during the 1930s, but these leisure opportunities arrived only once a year for smaller Black cities. Small-town Black churches would host holiday barbecues that enabled children and adults to exercise through leisure-time activities. For example, during a Memorial Day celebration in 1932, Shiloh Baptist Church in Des Moines, Iowa, offered to local Black residents "horse shoe pitching, races, and other games for both old and young," in addition to what appeared to be a highly anticipated "big girls base ball game."[67] One could imagine that this event attracted many community members and presented them with a rare moment of organized play and enjoyment. These moments afforded Black people a welcome distraction from the everyday deprivations of the Depression.

In the same spirit of momentary diversion, the Negro Civic League in North Carolina hosted a yearly "Reunion of Colored People" for African American residents of Salisbury. In 1933, organizers held various activities at Livingstone College Park, from reading the Gettysburg Address to singing the national "negro" anthem. Within the amusement portion of the day's events, schoolchildren performed "Physical Culture Exercises" and engaged in several sporting activities, including baseball, boxing, wrestling, the high jump, bicycling, and potato sack racing.[68] Similarly, in 1934 Mt. Olive Baptist Church in Iowa hosted a Fourth of July celebration that served "barbecued ribs, pork, and beef, ice cream, pop, and other refreshments" in addition to games and sports.[69] Since the early twentieth century, Black women had knitted together the ideological threads of exercise and citizenship. Implementing these activities with Memorial Day, the Fourth of July, and the Gettysburg Address as the backdrop shows how those threads adapted to Black recreational life in the 1930s. These fleeting, holiday-inspired opportunities for active recreation allowed Black churches and civic leagues to seamlessly blend patriotism, national belonging, and leisure during the Depression.

Holidays, however, come only a few times a year, and on the more uneventful days, Black communities contended with joblessness and idleness. The mere image of idle Black men perturbed some Black women, and they revealed their displeasure in print for Black readers. In 1932, Black columnist Alice Richards admonished Black men at the height of the economic crisis: "The unemployed man bluffs himself into believing that he could walk right into the job he says he seeks and work satisfactorily after wasting all the many hours of leisure he has had, sitting on park benches, lamenting to his fellow victims of woe the same old fairy tale, 'I am looking for a job.'" Richards imagined that this archetypal jobless man also wasted his "hours of leisure which he has at his disposal." She asked, "What better use can the unemployed man make of his leisure than to determine to improve himself?" Her advice to Depression-induced Black male unemployment and self-improvement was as follows: "After he has made a good self-examination . . . the next step would be to administer correction of his defects. . . .

Maybe it is simply to cultivate a good sense of humor, to drink plenty of fresh cool water, or to exercise vigorously. . . . He could seek wholesome amusement in public swimming pools, recreational centers and camps."[70] These steps, apparently, would reduce his "handicaps" and help him better compete for employment in an unusually tight labor market. Even if work could not be found, "his long hours of leisure will have been used more advantageously in that he will have improved his mental and physical health."[71]

Remarkably, Richards offered exercise as a gendered solution to Black unemployment and a more general corrective to African American male character flaws or so-called defects, as she put it. As historians of disability have noted, avoiding such defects enabled Americans to present themselves as employable, productive citizens, and Richards adopted this view.[72] Black women with Richards's mindset likely used the same reasoning when addressing their male loved ones and other male members of the community about the Depression. It is difficult to know if Black men followed this advice, but the impetus to engage in adult active recreation certainly came from Black women.

The Phillis Wheatley Association (PWA) in Cleveland, Ohio, also promoted the virtues of exercising during one's leisure time. Established in 1911, the PWA functioned as a settlement house whose primary objective was to provide a haven for young Black women who migrated to the North without families to receive them. The organization offered vocational training, music lessons, and recreational activities for its female residents and eventually raised enough funds to build an impressive nine-story building to run its operations. The mission statement read, "The purpose of the Phillis Wheatley Association shall be to maintain a home with wholesome surroundings; to afford colored girls and women an opportunity for fuller development; to promote growth in Christian character and service through physical, social, mental and spiritual training; to create a social understanding which operates unceasingly for the extension of the Kingdom of God."[73] Jane Edna Hunter served as the tireless founder and president of the PWA—a woman moved by a sense of Christian duty and reformer urges to protect young Black women. In the introduction to her autobiography, she was described as a "Negro woman who has pledged her life to . . . guide and protect the Negro girl in her search for decency and livelihood. The Phillis Wheatley Association was formed through her efforts and her spirit of consecration."[74] Apparently, active recreation proved vital in Hunter's pledge and in carrying out the PWA's mission, even during the difficult years of the Depression.

The PWA explicitly used recreational exercise to meet the organization's mission of physical, social, and civic training. Recreation, in general, was cited as a way to solve "boy and girl problems" and was also meant to target "domestic, business and professional women." The PWA instituted physical education to "develop in the girl and woman an appreciation for strong, clean bodies; correct habits of health, posture and exercise; a spirit of good sportsmanship." Association workers used playgrounds "to train [children] for citizenship" and to "decrease delinquency by providing leisure activities." Finally, summer camps enabled Black children to "develop through a program of supervised recreational, educational and social activities, the highest physical, mental and moral standards."[75]

Physical education, playgrounds, and summer camps provided amusement to Black people who may have struggled to find leisure outlets in Cleveland. But the PWA did not supply recreation for recreation's sake. The organization maintained larger goals of ensuring good health habits, law-abidingness, and morality—defining markers of "good" citizenship. A 1939 report stated, "The purpose and objectives of the Association remain much the same. The chief function is to provide a home with wholesome surroundings, find employment and train Negro girls and women to become self-supporting. The agency aims to develop leadership, good citizenship, inter-racial goodwill, economic independence, and family solidarity through a well rounded program, including activities of an educational, recreational, social and religious nature."[76] Although social welfare organizations like the Phillis Wheatley Association experienced profound financial barriers during the crisis, under the leadership of Black women, they continued to offer leisure programs that placed citizenship at the center of their ambitions.

Black women linked physical activity to various outcomes related to good citizenship and diminished criminality during the Depression. They used active recreation specifically to deter young people from a life of delinquency. The Southwest Harlem Neighborhood Council made a nod to this issue in 1937. Leah Lewinson, the council's president, lamented the lack of recreational facilities in southwest Harlem for African Americans. She noted that between 110 and 125th Streets and Fifth and Morningside Avenues, no YMCA, YWCA, Urban League, Utopia House, or settlement houses existed. Residents could rely on only one recreational center, which still failed to accommodate the more than 400 children who attended daily. Lewinson petitioned to the New York State Temporary Commission on [the] Urban Colored Population, "I cannot see any funds for [building a community center] coming from private sources and I recommend very, very strongly that the City government take over this project thus decreasing crime, disease, and juvenile delinquency through athletic games, public discussion and other wholesome activities."[77] A few of the activities Lewinson desired for the community included gymnastics, boxing, basketball, and swimming. Sports and other "wholesome activities" kept young people active and would help them avoid the trouble that seemed to tempt them even more during the idle times of the 1930s.

Lewinson also acknowledged that constructing or remodeling a new recreational center would produce other fringe benefits, like creating work for the WPA and allowing "delinquent" children somewhere to recuperate while their homes were improved. During the second New Deal, reformers began to agitate for more government support while private charities strived to keep afloat. With more young people out of work, the concern with idleness and criminality became increasingly entangled. Black women community leaders recognized that reducing youth crime during the Depression required more than traditional self-help methods.

The girls' gymnasium group of the Wharton Centre, a Black settlement house in North Philadelphia, also believed that recreation would discourage Depression-era delinquency and inculcate treasured civic virtues. Established in 1931, the center offered recreational outlets, a summer camp, housing programs, and a day care to Black Philadelphia residents. By organizing sports and other games through the center, Black women used athletic spaces as laboratories for teaching empathy, leadership, and teamwork through exercise. Organizers explained in reference to the 1939–40 girls' basketball team:

> There were usually about 12 girls who reported every Tuesday evening between 7 and 9 p.m. for gymnasium work. These girls when they first came seemed to be quite uninterested in the feelings of others, they were inconsiderate of their fellow players and seemed to care little about the rules of play. When a leader is confronted with a group of girls such as these the progress of the group is slowed considerably because it is necessary to have each member of the group realize that the only reason for playing is to have a little exercise and release pent up energy but that there is a far deeper and meaningful reason for participating in sports.[78]

The twelve girls may have merely sought some physical movement and a good time through their gymnasium work. But sports like basketball held

Figure 4.1. Black women continued to use settlement houses, open fields, Black YWCAs, and college campuses to exercise during the lean years of the 1930s. Although many Depression-era photos of Black people convey deprivation, active recreation images capture Black women's vigor, joy, and physical gratification. "Mass Gymnastics, Spelman College Founders Day," April 11, 1937, Atlanta University Photographs, Atlanta University Center Robert W. Woodruff Library.

too much potential for character development for the girls to waste the opportunity. Recreational leaders at the center would offer active recreation to permit the girls to "get a little exercise" and instruct them in more sacred lessons. Settlement workers used basketball to provide training in interpersonal relationships, cooperation, and following "the rules." It was even more critical to instill these civic lessons within the team, as Wharton struggled to finance travel for the girls to play other leagues outside of neighboring settlements during the Depression. Although economic conditions modified how Black girls and young women played, they continued to exercise their bodies with the larger goals of personal growth and civic betterment (see figs. 4.1, 4.2, and 4.3).

Figure 4.2. Images abound of Black women participating in sports and recreational activities on their college campuses during the Depression. "Dillard University, Long Jumper, 1936–1937." Kenneth Space Photographs of the Activities of Southern Black Americans, 1936–1937, Harmon Foundation Collection, 1922–1967, National Archives, photo no. 26174823.

Black women who believed in the civic benefits of active recreation carried these beliefs with them to the rural South through extension services. In 1914, Congress established the Agricultural Extension Service program that created jobs for women as southern "extension agents." Also known as home demonstration agents, extension workers formed clubs in rural areas and instructed women sharecroppers in homemaking, gardening, sanitation, and nutrition. Within these clubs, agents also created recreation programs for women and provided them with opportunities for exercise through games, physical education, and 4-H groups.[79] Extension

Figure 4.3. This photograph depicts group-based recreation in which Black women could forge a sense of belonging, collective pleasure, and sociality. "Howard University, Women's Swim Team, 1936–1937." Kenneth Space Photographs of the Activities of Southern Black Americans, 1936–1937, Harmon Foundation Collection, 1922–1967, National Archives, photo no. 26174876.

agents like Juanita Coleman, who worked in Alabama, emphasized the importance of active recreation in the 1930s.[80] While the photograph in figure 4.4, a 1939 image of Coleman with extension service recipients, might have been staged, it may realistically reflect the joy that recreation played in the lives of African American women who labored tirelessly as farmers, domestics, and homemakers. Images like this relay a forgotten reality: although Black people remained downtrodden during the Depression, they continued to carve out moments of pleasure and carried on with their recreational lives.

Figure 4.4. The original caption of this photograph reads, "Juanita Coleman helps during recreation time for adult class. In the church she teaches them to read and write and to discuss any interests and problems." Gees Bend, Alabama, 1939, Farm Security Administration–Office of War Information Photograph Collection, Library of Congress, LC-USF33-030355-M5.

While women like Coleman rolled up their sleeves and performed the hard work of promoting active recreation, others pontificated about the more frivolous aspects of exercise during the Depression. Perhaps naively, Madame Qui Vive of the *Atlanta Daily World* authored her column as if the crisis had not affected Black women's bodies and physical habits. The beauty columnist complained of young women who resembled "wraiths" and who did not "look like healthy, happy, spirited girls."[81] Qui Vive worried that throughout the 1930s, "carriage, posture and grace [got] little attention." Even with the extreme poverty and food shortage of the time, she believed that "there is no reason why the body of young women should not be strong [and] of muscle. She may have no occasion to use her muscles but for the sake of health and symmetry of body[;] they should be resilient and firm. The sensible thing is to devote a few minutes each day to exercises that will promote fiber vitality, and at all times to carry the body splendidly." Her final piece of advice proclaimed, "Don't waste anymore time. Do your daily dozen faithfully."[82]

The idea that one could "waste time" by not exercising reflects both the optics of inactivity and the productive value of exercise during the Depression. The "daily dozen," a set of twelve fast-paced cardiovascular exercises, would seem like a trivial concern considering the more exigent life circumstances Black people faced in the 1930s. But choosing to "devote a few minutes each day" to this activity was a serious matter. Making the conscious, intentional decision to exercise in one's free time held tremendous civic value to Black women who wished to be seen as productive citizens. Amid the joblessness and "idleness" precipitated by the economic crisis, women like Qui Vive used exercise to help position African American women in counterintuitive ways. Black women could project health, resilience, and the ability to "carry the body splendidly" during a time that seemed to foreclose these possibilities.

)(

This chapter displays how Black women, who were arguably on the outermost margins of the body politic in the 1930s, articulated the relationship between recreation, fitness, and citizenship in sophisticated ways that perhaps others could not. The "double jeopardy" of racial and gender discrimination compelled them to create unique spaces to express their vision of full citizenship. These expressions often fell outside of the arenas of electoral politics, suffrage, and military defense—arenas that became increasingly important to notions of citizenship in the first half of the twentieth century but were exceptionally difficult for African American women to access. Nonetheless, they used recreation to bind themselves and their communities to the nation's objective of producing healthy, industrious, and useful subjects for the twentieth century. In doing so, these Black women preceded Executive Order 10673—the establishment of Dwight Eisenhower's President's Council on Youth Fitness in 1956. In the post–World War II era, the council sought to curtail youth crime, bolster physical health, and increase Americans' ability to compete internationally by promoting active recreation.[83] With far fewer resources than a presidential agency, prescient African American women recognized the political value of instituting active recreation programs during the lean years of the 1930s.

Active recreation operated as a way for African Americans to exercise their bodies apart from the work that often left them physically depleted, emotionally drained, and economically disadvantaged. It served as an opportunity to present Black people as "good" citizens on terms that the African American middle class deemed respectable. Black women reformers believed their communities had much to gain from well-orchestrated leisure. They used active recreation to propose that white people did not have a monopoly on bodily exercise, thereby providing healthy amusement options to their communities while challenging problematic assumptions about Black recreational life. African American women articulated both their right to pleasure and their entitlement to citizenship in the language of physical exercise. Black women intensified this language in the postwar era, tying both diet and exercise to fit citizenship.

CHAPTER 5

34-24-36

BLACK WOMEN'S DIET, EXERCISE, AND FITNESS IN THE POSTWAR ERA

In 1959, Black fashion and marketing expert Elsie Archer published *Let's Face It: A Guide to Good Grooming for Negro Girls*, in which she offered advice on health, beauty, and comportment for young Black women. In the chapter "The Shape of Your Body," she explained, "Keeping in shape will be easy for you if you're careful about your diet, if your health is okay and you get enough exercise each day. Nothing pleases a girl more, or a fellow for that matter, than a shapely shape." This advice seems fair enough, but Archer's tone takes a more severe turn when she links thinness to "fitting in" and general success: "Once you start to slim down and your whole appearance begins to change, you immediately begin to feel better. You discover your feminine charm. Your clothes suddenly begin to look like something on you. You have a different outlook toward life. You know your chances are greater with a body that will 'fit' in. You heard somewhere that the slim, sleek gal is the one who gets all the breaks in this world. . . . The figures that are not overstuffed are the ones that are likely to succeed."[1] Archer promoted calorie counting and physical exercise, among other slenderizing behaviors, to attain such a figure. She reasoned that an exercised and dieted body opened several doors for Black women: higher self-evaluation, feminine allure, an enviable figure, and a greater likelihood of achievement. Although jarring, Archer's assessment was not unusual—it represented a growing trend in the postwar era to encourage both dieting and exercise not merely for the sake of health but as a route to Black upward mobility.

With perspectives like Archer's in mind, this chapter examines Black women's beauty pageants, newspaper and magazine articles, cookbooks, and advice literature between 1937 and 1960 to understand what constituted the ideal fit Black female body in the mid-twentieth century. It adds precision to chapter 1, which discussed how Black women in the late nineteenth century began imagining how the fit Black female body would literally take shape in the twentieth century. This chapter explores how those turn-of-the-century ideas of combined physical and civic fitness manifested in the actual and sometimes idealized bodies of postwar Black women. It demonstrates that the "ideal" body was not merely conceptual; rather, Black women quantified the ideal in pounds, measurements, calories, and exercise repetitions.

Intentional exercise became an urgent matter for the molding of bodies in the postwar period—a time Archer referred to as a "lazy era" in which "everything is made easy for you,"[2] an allusion to the proliferation of labor-saving devices and to convenience as a consumer good. As Americans bought cars, washing machines, televisions, and other commodities that reduced physical activity, deliberate exercise would need to compensate for a more sedentary population. Unlike previous eras, however, Americans could not achieve "fitness" with physical activity alone. They were expected to diet, too.

The turn to dieting in the postwar era reveals a paradox—Americans abstained from food as they seemed to consume more of it. The postwar period saw several developments that enabled Americans to eat more easily and in higher volumes, such as the exponential increase in the purchase of refrigerators, the availability of frozen meals and processed foods, and the rise of supermarkets and food advertising.[3] It is no wonder that between 1945 and 1950, national spending on food increased by 33 percent.[4] After the war, African Americans spent more money on food than on clothing, home furnishings, toiletries, medical remedies, and tobacco.[5] Unlike in the Depression and wartime eras, when food was scarce and having access to provisions held social, class, and material benefits, its abundance in the postwar period created a new relationship to food. To have it and actively resist it presented dieters as rational food actors and self-regulated citizens. Both diet and exercise advice aimed at Black women appeared regularly in Black beauty and print culture in the 1940s and 1950s, linking both behaviors to desirable civic qualities of health, beauty, willpower, and achievement. With close attention to these behavioral links, this chapter argues that through exercise and dieting practices, Black women portrayed themselves as ascending, successful, and ideal Black citizens in the postwar period.

The postwar era is often referenced as a time of prosperity, but the nation's good fortune did not spread evenly across all racial groups. While African Americans made some socioeconomic gains after the war, state

actors, real estate agents, employers, and everyday white Americans marginalized Black people from the markers of postwar prosperity (for example, government subsidies, suburban homeownership, mass ascendency
to white-collar jobs, and capital accumulation).[6] Working-class whites
achieved upward mobility through increased incomes, GI benefits, and
the trappings of middle-class life by purchasing suburban homes, cars,
appliances, and other domestic comforts.[7] Many Black women continued
to labor in low-wage domestic work, as they had done before the war, in
part to uphold the domestic comforts so many white Americans enjoyed.[8]

Even with disappointing economic gains, African Americans still cultivated an aspirational, middle-class consciousness after the war through
the consumption of material goods and services.[9] The scholarship on
Black postwar life has examined the inextricable relationship between
Black upward mobility, citizenship, and consumerism, noting for instance
that African Americans claimed middle-class citizenship "only when permitted to work, shop, and eat freely in the consumer sphere" and with
access to "the good life" and "the [American] dream."[10] Ideas of citizenship
and class status became tied to what Americans purchased, and this was
certainly the case for Black people who lacked the full civic and financial
freedom to consume.

Black print culture buoyed consumer culture. Magazines like *Ebony* and
Jet sought to show "the happier side" of Black life partly through the acqui-
sition of consumer goods and material accumulation.[11] As a primary vehicle of the civil rights movement, the Black press helped to frame the African
American citizenship struggle as a movement not just for legal rights but
also for consumer rights. In doing so, Black newspapers presented African Americans as good citizens via their right (and desire) to participate
equally in all marketplaces, including amusement venues, spaces of shopping, and the mostly white suburban housing market.[12] These print outlets
targeted a real and imagined upwardly mobile Black audience deserving
of full citizenship despite the barriers to financial security and obstacles to
civil rights that Black people faced.

While consumption and print culture reflected the intersection of
Black class formation and the citizenship struggle in the postwar years,
questions about the role of embodiment in this intersection remain
under-addressed. If the body functions as a historical indicator of class
and citizenship,[13] what role did the body play in African Americans' civic
aspirations in the postwar period?[14] Whose body, and what kind of body,
fit neatly into the narrative of an ascending, deserving, and model Black

citizen? Black women's culture of dieting and exercise in the mid-twentieth century helps to answer these questions. This culture shows us that although most African Americans lacked the purchasing power to participate fully in a consumer economy that prized shiny, new, and modern goods, they could use fitness practices to mold bodies that read as refined, sleek, and modern.

World War II and its aftermath created a new set of overlapping motivations for Black women to aspire to fitness. The war produced lingering anxieties about national security when the military rejected "frail" men and shunned "weak" women for their lack of fitness for the war effort. This anxiety prompted the creation of the first President's Council on Youth Fitness in 1956 and shaped a larger conversation about the meaning of civilian fitness in the Cold War era.[15] Other anxieties about bodies undergirded Black fitness efforts in the mid-twentieth century. As many considered demobilization and peacetime "a return to normalcy," putatively abnormal, overweight, and unfit bodies compromised the national desire for normality in all facets of life. Attaining ostensibly normal bodies became "a way for Americans to imagine a perfect postwar citizenship."[16] African American women, and Black communities more broadly, engaged in their own fantasies of ideal corporality as they continued their quest for citizenship. Part of this fantasy entailed the unrealistic expectation that Black women would be responsible for the fitness of the race. Women's retreat from war industries and return to the domestic sphere created gendered pressures for women to uphold personal and family fitness. Confronted with headlines in the Black press like "Wives' Help Needed to Reduce 'Softies'" and "Saving Bulging Males Wives' Job," Black women faced real demands to ensure the healthy diets and regular physical activity of their family units.[17] This chapter is situated within these postwar crosscurrents.

The following pages examine Black women's new and more robust definitions of fitness in the 1940s and 1950s. I chronicle African American women like Mabel Alston and Bernice Harrison who used exercise and visual portrayals of fitness to influence postwar Black body ideals. The chapter also reveals that what Black women put in their bodies—or more accurately, what they resisted putting in their bodies—became an essential element of Black fitness culture. Black women who had a strong association with food, like cookbook authors, newspaper diet advisors, food journalists, and culinary tastemakers, became pundits of food and fitness. The discussion of these fitness cultures is divided into three parts, with sections on World War II, exercise, and dieting.

Wartime Fitness

In order to examine postwar fitness culture, it is vital to understand first how World War II influenced ideas of citizenship and the fit body. Although the U.S. government expected all Americans to exhibit some version of "fitness" during the war through calls for strength and self-restraint, Black women found it difficult to demonstrate their fitness through official government channels. A select few, though, defied this trend. Major Charity Adams Earley and her unit of 855 Black servicewomen underwent rigorous physical and psychological fitness assessments for the war effort.[18] Earley served as the commanding officer of the 6888th Central Postal Directory Battalion—the only unit of Black servicewomen deployed overseas during World War II. Major Harriet M. West, the only other Black woman promoted to the rank of major during the war, revered the women of the 6888th Battalion for their stamina, remarking, "Aside from doing an excellent job as a postal unit, this group of women was not idle either physically or mentally during off-hours."[19] The battalion was a notable exception, however, as Black women's involvement in wartime physical fitness regimes occurred primarily outside of military enlistment.

Racial and gender discrimination limited the number of Black women who could enlist in the military or work in defense industries. During the conflict, Black women constituted only 3 to 5 percent of corps personnel.[20] Even for those who did enlist, the military funneled most African American Wacs (members of the Women's Army Corps, or WAC) into "unskilled" assignments like laundresses, kitchen staff, and hospital orderlies. They often received similar treatment in defense industries, working in the "dirtiest and most taxing jobs" in steel mills, munitions factories, and other industrial plants.[21]

Some Black women sought to spread a war-induced gospel of fitness on the home front. Charlotte Moton, a representative of the "colored unit" of the Office of Civilian Defense, served as a Black fitness spokesperson. In Atlanta, she addressed a packed auditorium of African American community members about government efforts to improve American fitness just four months after the United States entered the war. A "fitness clinic" accompanied Moton's talk, which included bodybuilding and aerobics demonstrations, dance presentations, table tennis exhibitions, and self-defense exercises.[22] Similar wartime programs led by Black women took place in schools, such as the "Victory through Fitness" exercises at the historically Black Cheyney Training School for Teachers (now Cheyney

University of Pennsylvania). Led by "May Queen" Gladys I. Purnell, Cheyney students played war games, navigated obstacle courses, participated in military drills, and performed "mass conditioning exercises."[23] Although propagandist in nature, these fitness clinics allowed Black people who lacked access to official military training the opportunity to exercise in militaristic fashion, demonstrate their patriotism, and show their commitment to physical fitness. They could, at the very least, act out the nation's war-produced vision of citizenship.

The war seemed to have a more visible imprint on white women's fitness endeavors, providing white women, in the name of national duty, with the opportunity to do "men's work" without compromising their femininity. Government officials felt compelled to quell public fears of masculinization, homosexuality, and disruptions to gender norms that white women's war participation would trigger.[24] For instance, the military designed "a course of planned exercises" that enabled Wacs to use their bodies to their optimum capacities while "visibly expressed in a correct, attractive carriage."[25] The armed services attempted to deny the ruggedness required of its servicewomen through allusions to their domestic inclinations and delicate features.[26] Military officials like Colonel Oveta Culp Hobby, the WAC director, worked especially hard to create an image of feminine, heterosexually inclined but virtuous white female soldiers.[27] Black servicewomen, who worked in traditionally "male-employing industrial fields" and performed "heavy labor for the railroads" during the war, did not receive such government consideration.[28]

A study of white women's wartime fitness reveals how the army placed unique gendered pressures on Wacs and the additional ways in which the War Department created nonthreatening ideas of physical fitness for some women. White Wacs were warned that "the eyes of the Army—and of the Nation—are upon you" and that they needed to remain in prime physical shape to fulfill their patriotic duty.[29] The WAC field manual noted that the mere presence of women would not help the war effort; rather, the country needed supremely fit women: "The war will not be won by women alone. But victory in total war will go to the side which utilizes the most women, and the fittest."[30] The armed forces' endorsement of fit and presumably brawny women created a tightrope of fitness and femininity for Wacs to walk. The military, however, performed the careful rhetorical work of shifting ideas of femininity and strength by emphasizing that "none of your duties will be beyond the capacity of a woman in fit condition. But nearly all military duties will be beyond the ability of a woman who lacks strength,

Figure 5.1. The army's vision of women's wartime fitness. U.S. War Department, *W.A.C. Field Manual: Physical Training* (Washington, DC: U.S. Government Printing Office, 1943).

YOU MUST BE FIT

who tires easily, whose mind and body do not work in swift accord, who is constantly prey to illness and moods."[31] For white military women, fitness and womanhood became synonymous, and they could embody physical fitness without its social and gendered risks. Even for those not enrolled in the military, the war set new standards of health, strength, and bodily resilience for white American women.[32]

The War Department's motto for white women was simple and explicit: "You Must Be Fit" (see fig. 5.1). "Fitness" encompassed women's physical and mental faculties, even outside direct combat. The department noted to its female contingent, "You are a member of the first Women's Army in the history of the United States. You are one of the small percentage of women qualified in mind and body to perform a soldier's noncombatant duties. These duties are many. The demands of war are varied, endless, and merciless. To satisfy these demands, you must be fit."[33] Fitness, for the War Department, constituted an absolute quality free from ambiguities. The department asserted that one either embodied strength and vigor or did not, and admonished those who "faked" their fitness. The War Department cautioned Wacs against the "shortcuts" women took to appear fit, like wearing foundation garments instead of developing "firmly toned abdominal muscles" or using laxatives instead of relying on a well-functioning gastrointestinal system.[34] A sound diet and "planned exercise," the army declared, improved several bodily functions and attributes, including muscular tone, stability, elimination, posture, stamina, coordination, and resistance to illness and extreme weather. White Wacs seemed to embody the shining example of female fitness during the war.

World War II also produced heightened scrutiny of Black male fitness. Both white government officials and Black health advocates capitalized on the urgency of the war to survey the state of Black men's bodies. Jack Kelly, the U.S. director of physical training, instituted a fitness campaign named "Hale America" that sought to increase the "physical fitness quotient of the manpower of America."[35] A key element of the campaign involved enlisting the help of Black athletes like Jesse Owens to encourage exercise and fitness training among Black men. This "fitness drive" was not concerned with the intrinsic value of African American health; instead, it sought to "spread the gospel of physical fitness among the men whom the country expects to depend upon in future emergencies."[36] In later iterations, the Office of Civilian Defense expanded the program to "emphasize the need for systematic daily exercises and exertions" among civilians.[37] This specific program made no promises of citizenship to African American participants, but it did create a clear relationship between physical fitness, civic responsibility, and national belonging. World War II provided a new opportunity to bring issues of race and fitness to the fore.

Historians and political scientists have documented the ways in which international wars enabled African Americans to envision themselves as citizens.[38] Fighting on behalf of the United States presupposed "good" citizenship through sacrificing life and demonstrating patriotism. During World War II specifically, the Double V campaign intensified African Americans' demands for full-fledged citizenship. But to achieve victory at home and abroad, Black troops first needed to be fit. One Black writer believed that the war produced "New Negroes" because Black troops underwent new health and fitness regimens:

The Selective Service Act is giving this country tens of thousands of New Negroes annually. They are New Negroes PSYCHOLOGICALLY as well as physically. A few months ago, a disproportionate number of these young men took improper care of their HEALTH, lived in unhealthful SURROUNDINGS and had a non-cooperative point of view. . . . With the exception of the athletically inclined, few of these young men bothered to take any EXERCISE and were stiff and flabby. They now take exercise every day except Sunday. This DAILY regimen of exercise, deep breathing, perspiration and sunshine is making NEW MEN out of these draftees.[39]

For some Black supporters of the war, the stakes of wartime citizenship hinged not only on the existence of Black male soldiers but on their exercise behaviors, their fitness levels, and the potential to remake themselves anew. Ignoring the fact that losing life and limb in the war would make fitness moot, some relished the idea that World War II bestowed Black men with a new kind of physicality and helped them change unhealthful behaviors. Another Black writer for the *Philadelphia Tribune* celebrated the Hale America program for its potential to alter the physical habits of Black men. The article stated, "[Jack Kelly's] greatest obstacle is going to be the changing of minds of thousands of our men who figure that lifting a beer mug and throwing darts at a board is the best kind of physical exercise possible."[40] While these perspectives seemed akin to war propaganda and served a less than progressive agenda, they may have stemmed from a deeper public health concern.

Health surveys revealed stark racial health disparities during wartime. For example, one study found that between April 1942 and March 1943, the top two reasons that the Selective Service denied African Americans entry into the military were cases of syphilis and "educational and mental deficienc[ies]," both of which accounted for 51.6 percent of rejections.[41] These statistics alarmed health workers and researchers. Gladyce H. Bradley, a Black woman professor of education at Morgan State College and the author of the study, suggested that health education would mitigate this problem:

There is a definite need for more and better health education and education among Negroes. This program must include all age groups and extend into all communities. While many of the persons examined had not had the opportunity to attend school for even four years there were many others who were rejected who had not been so unfortunate.

How can we account for this failure? A major part of it can be laid directly at the door of the school in that, by and large, the curriculum is still dominated by the classical. It is still difficult to obtain a reasonable allotment of time for those activities that can provide and produce physical fitness.[42]

These results are what early twentieth-century reformers feared— inadequacies in physical education that would manifest in physical examinations decades later. As for the particular problems of syphilis and educational deficiency, Bradley argued that health education alone would not solve the problem. "Social conditions," including insufficient housing, unemployment, racial discrimination, and lack of wholesome recreation, accounted for the more intractable reasons for fitness deficiencies. In her final recommendation, Bradley suggested that "the important message which comes to every Negro from the findings of the physical examination is this: Find out what the health and physical fitness program is in your community from your doctor or the physical education director, health department, school, YWCA, YMCA, voluntary organizations, or other groups and then take an active part in it."[43] Bradley used the results to encourage all African Americans, regardless of gender or military background, to utilize their community exercise programs to improve Black physical fitness rates.

Although Bradley made these conclusions in the context of physical readiness for war, she framed the military rejections as a call to fitness for the general welfare of African Americans. She believed Black fitness was "of sufficient importance to warrant discussion" as opposed to a duty to the state. Nevertheless, since World War I, participation in war symbolized national belonging and particularly allowed men to assert themselves "as courageous and capable, independent and deserving of honor."[44] Even with the disappointments of the Great War, World War II offered yet again another occasion to earn citizenship through demonstrations of the fit Black body. Afflicted with sexually transmitted infections and mental "deficiencies," Black men seemingly relayed their physical and mental weakness, which marked the Black body as militarily and civically unfit. Black people used the postwar years to rewrite this narrative and project new ideals of fit citizenship. No longer concerned with the male-dominated war effort, the intra-racial onus of fitness shifted from Black men during World War II to Black women in the postwar years.

Black Women's Postwar Exercise Culture

In the early twentieth century, Black women's exercise took place in seg-regated YWCA gyms, parks, schools, community centers, and homes. But in the mid-twentieth century, Black women began to exercise on more public stages, including beauty pageants. Local and regional Black beauty contests in the late 1930s and 1940s allowed Black women to display their physical fitness in two ways that were less common in previous eras. First, they sometimes required a swimsuit portion that showed the shape of contestants' bodies, and second, they involved a display of fitness in which judges asked contestants to perform physical acts as a part of the compe-tition. The "first Negro beauty contest" in Phoenix, Arizona, held in March 1937, required contestants to perform a "hot-cha" dance (see fig. 5.2). The talent segment of the contest was not a mere addendum to the pageant—it operated as a key metric for how judges evaluated Black women's physical beauty. The *Des Moines Register* explained, "Going white-folks one better, this contest required that the girls not only be pretty, but that each do a hot-cha dance before the judges' stand. Beauty of figure and face, and dancing ability, were taken into consideration in awarding the prizes."[45] The con-test implied that Black women could perform physical feats that white women contestants either could not or found challenging, highlighting the ways in which African Americans envisioned pageantry through ide-als of Black ability and fitness. Although earlier Black contests intimated that bodily assessment factored into judgments of comeliness, by the late 1930s, beauty of the body and what it could do became a more determina-tive attribute of attractiveness.[46] The first Black pageant in Phoenix linked Black beauty specifically to physicality and suggested that bodily and per-formative "fitness" was essential to judging Black women's corporal value.

Beauty contests were not the only venue for Black women to present various kinds of fitness. The same women who entered beauty pageants also vied for a place in Black print culture as models. With a growing media and consumer culture in the mid-twentieth century, everyday Black women turned to magazines and newspapers, and to the models featured in these print outlets, for examples of aspirational African American wom-anhood.[47] Black commercial models encouraged their readers to exercise and championed what historian Laila Haidarali terms "efforts to stay fit."[48]

Before the postwar era, Black women claimed that exercise created the ideal Black model body. Beauty and charm schools made exercise central to how they trained Black models.[49] Mabel Alston, a self-described "expert

Dusky Belles Parade in Negro Beauty Contest

Figure 5.2. The first Black beauty contest held in Phoenix, AZ. "Dusky Belles Parade in Negro Beauty Contest." *Des Moines Register*, March 21, 1937, 66. © USA TODAY NETWORK.

cosmetologist" of Mabel Alston's Charm School, issued beauty advice in 1940 that encouraged readers of the *Baltimore Afro-American* to practice "controlled exercise" that would promote weight loss. Alston differentiated between exercise performed through housework and "controlled" exercise:

> In a survey made by the Northwest Public Service it was found that the average housewife washes an acre of dirty dishes, scrubs three miles of floors, and washes three miles of clothes, hung close together, each and every year. In view of these statistics it's no wonder that housework makes you so tired that you think you have more exercise than you need. But here's the difference: You get exercise, but you need controlled exercise, which will affect certain muscles.[50]

It was not enough that Black women often performed backbreaking work; this labor did not count as exercise. Black women were compelled to follow a prescribed regimen of physical activity to achieve true beauty and fitness, including repetitive "bicycle movements" and abdominal maneuvers to "reduce hips and keep [the] figure" and "reduce the stomach" (see fig. 5.3). These exercises seemed to be the only way to mold the body into Mabel Alston's vision of ideal corporality. This category of beauty advice, stemming from the Black press, was critical to shaping the postwar Black female body and promoting new concepts of the ideal Black female form.

In the 1950s, Black print culture became even more specific about ideal body shape and measurements and continued to tout exercise as an essential way to attain a desirable figure. In 1953, *Jet* featured an article on ballet exercises that targeted "women with figure problems [who] could well afford to take a tip from ballerinas whose slim and graceful physiques are the result of daily exercise."[51] Like the aforementioned *Baltimore Afro-American* article, *Jet* advised housewives to avoid relying on the physical activity of domestic work for exercise. Instead, the magazine directed its readers to schedule thirty minutes of daily, intentional exercise. The model for these exercises, Bernice Harrison, is pictured bent over in a leotard to demonstrate the recommended ballet poses (see figs. 5.4A and 5.4B). Adding to this svelte and flexible visual, the magazine revealed Harrison's weight and body proportions: 115 pounds with a bust-waist-hip measurement of 34–24–36 that the writer described as "ideal" for a woman who stood at 5′3″. This kind of bodily quantification offered Black women concrete goals to which they could aspire in the postwar years. Black women exercisers provided specific exercise routines, exact workout durations, and precise body measurements for fitness hopefuls.

Harrison's measurements, her sexualized appearance, and the suggestion to add thirty minutes of extra physical activity to the day's agenda were likely out of alignment with the material realities of most Black women's lives in the early 1950s. Nonetheless, by the mid-twentieth century, "too large hips" and "soft and flabby" muscles, as *Jet* proclaimed, indicated a personal and moral failing as well as a collective liability that some Black women sought to avoid. While Harrison's figure may have been difficult to achieve and the exercises challenging for the average woman, *Jet* assured readers that they could perform the fitness poses "in the home" and that the exercises became "easier with repetition." This assurance represented the magazine's earnest if failed attempt to speak to readers who experienced physical barriers to achieving the model's "supple, healthy and shapely"

Mabel ALSTON'S
CHARM SCHOOL

AN INSTITUTE OF BEAUTY ADVICE
Conducted for AFRO Readers by an
Expert Cosmetologist

EXERCISE TO REDUCE
HIPS AND KEEP FIGURE

In a survey made by the North-west Public Service it was found that the average housewife washes an acre of dirty dishes, scrubs three miles of floors, and washes three miles of clothes, hung close together, each and every year.

In view of these statistics it's no wonder that housework makes you so tired that you think you have more exercise than you need. But here's the difference: You get exercise, but you need controlled exercise, which will affect certain muscles.

LIE ON FLOOR

To avoid possibility of strain while taking exercises the very heavy persons should lie on the floor. Most people would prefer to lie on a mattress or something soft but it is always better to take exercise of this type on a hard surface such as a mat or blanket spread on the floor. A weak spine will sag into faulty position on a pliable surface. Also the non-giving surface calls for a higher degree of muscular resistance which increases the value of the exercises on the floor.

FOR THE HIPS AND
THE THIGHS

Exercise 1. Position: Lying on the back on the floor, hands on hips, body stretched out full length. Movement: Raise one leg toward chest as far as is convenient. Next stretch leg forward on floor as far as possible. Now raise this leg and go through same movement with the other leg. Repeat this movement five to ten times and gradually increase the number day by day.

Exercise 2. This exercise is known as the bicycle movement, and is particularly good for reducing the thighs. Position: Lie down on the back and place the palm of the hands over the thigh, the legs stretched out straight. Now raise the thigh, as if pumping bicycle, keeping the hand on thigh. Alternate the thighs, using first one then the other as was done in the previous exercise. Repeat this movement five to ten times the first day and increasing the number of times gradually day by day.

MISS THELMA JACKSON, who is demonstrating the correct position for an abdominal exercise, which reduces the stomach.

End the routine with the deep-breathing exercise. Lying on floor, hands on hips, knees up, the feet on the floor; take a deep inhalation through the nose, pushing the abdomen outward, exhale

Figure 5.3. Thelma Jackson models an abdominal exercise in Mabel Alston's beauty advice column. *Baltimore Afro-American*, January 27, 1940, 15. Courtesy of the AFRO American Newspapers Archives.

BALLET EXERCISES FOR REDUCING

Sure-fire method for paring off unwanted inches is to adopt the ballet exercises which well-known dancers like Los Angeles ballerina Bernice Harrison perform daily. They keep the body supple, healthy and shapely. They can be done at home and become easier with repetition. (See "Modern Living.")

Figure 5.4A. Bernice Harrison models weight loss exercises through ballet poses. "Ballet Exercises for Reducing." *Jet*, March 26, 1953, 2. Courtesy of EBONY Media Group.

MODERN LIVING

Stretching and bending exercise limbers Bernice Harrison's leg muscles, subtracts inches from waistline.

Exercise For A Ballerina Figure

Women with figure problems could well afford to take a tip from ballerinas whose slim and graceful physiques are the result of daily exercise. Not only does it keep their bodies supple, but healthy and shapely. Many of the exercises they perform can be done in the home

Figure 5.4B. "Exercise for a Ballerina Figure." *Jet*, March 26, 1953, 33. Courtesy of EBONY Media Group.

body.[52] This article represents just one of the ways in which *Jet* targeted a growing Black middle class as well as blue-collar African Americans with middle-class aspirations. The magazine assumed a leisured, able-bodied, and amenable Black female reader who would undoubtedly want Bernice Harrison's body. *Jet*, therefore, both reflected and stoked Black women's desire to exhibit models of postwar bodily fitness through exercise.[53]

The Finest Frame

Black magazines used various methods to present seemingly unattainable fit Black female bodies as both accessible and aspirational. In 1947, *Ebony* magazine reported on the unusual outcome of the "Miss Fine Brown Frame" beauty contest—one that ostensibly challenged Black aesthetic norms and offered beauty to a larger segment of the African American female population. The title of the contest relayed normative expectations of African American beauty, bodies, and especially skin tone. Although judgments of skin color are and were subjective, "brownskin" women dominated the postwar Black commercial model and advertising markets. They represented a "happy medium" in terms of skin tone, falling somewhere in the "middle" of the complexion scale and garnering favor in Black print culture.[54] Black market researcher David J. Sullivan even encouraged white advertisers to "use brown-skinned girls for illustrations" as they would "satisfy all."[55]

The 1946[56] Miss Fine Brown Frame contest, however, upended this trend by crowning Evelyn Sanders, whom *Ebony* described as "probably the darkest—and one of the most exotic—beauty contest winners in Harlem in a decade."[57] The judges and Sanders herself expressed shock at the results, as she "had a hunch this body-beautiful contest would be won by some nearly-Caucasian face atop a light brown frame."[58] In essence, the audience demanded Sanders's win and overturned the judges' initial choice, a woman whom the magazine described as "a light-skinned Dixie belle." The crowd asserted that "white standards of beauty would not be forced upon them."[59] Arguably, the pageant ruptured these standards on the basis of skin color. A writer for *Jet* claimed that generally speaking, "most Negro beauty contest winners usually turn out to be fair-skinned girls" and explained that judges often eliminate darker-skinned women in the first rounds of pageants.[60] Many agreed not only that Sanders was deserving of the crown but that she rightly breached these troubling norms in Black beauty contests. Nevertheless, pageant "body standards" remained firmly in place. In the end, Sanders's bodily proportions aligned with traditional Black calculations of corporal beauty (see fig. 5.5).[61]

The attempt to determine who could claim the most beautiful Black body in America proved a high-stakes affair. Hundreds of women coveted the Miss Fine Brown Frame title. Organizers poured innumerable resources into the contest, and the pageant finale received a great deal of press coverage.[62] The fact that Sanders's success posed a challenge to "white standards of beauty" resonated deeply for African Americans across the country, many of whom felt excluded from beauty criteria established even within their own communities. Black beauty stakeholders in numerous U.S. cities vied to place a hometown contestant in the pageant. The event drew interest from "bronze beauties" in Puerto Rico, Hawaii, Alaska, Cuba, and Brazil.[63] Ohio journalist John Fuster lamented his state's lack of representation in the contest: "To this writer, this state of affairs is sad and touching. Think of all those beautiful 'fine brown frames' walking and riding up and down Cedar Avenue in Cleveland, down the length of E. Long Street in Dayton, and around the corner of Fifth and John Street in Cincinnati!! . . . We are prejudiced in favor of the fine brown frames on evidence throughout the Buckeye State."[64] Indeed, enthusiasm for the contest ran deep and wide. Pageant officials held preliminary contests in over 150 locations throughout the country, and hundreds of women, including college "campus queens," competed for the crown.[65]

The prizes attached to the contest reveal some of the material motivations for the high participation rate. The founder and sponsor of the pageant, Maestro Buddy Johnson, sought to broaden the appeal of the event by offering a $300 cash prize (approximately $4,000 in 2022 dollars), a trophy, a film contract with the Association Producers of Negro Pictures, commercial endorsements, and a tour with Johnson's band. Johnson also invited celebrities, including Lena Horne, Joe Louis, and Paul Robeson, to serve as judges.[66] But the search for the most exquisite Black body also invited unforeseen controversies and impassioned reactions.

The local qualifying contests that preceded the final pageant revealed the inordinate emotional charge of the competition. In South Florida, two contestants "were of the opinion that their anatomy was superior to that of the young lady who was crowned 'Miss Fine Brown Frame of Ft. Lauderdale,'" and in protest they physically assaulted both Buddy Johnson and the winner of the title.[67] In Raleigh, North Carolina, a married couple found themselves in a serious legal predicament because of the pageant— one that threatened their freedom and the well-being of their marriage.

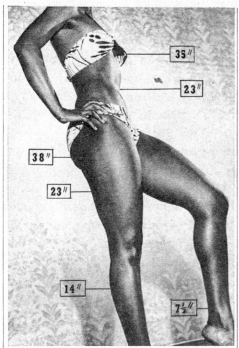

Long-legged, deep-hipped, satiny torso that won Miss Fine Brown Frame title for Evelyn Sanders scales 130 pounds. She's 24, wants to be a model.

MISS FINE BROWN FRAME
Darkest girl in contest wins first prize

FOR MANY months the juke boxes in Harlem had been blaring out the lyrics of *Fine Brown Frame*. The expression began to make gossip columns with regularity. It was too good a bet for a press agent to pass up and a nation-wide contest to select Miss Fine Brown Frame was cooked up for Buddy Johnson's band.

For vivacious Evelyn Sanders of Freeport, Long Island, the finals of the contest began inauspiciously at the Golden Gate Ballroom. Her smart chartreuse dress was too tailored to bowl over the judges and she felt lucky to squeeze through the preliminaries. She had a hunch this body-beautiful contest would be won by some nearly-Caucasian face atop a light brown frame, unless Miss Freeport, the darkest entrant, could think fast. Then she made a mad dash to a nearby fabric shop.

In the finals that night, a few of the 25 contestants also had ditched their gowns for bathing suits, but none could equal the vest-pocket model Evelyn had stitched up an hour before. The audience instantly and noisily voted her the finest brown frame seen in many years.

But the judges demurred, as Evelyn had feared, and started to crown a light-skinned Dixie belle. The audience would have none of it, however, and articulately let Maestro Johnson and his judging board know that, for once, white standards of beauty would not be forced upon them. The judges tried a compromise, awarding Evelyn the cash and a light girl the title. Fists shot up threateningly from the audience. So finally, to tremendous acclaim, Evelyn Sanders was crowned Miss Fine Brown Frame, probably the darkest—and one of the most exotic—beauty contest winners in Harlem in a decade.

Mrs. Wilson entered the contest, and her husband, Albert Wilson, served as a judge who was primed to vote in her favor. All seemed to go as planned until Mr. Wilson reevaluated his wife's deservingness of the title. When Mrs. Wilson realized that Albert did not support her, she slapped him, and he responded by physically assaulting her. Authorities subsequently arrested Mr. Wilson for assault and battery, and he received a sixty-day jail sentence.[68] Why did the Miss Fine Brown Frame pageant produce such vehement responses?

Black people across the country invested greatly in this contest and Sanders's win because of the pageant's racial and civic significance. African Americans celebrated Sanders as a certified beauty representative and an agent in diversifying ideas of Black beauty. This specific contest crowned the *best* (that is, finest, fittest, most beautiful) *Black body* in the United States, which held great meaning for Black people seeking to dispute ideas of racial inferiority and disgraced Black womanhood through corporal representations. In response to the contest, *Ebony* readers wrote to the editor that "such articles will diminish the high percentage of inferiority complexes that exist within our race," and "the poses of Miss Fine Brown Frame are wonderful examples of Negro womanhood. Yes, the gorgeous shape of Miss Sanders is really a work of art."[69] While beauty pageants were ostensibly counterproductive and imperfect venues to wage gender and racial justice battles, they nevertheless transmitted powerful visuals of social and political value.[70]

Beauty contests were especially consequential in the postwar context, when Black political agents, image makers, the press, and laypeople linked Black progress to an expanding media culture.[71] Portrayals of Black women's beauty, particularly in the visual mediums of pageants, magazines, film, and television, served as a venue to cultivate postwar racial pride.[72] Black-owned and Black-operated media outlets of the postwar era also "offered African Americans new resources to define themselves anew to national audiences through media representations that reinforced their citizenship demands."[73] By attaching civic value to beauty, the Miss Fine Brown Frame contest, *Ebony*, and Black newspapers performed various kinds of cultural and political work that aligned with new forms of racial representation and citizenship seeking.

Historically, pageants have operated as "site[s] to witness the gendered construction of national identity," and the Miss Fine Brown Frame contest was no different.[74] Pageant organizers sought to present the pageant as a patriotic enterprise. They firmly connected the event to the aftermath of

World War II, particularly reintegrating veterans into civilian life and funding the war effort. During the pageant's finale, Buddy Johnson requested that the Philadelphia Veterans of World War II participate by hosting the dancing and entertainment portion of the evening's events.[75] At one point in the preliminary competitions, Johnson offered a $100 victory bond as part of the winnings.[76] This prize must have been an intentional strategy on Johnson's part, given the symbolic power of war bonds. War bonds allowed rank-and-file Americans to demonstrate "fiscal citizenship" and their commitment to the state.[77] In an apparent effort to add nationalistic meaning to the Miss Fine Brown Frame contest, Johnson sought to enter the winner into the then exclusively white Miss America pageant. Johnson, however, was unaware of the official white-only policy, but once he realized that he faced this formidable barrier, he vowed to "carry his case to the highest courts of justice to win recognition in the 'Miss America' pageant for the girl crowned 'Miss Fine Brown Frame of America.'"[78] The participants, especially the front-runner of the pageant, reflected ideals of American citizenship through Johnson's hard-fought efforts.

The titleholder of Miss Fine Brown Frame, then, would simultaneously embody Blackness, beauty, and civic virtue. At 5'6" and 130 pounds and with measurements of 35-23-38, Sanders's body aligned with postwar prescriptions of Black middle-class beauty standards (that is, her measurements were just an inch or two smaller or larger than *Jet*'s Bernice Harrison). While the magazine mentioned that Sanders ate "a whole lot" and avoided exercise, the fact that she aspired toward modeling and professional dancing suggests that exercise likely factored into her beauty regimen.[79] Regardless of her physical training (or lack of) for the pageant, she performed essential representational work by projecting a vision of a fit citizen. Although her scantily clad image may not have reflected traditionally "respectable" corporality, Sanders's body, particularly her headless body, provided a textbook-like demonstration of the kind of "frame" that some African Americans deemed ideal. Women like Sanders set quantifiable standards for the "frames" to which Black women should aspire in the postwar period.

Black Women's Food Consciousness, Dieting, and Fitness

Before the emergence of a distinct "diet" culture in the mid-twentieth century, some Black women intentionally restricted their food intake in the early twentieth century. Spelman Seminary placed limits on off-campus "food boxes" that students often preferred in the 1910s.[80] As noted in chapter 3, Black women likely took advantage of emerging diet technologies of the 1910s and 1920s, and some participated in calorie counting during that time. In the 1930s, women of the Allah Temple of Islam embraced smaller figures by actively avoiding fattening foods, despite the food scarcity of the Depression. According to historian Ula Taylor, "a fit physique," a low body weight, and an abstemious diet indicated high moral character for women of the Allah Temple.[81] By creating distance between themselves and calorie-laden foods, Black women also distanced themselves from ideas about the overindulged, zaftig body. But this history has gone underexamined in the historical scholarship on race, gender, and food.[82]

Food studies, particularly the scholarship on African American food traditions, have proliferated in the past two decades. This body of work usually examines Black food production and consumption as a rich, ambrosial experience of resourcefulness and creativity. Historian Frederick Douglass Opie, for example, defines soul food as a "cultural mixture of various African tribes and kingdoms" or, more plainly, "fabulous-tasting dish[es] made from simple, inexpensive ingredients."[83] Psyche Williams-Forson reminds us that although Black people's association with chicken has an overdetermined, sexist, and racist past, when they did cook the bird, it was an "art form."[84] Food studies scholar Jessica Kenyatta Walker explains that in popular culture and especially television, even "amateur" culinary demonstrations by Black women "[presuppose] a natural affiliation between Blackness, motherhood, and exceptional cooking."[85] Black historical food actors and their chroniclers assert that when Black women were at the helm of cooking, the food was certainly well seasoned, delicious, and enticing. This association between Black women and savory food has been at the same time materially true, overrepresented, and imagined. The following discussion, though, takes a different turn, looking at the denial of this food as also part of that history.[86] It explores what happened when Black people and especially Black women, who have been the primary cultivators and cooks of these seemingly irresistible dishes, resisted the very food they created in the name of fitness. This refusal stemmed from a more general consciousness about food, food value, and the political meaning attached to eating in the mid-twentieth century.[87]

This consciousness that tied food to fitness was national in scope. Under the auspices of the National Research Council in 1941, policy reformers and home economists worked together to form a recommended dietary allowance (RDA) for foods to "instill the idea that every American needed to strive for better eating habits, improved health, and more vigor" while the country mobilized for war.[88] After the war's end, the U.S. Department of Agriculture issued the National Food Guide in 1946 that followed RDA guidelines. It advised American families to consume various leafy green vegetables, fruits high in vitamin C, potatoes, milk and other dairy products, meat, bread, and butter. The guide reminded Americans, "This is the Basic 7 guide for well-balanced meals. In time of emergency, you need to eat less of the scarce foods, more of the plentiful. FOOD IS NEEDED TO FEED THE HUNGRY — DON'T WASTE IT."[89] Making revisions to the 1946 guide, the USDA in the 1950s created four food groups, including meat, milk, vegetable/fruit, and bread/cereal. In 1958, the agency premiered a chart with examples of these food groups, including beef and veal, cottage and cream cheeses, grapefruit and cantaloupe, carrots and spinach, and wholegrain bread and macaroni.[90] The USDA promoted this guide as "food for fitness" and detailed what each food group did to and for the body (for example, protein repaired the body, vitamins helped the body grow, carbohydrates provided energy, and so on). American institutions and individuals adhered to these guides in an effort to practice healthy and balanced eating sanctioned by the U.S. government.

African Americans exhibited a similar food consciousness around the idea of "fitness" in various ways during World War II. Through domestic science, nutritional education, and social uplift programs, they engaged in meal planning so that members of the community would make sound food choices. The Grand Rapids Study Club, a Black women's reading and discussion group for "civic-minded citizens" in Michigan, made "dietetics," "food values," "nutrition," "vitamins," "calories," and "what we should eat" the topic for one of its meetings in 1942.[91] Group members asked the discussion leader questions about what constituted a balanced diet and noted foods that would help them avoid diseases like pellagra. Similarly, at the Friendly Inn Social Settlement, a settlement house in Cleveland, Black women taught nutrition classes in 1942 that helped other Black women in the community to "plan well balanced meals."[92]

"Well balanced meals" during World War II enabled Black people not only to project good habits, health, and vigor, as aforementioned, but to demonstrate that they could resist the temptations of overly pleasurable foods. A "well-balanced" meal usually included less-tantalizing cooked vegetables or salads. Black women chefs like New Orleanian Lena Richard proclaimed in her 1939 cookbook that "salads are very rich in minerals and vitamins and should be included daily in the menu," tying green salad in particular to "modern recipes as well as those used for generations in the South, the home of famous Creole cooks."[93] The decisive inclusion of high-mineral and high-vitamin vegetables on African American plates evoked ideals of a balanced meal, a balanced diet, and moderation. Various historical actors espoused these ideals of moderation during and after the war, including government officials, local Black cooks, settlement house dieticians, and ordinary Black people.

Moderation in diet required attention to ever-shifting national food guides. The idea of a "balanced meal" was not static—between 1943 and 1956, the recommended food groups changed from the "Basic 7" to the "Basic 4." To claim a commitment to preparing and consuming well-balanced meals signaled a close study of the most up-to-date nutritional science and national food recommendations. Understanding "newer nutrition," particularly through an actual nutrition class during the war, "depicted a direct relationship between good diets and good wartime citizenship."[94] These food politics likely shaped everyday decisions about diet in the war and postwar periods.

A government-informed food consciousness was also important to the mission of African American home demonstration agents in the 1940s. Black demonstration agents linked specific provisions to citizenship and framed certain food practices as patriotic acts during wartime. Demonstration workers focused on food conservation, nutrition, and rationing regulations. While both white and African American agents performed this work, Black agents' efforts conveyed critical messages about race, food, and citizenship. A Black home demonstration district agent explained in 1946:

> I visited Rachel Anthony, a demonstrator in L— County on the 11th of November. I found growing in her garden carrots, parsnips, beets, onions, spinach, turnips, snap beans, butter beans, eggplant, sage, pepper, mustard, parsley, rutabaga, and flowers. Just across the driveway was a well-kept orchard. I entered a living room and found it furnished neatly and simply, but well. The kitchen had a spacious pantry adjoining it, filled with canned products. I found the owner had worked out a canning budget to meet the needs of her family. Mrs. Anthony has been working [as a] Negro home demonstration agent for 8 years. The results speak for themselves.[95]

Although the laundry list of vegetables, the mention of an orchard, and the evocation of a kitchen with a "spacious pantry" seem mundane, these food conventions proved symbolic of larger civic aspirations for rural Black families. These conventions represented a departure from the turn-of-the-century diets of African American Black Belt residents who consumed mostly pork, corn fare, and molasses with less access to fresh foods.[96] The short description of Mrs. Anthony's home implied an embrace of scientific nutrition and demonstrated respectability through home economics and "dignified" food practices. Her robust garden, well-organized kitchen, and presumed balanced diet aligned with current and future government guidelines that connected particular foods to good citizenship.[97] Rural Black women used food and its trappings (such as kitchens, gardens, canning, and the like) to signal modernity, a commitment to health, and patriotism.

Differences abounded in how Black and white women performed their demonstration practices. Although all agents conducted most of their work through small clubs, Black girls and women who assembled under the auspices of home demonstration work took the opportunity to discuss race "problems." The USDA noted, "One of the greatest single factors contributing to the success of Negro extension work has been the *tact with which Negro agents attack the problems of their race.* Possessed of an innate good judgment, the Negro home demonstration agent has not only influenced better farming and better homemaking practices, but has helped to give white people a new understanding of Negro problems" [emphasis added].[98] "Good judgment," better farming, and improved homemaking denoted wartime patriotism tied to food resourcefulness and postwar ideas of responsible citizenship.[99] After all, the larger extension program for rural families of all racial stripes explicitly concerned citizenship training. The USDA stated, "Home demonstration club programs have included the study of government, citizenship responsibilities, international relationships, and the cultures of other lands."[100] It is unclear how "tactful" Black agents actually were, but "attack[ing] the problems of their race" likely involved explicit discussions of the Black citizenship struggle. Food and "citizenship responsibility" overlapped for these Black women working in the rustic South. These civic food practices served as a rural analog, or perhaps a modification, to the more direct engagement in dieting that emerged in an urban Black consumer culture.

We Are What We (Do Not) Eat: Black Women's Dieting

Like the rest of Americans, African Americans dieted in greater numbers in the postwar era. As the modern diet food industry, composed of specially made "lite" foods and low-fat substitutes, did not emerge until the 1960s, most dieters sought to lose weight through simple food and calorie restriction.[101] Black women turned to the Black press for advice on reducing their caloric intake in the same way they did for exercise instruction in earlier periods. Several Black newspaper columns endorsed dieting in addition to or in place of exercise after the war. Black female journalist Elta Arnold clarified, for example, in 1950, "The people who inquire about exercise as a method of reducing . . . want a way to keep on eating as much as usual and to reduce at the same time. Exercise plus diet can accomplish wonders. Exercise without diet is in vain."[102] Arnold not only advocated dieting because it accelerated weight loss but also aimed to discourage those who wanted to simply "keep on eating." The growing popularity of dieting and exercise enabled Black women like Arnold to shape, or at least attempt to shape, Black bodies from the inside out. African American diet counselors embraced abstemiousness as beneficial for both character and bodily development. Getting fit through dieting, it appeared, required more self-restraint than exercise alone and spoke volumes about one's commitment to total fitness.

One article from the *Chicago Defender* titled "Attention Diet Watchers" explained the advantage of dieting over exercise with numerical precision. The article claimed that if a person (presumably a woman) ironed clothing for one hour, she would burn 140 calories, and if she ate a slice of apple pie after the task, she would then consume 330 calories, resulting in a net gain of 190 calories.[103] The author suggested having "a glass of skim milk or fruit juice" instead of dessert to avoid extra caloric intake. The focus on food made readers more aware of the labor involved in burning calories and the ease of ingesting them with the increasing availability of higher-calorie foods.

Unsurprisingly, diet advice offered to Black readers was decidedly gendered—Black women were the assumed Black dieter. They overwhelmingly wrote to the press for guidance, and the press targeted them in a mutually reinforcing relationship. "Housewives" columns presumed that Black women would prepare a special diet for themselves while simultaneously preparing a different meal for their families. The *Defender*'s "Housewives Corner" published a split menu for Black women to follow. One side listed a daily diet "for the family," which included cinnamon rolls, chop suey, brown rice, and fruit. The side "for the dieter" entailed a sample menu of warm lemon water, two cinnamon rolls, and coffee for breakfast. A "housewife" could have minestrone for lunch, and a "working girl" could enjoy a cheese sandwich, milk, and applesauce. Dinner consisted of lettuce with low-calorie dressing, fruit, and "one cookie only." The column promised that the reader would find this food plan "fun and plenty filling."[104] The paper also suggested that diet seekers bake their own bread from scratch, apparently to have some measure of control over the ingredients the dieter would ingest and to avoid "synthetics" in store-bought bread. The *Defender* assumed that Black homemakers would prepare two separate meals, partly from scratch, until they achieved their desired weight loss and provided for their families.

In Black dieting columns, journalists framed the overindulgence of food as aberrant. In the 1950s, the *Chicago Defender* published a "Foodaholic" series written by Mrs. Mendenhall, a psychiatrist. In advertising the series, the *Defender* explained to the reader, "Follow these weekly stories and see which one might fit your case." The column deployed the term "foodaholic" in various ways. Writers used the term at times in a medical sense to define it as one "addicted to overeating" and at other times in more denigrating ways. One writer commented that "the conditioning diets are extremely important psychologically. You can't just take food away from a 'fatty' except when you can replace it with something else."[105] While intended to help those struggling with weight loss, such language further stigmatized individuals perceived as overweight. Although these articles offered sound advice about food consumption, like replacing lard with vegetable oil and swapping carbonated beverages with fruit juice, they also used derisive terms like "fatty" and presented overweight people as deviant. Similarly, the *Crisis* published an extensive article on dieting and "weight control" and argued that "the difficulty in losing weight usually arises from a psychological rather than a physical need to eat. . . . Psychotherapy may, therefore, be a necessary adjunct to a reducing diet."[106] In essence, so-called foodaholics did not receive sympathies from Black health editors and diet advisors. Agents of the African American press portrayed food addiction as a moral, physical, and even psychological shortcoming. They wrote in ways that merged categories of Black eating, bodies, minds, and character.

Black dieting reveals both vain and serious motivations for losing weight. Some dieters admitted that they simply wanted to look more desirable. Others experienced heart attacks exacerbated by excess weight and turned to dieting as a lifesaving measure. Whether they resorted to food denial for serious or frivolous reasons, African American diet advocates presented food abstinence as valuable for both body and personality while eschewing food indulgence as shameful. These dieting imperatives likely stemmed from the understanding that food informed stereotypes of Black women as unhealthy, sensuous, and overindulgent, which further challenged their postures as fit citizens.

In the 1940s and '50s, before-and-after weight loss photos in Black newspapers featured Black women who expressed their commitment to dieting and, consequently, their dramatic bodily transformations. In 1947, Mrs. Charles Pernell of Pittsburgh provided *Pittsburgh Courier* readers with the steps for a diet plan designed for a pound-a-day weight loss. The article that featured Mrs. Pernell's story targeted an audience who disliked exercise or were "too lazy" to take "brisk reducing walks."[107] At 5'5" and 163 pounds, Pernell calculated that she had 28 pounds to lose, and she began her weight loss journey with the *Harper's Bazaar* nine-day diet, which consisted of black coffee and grapefruit for breakfast; a chicken sandwich, an omelet, steak, or lamb chops for lunch; and salad with a choice of lamb chops, steak, hamburger, or eggs for dinner. Pernell explained that the diet in and of itself would not produce desired results: "Keeping busy is the best way to keep on your diet. If you're too busy to think about food, you won't want it." She added, "Keep determined to win. Use your will power and if you haven't got any, develop some!"[108] Pernell's rhetoric of busyness and willpower reflected themes of self-control reminiscent of war-induced notions of patriotic food restrictions, as well as newer postwar indictments of overconsumption.[109] By Pernell's estimation, losing weight through diet was not merely about achieving thinness. Dieting displayed character traits that indicated attributes of self-sacrifice and productivity. By adopting these principles and publishing their before-and-after photos, Black women like Pernell could tether themselves to a model Black body through both the act and the results of dieting.[110]

While some Black women displayed their dieting success, others demonstrated a desperate search for diet programs and slimmer bodies. One 1952 letter from Mrs. Davis of New Jersey to the *Baltimore Afro-American* "Diet Editor" read, "I am quite fat. I would like to try the Fat Boy's diet plan. Please send me one at once. I weigh 190 lbs. I am 5 ft. 4 in. tall. I stay very tired. I am 46 and can't walk very much. Would you help me?"[111] Another from Mrs. Lillian Johnson of Virginia read, "Enclosed please find a self-addressed, stamped envelope. Please send me the calorie chart at once. I am 5 feet 2 inches tall and weigh 175 pounds which I think is too much."[112] Naomi Yelverton of North Carolina requested calorie charts for herself and her daughter for different reasons—she wanted to lose weight while her daughter wanted to maintain her weight, or as Yelverton put it, "She doesn't want to get any fatter."[113] The letters-to-the-editor section where these requests appeared only included correspondence from readers with traditionally female names, except for one from an unidentified reader. Some Black women wanted to educate themselves on calorie counts and used dieting to achieve a certain weight they judged appropriate for their height. Even though the 1950s saw innovations in labor-saving kitchen appliances and faster meal preparation with processed foods—innovations that would make eating more convenient—some Black women simply opted to reduce their food intake.

In addition to newspapers, Black women's cookbooks served as a viable, albeit ironic, venue for information on moderation. Some postwar Black cookbooks focused on nutrition, daily calorie recommendations, and the political meaning of cooking at a time when Americans were still adjusting to life without wartime food scarcity. Marvene Constance Jones's *Eating for Health: Food Facts and Recipes for Pleasant Eating and Better Health*, published in 1947, built a direct relationship between food and citizenship.[114] The book explained, "The stressing times in which we live demand the best of us. Without good health one cannot give his best to his God and his country."[115] "Stressing times" may have referred to the period in which Jones was writing, just two years after the end of World War II. The country had experienced high economic growth, but African Americans found it difficult to access this boon. It is not clear if this statement referred exclusively to Black people, but as a Black author, Jones folded African Americans into patriotic, God-fearing, and health-conscious readers who would give "the best" of themselves through their eating behaviors.

Figure 5.6 offers more convincing evidence that Jones directed the statement to her African American audience. She featured the moralizing assertion as a caption underneath an image of a young Black woman pointing to a propaganda poster that read, "The U.S. Needs Us Strong." In a cookbook on health, this iconography connected Black women to habits of salubrious eating and national belonging. Black women's food consumption and cooking were not detached from the national trends in nutrition and the model of "cook as citizen." More to the point, Jones noted that "good cooks can contribute much to the building of better bodies for the citizenry of our country." Emphasizing "vitamins and minerals," "savory soups," "healthful breads," and vegetables, Jones explained that

Figure 5.6. Photo from the book *Eating for Health: Food Facts and Recipes for Pleasant Eating and Better Health* by Marvene Constance Jones (Nashville: Southern Publishing Association, 1947), 14. Janice Bluestein Longone Culinary Archive, University of Michigan Special Collections, Ann Arbor.

The stressing times in which we live demand the best of us. Without good health one cannot give his best to his God and his country.

"better bodies" for the citizenry required low-calorie and high-nutrient foods.[116] Food selection and menu building assumed a prominent role in Black women's postwar understandings of citizenship and their stances as rational, as opposed to carnal, eaters.

Jones placed Black women prominently in the book as the arbiters of Black family health. They "plan the family meal" and prepare a "balanced diet" that "furnishes the body with proper proportions of vitamins and minerals," which acquired new civic significance in the war and postwar eras. Black women bore the burden of projecting civic virtue in themselves, their families, and the larger racial collective through healthy meal preparation. If Jones actually believed that "it has been wisely stated that our physical body is in reality the food that we eat," then Black women's centrality in the book indicated the vital role African American women played in shaping that civically fit physical body.[117]

The postwar period presented an opportunity for Black culinary actors to redefine Black eating habits and appetites. Freda De Knight's 1948 cookbook, *A Date with a Dish: A Cook Book of American Negro Recipes*, did just that. In the section on "Vitamins and Calories," De Knight explained, "A well-balanced diet is a 'must' in your daily routine. And if you want to keep your weight down along with your doctor's advice, eat regularly, wisely and well. Eat sparingly of starches, sugar and fats. . . . That plate of vegetables should be green. Not potatoes, macaroni, rice and spaghetti."[118] Throughout the book, De Knight, who also served as the first food editor for *Ebony* and as a well-respected culinary expert, endorsed low-calorie foods like salads with "just a tiny bit of dressing" and generally advocated moderation. As a powerful figure in African American food culture, De Knight used her cookbook to influence postwar Black culinary practices and impose stipulations on what her Black readers should *not* eat. She presented Black women, her primary audience, as not just food producers, consumers, and culinary geniuses but also regulators of food.[119]

De Knight's corporality and personality played an important role in defining Black food culture in the book. Described as a "slender, bright-eyed, and charming young woman with a fine zest for living" as well as a "cultivated Negro woman" in the foreword, De Knight's slim body and urbanity signaled a new era of Black aesthetic and culinary culture. Even by the late 1940s, Black women cooks were still haunted by the trope of the overweight, edacious, and provincial southern "mammy cook," and De Knight sought to break away from this image and redefine Black women's often pejorative association with food and cooking.[120] Just a year before *A Date with a Dish* was released, *Ebony* published an article titled "Goodbye Mammy, Hello Mom," which argued that World War II and "modern industrial life" had "interred" Mammy and introduced a new, sophisticated postwar version of Black female domesticity.[121] De Knight supported this logic. She entreated her readers not to limit themselves to "fried chicken, greens, corn pone, hot breads, and so forth" and instead to "branch out" to fare from Spain, Italy, France, Indonesia, and India.[122] De Knight encouraged the art of good hosting and aesthetically pleasing tables filled with colorful vegetables. She touted a sensible diet and warned that without one, overconsumption and regrettable weight gain would be the result.[123] *A Date with a Dish* seemed to usher in a new genre of African American cookery that influenced both culinary tastes and bodily aspirations. By espousing these ideas in a designated "Negro" cookbook, De Knight connected not only certain foods and cooking methods to Blackness but also the intentional moderation of food to Black culinary culture.

Moderation, or lack thereof, continued to serve as a recurring theme in Black-authored texts aimed at Black women and girls. Elsie Archer's aforementioned 1959 advice book *Let's Face It* provided detailed information on the methods to achieve an ideal Black female body and on how to avoid overconsumption. Part of Archer's objective was to encourage body consciousness among Black girls and urge them to think twice about fat acceptance. She questioned her readers:

> How did you get fat anyway? . . . The most familiar one is overeating. You are bound to gain weight if you stuff yourself with the wrong foods. Gooey sweets and desserts piled high with whipped cream will make you fat if you overdo them. You may think you have to be fat, just because everyone else in your family is. Well, if they are, and you are, too, you've fallen into the same pattern by following their bad eating habits. Starches, rich foods cooked and seasoned with fat meat and bacon are pound builders.[124]

Archer implied that the "fat" and presumably complacent Black family was detrimental to young Black women's figures. Avoiding "bad eating habits" and rejecting the "wrong foods" would allow young African American women to create new generational dietary trends—but they needed the correct nutritional information to do so. In the tradition of earlier Progressive Era advice manuals, *Let's Face It* served this purpose. It functioned as an etiquette guide for young Black women to educate themselves on exemplary Black behavior, including "correct" eating. In other words, if Black girls did not understand the health and social risks of eating high-calorie foods or even what qualified as calorie-laded fare, *Let's Face It* provided the answers. By attempting to mold Black girls' eating habits and bodies, Archer also sought to shape Black women's futures. With the knowledge that Black girls eventually matured into Black women, Archer acknowledged that "fit" African American female bodies had a vital role to play in late twentieth-century Black life.

)(

While the fit Black body held civic value throughout the Progressive Era, Jazz Age, and Great Depression, World War II and the exigencies of the postwar period renewed older motivations for fitness. The pressures of self-surveillance, bodily transformation, moderation in eating, and productive physical activity prevailed in the postwar period as markers of good American citizenship. The turn to diet and exercise represented the ambitions of a constellation of Black historical actors who strived to portray African Americans as rational, abstemious, and disciplined citizens with extraordinary willpower. Abstaining from sumptuous foods and engaging in intentional exercise became essential behaviors for a Black postwar generation seeking achievement, upward mobility, and full citizenship.

The linked enterprise of dieting and exercise may have given Black women some sense of autonomy over their bodies—bodies that the public sphere often manipulated and distorted. Conversely, the pursuit of physical fitness may have also imbued Black women with distress and negative self-evaluation. Nonetheless, to fully understand what it meant to be a fit citizen, it is necessary to confront this fraught and sometimes uncomfortable history of Black women's desire for bodies made healthier, thinner, lovelier, and more ideal through diet and exercise.

) (Epilogue

THE POSSIBILITIES
AND PITFALLS OF
BLACK FITNESS

This book uses exercise to chart Black women's experiences with "fitness" from the post-Reconstruction period to the postwar era. Although ideas of fitness shifted through two world wars, increasing government investment in population health, and an expanding media culture, fitness remained a consistent aspiration for Black women. African American women derived some liberation from fitness culture, as they endeavored to lower mortality rates, created collective bonds, and contested damaging stereotypes through exercise. They also found the pursuit of fitness challenging, as racism and sexism hindered their exercise practices and questioned their civic value. In the first half of the twentieth century, Black women's assertions of citizenship became entangled with affirmations of fitness.

"Fitness" continued to offer possibilities and present pitfalls for Black women in the latter half of the twentieth century and into the twenty-first. Taking these possibilities and pitfalls into account, I end this book by offering novel ways to think about the civil rights movement, the welfare queen trope, and First Lady Michelle Obama through the lens of Black women's exercise and (un)fitness. These three "sites" of inquiry may prompt us to ask new questions about Black women's health, physicality, and bodies in studies of the Black freedom movement, in cultural studies, in politics, and even in our own family histories.

Exercise in the Civil Rights Movement

A framework of exercise may allow us to think differently and more expansively about the physical conditions of the modern civil rights movement. While some forms of Black protest during this era included sedentary acts like sit-ins and freedom rides, the movement was marked by an abundance of physical activity in which activists walked, marched, and picketed for freedom. Rich opportunities remain for the examination of the physical movement *within* the movement and the ways in which exercising citizenship necessitated actual physical exercise. For example, between December 1955 and December 1956, around 40,000 Black Montgomery residents sacrificed the convenience of public buses to boycott the city's segregationist policies, which required Black riders to privilege the seating of white patrons. While the boycott included the organization of private carpools and taxis, many participants simply walked to reach their destination.[1] Collectively, participants walked tens of thousands of miles during the length of the boycott.[2] Rosa Parks recalled that boycotters "who had jobs wore out many pairs of shoes walking to and from work," and Parks herself vowed that she "would never, never ride another segregated bus, even if I had to walk to work."[3] Walking came to represent more than just another form of mobility—it was "an act of protest."[4] Boycott participants walked with their heads "held high," while praying, and "with God."[5]

Black women played a vital role in the boycott. One reporter admitted, "Women are the backbone of the protest," noting that they made up 90 percent of the attendees of the biweekly boycott meetings.[6] Black domestic workers accounted for a large contingent of the boycotters and often walked to their employers' homes for work. One domestic worker explained that she walked to her employer's residence each day, traveling an hour each way (likely three to four miles). She remarked that she was "glad to walk" and would rather journey on foot, even in the rain, than endure the insults of "mean" bus drivers.[7]

This particular moment in the civil rights movement may be interpreted as not just an exercise *in* citizenship but also exercising *for* citizenship. It might be documented through collective miles walked, calories burned, blisters sustained, and number of threadbare shoes accrued. Other iconic moments in the civil rights movement, like the fifty-four-mile protest march from Selma to Montgomery in 1965, James Meredith's 1966 March Against Fear in Mississippi, and the registration of Black voters by the Student Nonviolent Coordinating Committee's door-to-door efforts can be examined for the ways in which they displayed the double meaning of "civic fitness." Within the framework of Black physical culture, these moments may reveal how exercise (particularly Black women's fitness activities) has been critical to Black politics, direct-action strategies, and expansive ideas of Black citizenship and freedom. African American civil rights history is essentially a history of bodily movement. Black exercise can be found almost anywhere that movement took place.

Fatness, Fitness, and the "Welfare Queen" Trope

As African Americans began to reap some of the legislative victories from the civil rights movement in the late twentieth century, they contended with emerging stigmas that continued to call into question their "fitness" for citizenship. Black women had grappled with controlling images of mammies and jezebels in the first half of the twentieth century—images that positioned them as unfit citizens. But in the 1970s and 1980s, a new and equally destructive trope emerged: the welfare queen.[8] In his 1976 presidential campaign, Ronald Reagan popularized the welfare queen trope while making his rounds on the campaign trail. Although that presidential bid proved futile, the image of the duplicitous and undeserving welfare crook endured. The presidential hopeful explained, "There's a woman in Chicago. She has 80 names, 30 addresses, 12 Social Security cards and is collecting veteran's benefits on four nonexisting deceased husbands. . . . She's got Medicaid, getting food stamps and she is collecting welfare under each of her names. Her tax-free cash income alone is over $150,000."[9] Presented as irresponsible, indulgent, and a threat to American values, this mysterious woman seemingly embodied the faults of the welfare system.[10]

"The woman" in Reagan's speech (later identified as Linda Taylor) became a source of public scorn and even disgust.[11] Reagan had grossly exaggerated Taylor's case, but his overstatement proved politically useful. His rhetoric incensed members of the conservative base and incited widespread castigation of big government, public housing, and extant welfare programs.[12] Although Reagan never mentioned a name, race, temperament, or body size when discussing the Chicago woman, he forcefully implied that she was a lazy Black welfare recipient getting "fat" from government assistance. This powerful trope framed Black welfare mothers as greedy, undeserving, and overweight and further marginalized them from categories of good mother, worker, and citizen.[13]

The political castigation of the oversized, indolent Black welfare mother heightened Black fat shame in the late twentieth century and may have influenced Black women's fitness activities and weight loss behaviors. In 1989, *Essence* magazine published a poignant essay by Retha Powers titled "Fat Is a Black Woman's Issue."[14] Powers recounted her struggle with disordered eating and the personal, familial, and social pressures to lose weight. She positioned herself as "one example of the many Black women who are seen as merely fat and greedy." Fatness, she argued, produced a "persistent mammy-brickhouse Black woman image." Despite prevailing notions of Black fat acceptance, fatness, Powers insisted, was indeed a Black woman's issue. As shown in chapter 3, fat had been "a black woman's issue" for several decades before Powers published her essay, but newer tropes of Black women as overweight burdens on the state exacerbated long-standing disdain for "excessive" Black female bodies. The magazine followed in 1990 with an essay titled "Fat War: One Woman's Battle to Control Her Weight," written by Georgiana Arnold.[15] Arnold resorted to various calorie-restrictive diets, pills, and exercise regimens to lose weight in the 1970s and 1980s. Although in some parts of the essay, she categorized weight loss as a "right to health," Arnold's exercise and diet behaviors were inextricably tied to bodily shame.

We may situate Powers and Arnold in a political moment in which supposed "fat and greedy" Black women became conflated with the despised figure of the Black welfare recipient. An imagined welfare receiver who was African American, fat, and female garnered public and political animus during the rising conservatism of the 1970s and 1980s. During this time, fatness signified much more than a metric of beauty or health. It marked Black women as state-dependent, downwardly mobile, and shunned members of society. African American women found themselves at the tangled intersection of anti-welfare sentiment *and* increasing fat rejection. These sentiments also emanated from African Americans themselves.[16] Literary scholar Margaret K. Bass suggests that meanings of fatness in Black communities "changed" in the 1980s and 1990s and "now not even blackness provides that comfortable space that it once claimed for a fat black girl."[17] Indeed, something had changed, or perhaps intensified.

During the last few decades of the twentieth century, welfare and its negative associations became embodied as Black, female, and fat, among other characterizations. The feminization, racialization, and "fattening" of presumed welfare recipients provided additional rationales for Black women like Powers, Arnold, and Bass to reject fatness and pursue weight loss through diet and exercise. As political scientist Rachel Sanders put it, the Black welfare queen archetype "lacks the self-motivation to exercise, the willpower to control her appetite, and the work ethic to contribute positively to society."[18] It would seem difficult, if not impossible, for Black women to escape these newer sociopolitical denigrations of fatness and the challenges they posed to ideas of Black women's fitness. Black women's modern exercise and dieting practices, disordered eating, and negative feelings about their bodies, therefore, cannot be extricated from this political moment.

Let's Move! and Impossible Fitness

When First Lady Michelle Obama announced in 2010 that she would roll out the "Let's Move!" campaign—a national public health program created to reduce childhood obesity—she became the most prominent Black fitness advocate in America. Let's Move! seemed like a suitable platform for a visibly "fit" First Lady with a vested interest in children's health. Nevertheless, enduring ideas of Black women as eternally unfit challenged her campaign of fitness. Critics attacked both the merits of the program and Obama's role in the campaign. Conservative radio talk show host Rush Limbaugh stated of her involvement with Let's Move!, "Our First Lady does not project the image of women that you might see on the cover of the Sports Illustrated Swimsuit Issue or of a woman Alex Rodriguez might date every six months or what have you."[19] Dr. Keith Ablow, a psychiatrist and occasional medical commentator on Fox News, harbored similar doubts. In reference to Obama's healthy school lunch program, he claimed, "She needs to drop a few. . . . Why are we taking fitness advice from her? Let's be honest, like there are no French fries happening there? Like that is all kale and carrots? I don't buy it."[20] Limbaugh's and Ablow's comments reflected centuries-old critiques about Black women's bodies, health, desirability, and political value. They revealed racialized and gendered misgivings about a Black woman serving as the nation's most powerful and visible proponent of physical activity.

Although she "actively worked to dispel the overweight image of Black women through her 'Let's Move!' fitness campaign,"[21] Michelle Obama could not evade long-standing notions about Black women's inherent unfitness. Regardless of the healthy food that Obama ate, how much she exercised, or her public demonstrations of physical capability, she could not fully inhabit fitness. For some, Obama represented *impossible* fitness. If Michelle Obama, who appeared "fit" in every way possible, could engender doubts about her fitness, was fitness reachable, or ever possible, for other African American women?

Considering the fraught history of Black women's exercise chronicled in this book, one could argue that "fitness" was indeed impossible for Black women. African American women experienced recreational segregation, state neglect, and insults when they attempted to exercise. Many Black women succumbed to infectious and chronic diseases before they could ever have the chance to participate in fitness culture. Within their communities, they endured unrealistic pressures to keep themselves, their families, their communities, and, by extension, the entire race healthy through proper diet and exercise. Ideas of Black women's moral and physical unfitness tainted their exercise campaigns in the twentieth century. This historical context created a nearly impossible situation for the First Lady as the lead representative of Let's Move!

In the face of impossibility, however, Michelle Obama continued to advocate for children's health and well-being through the campaign. She improved the nutritional value of school lunches for over 50 million students, helped to increase physical activity for over 12 million schoolchildren, and updated the President's Challenge Youth Fitness Test.[22] At the dedication ceremony of the White House Kitchen Garden in 2016, Obama reflected, "I took [on Let's Move!] because I'm a citizen who loves this country and cares deeply about the future of all of our kids. So I intend to keep working on this issue for the rest of my life," affirming both the validity of the program and her citizenship.[23] While Obama may have represented impossible fitness in the eyes of her critics, she nevertheless asserted her stance as a fit citizen and the right to fitness for others. In this way, she followed the tradition of the Black physical culturists who preceded her—women who met impossibility with aspiration.

Aspirational Fitness

In writing this book, I spoke to several Black family members, colleagues, and friends about their family histories of exercise. I asked if they had memories of their mothers, grandmothers, aunts, and neighbors engaging in intentional physical activity. Most expressed that they had, and they shared stories with me of their relatives taking Jazzercise classes, attempting yoga, joining YWCAs, and purchasing exercise bikes, workout tapes, and other fitness equipment they were often too tired to use. They remembered their mothers wearing sneakers on their work commutes and taking "power walks" with fellow church members. Some told stories of their female loved ones playing golf and tennis at historically Black colleges as young women.

Personally, I have vivid memories of my mother trying different methods to lose weight and live a healthier life before she died at the age of forty-two. My mother was a single parent who worked the night shift in a low-paying job. She was usually exhausted and sleep-deprived. We lived in a high-crime neighborhood where it was unsafe to exercise outdoors. Needless to say, she experienced significant barriers to achieving physical fitness. Nevertheless, I remember tagging along to an aerobics class with my mother, although she attended only a few sessions. At another point, she purchased a home exercise machine complete with resistance bands, a stair-stepper, and a bench-press contraption. I played on the machine much more than my mother used it for exercise. Still, she strived for fitness. My mother aspired toward an ideal that remained largely unavailable to her.

Aspiration, as a concept, may appear inconsequential since it does not account for measurable results. It matters, however, because aspiration unveils the possibilities and limitations of American fitness. A focus on aspiration allows us to thoroughly examine the structural barriers to exercise for Black women. In other words, when we study what Black women longed for, we can better assess the forces that squelched their desires. Aspirational fitness exposes the truths of exercise—that its promises of health and citizenship fell short for African American women. Aspiration also illuminates how Black women fantasized about health, dreamed of longevity, and imagined a future of Black wellness. It brings to bear how Black women sought physical movement outside of labor and practiced a form of healing and self-care through exercise.[24] This book commemorates Black women who did not necessarily accomplish fitness but aspired toward it.

Notes

Abbreviations

CHM   Chicago History Museum, IL
HJLSCPC   H. J. Lutcher Stark Center for Physical Culture and Sports, University of
            Texas at Austin
MARBL   Manuscripts, Archives, and Rare Books Library, Emory University,
            Atlanta, GA
RWWL   Robert W. Woodruff Library, Atlanta University Center, GA
SCRBC   Schomburg Center for Research in Black Culture, New York, NY

Introduction

1. Crystal Bird, "Colored Girl Reserves," *Southern Workman* 50 (August 1921): 353–56.

2. Bird, 356.

3. Evelyn Glenn uses the framework of "substantive citizenship" to illuminate how people who were citizens in law could not realize citizenship in practice. Glenn, *Unequal Freedom*.

4. While out of the scope of this book, I recognize that there are fertile opportunities to examine how the physical "exercise of citizenship" resonated with other ethnic groups. A 1925 issue of *La Prensa*, a Mexican American newspaper based in South Texas, promoted "cultura física" and urged its readers, "Let's be actors in what refers to physical exercise and not only spectators." The paper warned that a lack of exercise would simultaneously atrophy one's muscles and one's will. Historian Nayan Shah indicates that young Chinese Christians in San Francisco joined the YMCA, in part, to learn the tenets of health, hygiene, and physical fitness as a form of citizenship training from the 1910s to the 1930s. Likewise, Native American children at the Carlisle Indian School engaged in physical education as an "assimilation" project. See, in order of mention, "Cultura física: Ejercicio y diversión," *La Prensa*, July 7, 1925, 8; Shah, *Contagious Divides*, 209; and Bloom, *To Show What an Indian Can Do*, 77–96.

5. In order to reduce confusion, I avoid using "exercise" in the manner mentioned here.

6. In the book, "exercise" describes repetitive forms of physical exertion that human beings perform to manage their health, improve their bodily capabilities, achieve physical attractiveness, and engage in recreation. I examine exercise as an intentional physical activity that increases the heart rate, such as walking, calisthenics, gymnastics, hiking, and swimming. Intentionality is essential to the premise of the project, as the book looks outside of compulsory modes of physicality to understand how Black women attempted to expand categories of Black movement. A framework of intention helps to uncover how Black women endeavored to move their bodies apart from manual labor and service to others.

7. "Physical culture" also appears in the book and is a much broader category than exercise, as it captures a variety of behaviors. I consider physical culture a health-seeking ethos of the late nineteenth and early twentieth centuries marked by

nutrition, cleanliness, ventilation, proper clothing (i.e., avoiding corsets and other restrictive attire), and especially exercise. Similarly, the term "physical culturist(s)" refers to women and men who put these principles into practice in their personal lives, professions, homes, and communities. The book inquires how Black women practiced other components of physical culture while centering exercise to explore how and why they invested specifically in physical activity. At times, I use "exercise" and "physical culture" interchangeably.

8. Marshall, "Citizenship and Social Class."

9. Canaday, *Straight State*; Glenn, *Unequal Freedom*; M. Jones, *Birthright Citizens*; Molina, *How Race Is Made in America*; Thuesen, *Greater Than Equal*; Warren, *Quest for Citizenship*.

10. Kymlicka and Norman, "Return of the Citizen," 353.

11. Kymlicka and Norman, 353.

12. Citizenship as "status" and "activity" sometimes overlap, such as voting functioning as a right afforded to citizens as well as a perceived responsibility of citizenship.

13. Spires, *Practice of Citizenship*, 3. Martha Jones also contends that African Americans in the antebellum period sought citizenship by "comporting themselves like citizens." M. Jones, *Birthright Citizens*, 10.

14. Jessie T. Payne, "Physical Fitness: A National Program," *Southern Workman* 48 (July 1919): 348.

15. Stephen Berrey's conceptualization of racial "routines" is instructive here. See Berrey, *Jim Crow Routine*.

16. K. Mitchell, *Living with Lynching*, 16.

17. I thank Ula Taylor for suggesting the framework of embodied citizenship.

18. Elliot, "Big Persons, Small Voices"; E. Russell, *Reading Embodied Citizenship*.

19. Nannie Helen Burroughs, "Anniversary Echoes: Nannie Burroughs," *Southern Workman* 50 (September 1921): 413-14.

20. E. Russell, *Reading Embodied Citizenship*, 4.

21. Bacchi and Beasley, "Citizen Bodies."

22. In addition to cited works on embodied citizenship in fat studies and disability studies, several historical texts have influenced my understanding of citizenship as a racialized, gendered, and particularly embodied concept: Baldwin, *Chicago's New Negroes*; J. Brown, *Babylon Girls*; Greer, *Represented*; R. Kelley, *Race Rebels*; Mckiernan-González, *Fevered Measures*; Molina, *Fit to Be Citizens?*; Ngai, *Impossible Subjects*; Shah, *Stranger Intimacy*; Wolcott, *Remaking Respectability*.

23. Putney, *Muscular Christianity*, 25-39; Verbrugge, *Able-Bodied Womanhood*, 108-10.

24. What I term the "modern American exercise movement" is the rise in health culture, exercise facilities, and fitness innovation that began in the 1890s and continued to the mid-twentieth century. While other historians have not used this term specifically, they note a similar timeline in Americans' zeal for exercise. See Harvey Green, *Fit for America*; Grover, *Fitness in American Culture*; and Verbrugge, *Able-Bodied Womanhood*.

25. J. W. Chambers, *Tyranny of Change*, 81-88; V. Smith, *Clean*, 297-302.

26. Stage and Vincenti, *Rethinking Home Economics*.

27. Todd, "Bernarr MacFadden."

28. V. Smith, *Clean*; Verbrugge, *Active Bodies*; Whorton, *Nature Cures*.

29. Cahn, *Coming on Strong*; Verbrugge, *Active Bodies*, 49-51.

30. Hult and Trekell, *Century of Women's Basketball*, 5–8; Patterson, *Beyond the Gibson Girl*.

31. Oliver, *Fat Politics*; Vertinsky, "'Weighs and Means.'"

32. "History," YMCA; "History," YWCA. The YMCA was originally founded in England and the YWCA was founded in New York City. A formerly enslaved man named Anthony Bowen founded the first Black YMCA in Washington, DC. There is confusion about the founding date of the first Black YWCA. The official YWCA website states it was founded in Dayton, Ohio, in 1889, while historian Paula Giddings cites the same location but refers to the year 1893. Giddings, *When and Where I Enter*, 155.

33. Helen A. Whiting, *Booker T. Washington's Contribution to Education* (Charlotte: Kluttz Mail Adverting Service, 1929), 57–58, box 1, folder 11, Helen Adele Johnson Whiting Papers, Auburn Avenue Research Library on African Culture and History, Atlanta, GA.

34. Alice M. Richards, "Leisure and the Unemployed Man," *Washington Tribune*, July 8, 1932, 8.

35. Richards, 8.

36. In chronological order: Whorton, *Crusaders for Fitness* (1982); Harvey Green, *Fit for America* (1988); Grover, *Fitness in American Culture* (1990); Todd, *Physical Culture and the Body Beautiful* (1999); Black, *Making the American Body* (2013); McKenzie, *Getting Physical* (2013).

37. Moran, *Governing Bodies*.

38. Dworkin and Wachs, *Body Panic*; McKenzie, *Getting Physical*.

39. Some of these texts from the past twenty years include Chapman, *Prove It on Me*; Hendricks, *Gender, Race, and Politics in the Midwest*; Higginbotham, *Righteous Discontent*; T. Hunter, *To 'Joy My Freedom*; M. Mitchell, *Righteous Propagation*; White, *Too Heavy a Load*; and Wolcott, *Remaking Respectability*.

40. Photography also provides a way to understand how poor and working-class women, who left fewer written records, might have sought physical exercise.

41. Mary P. Evans, "Health and Beauty from Exercise Paper No. 3," *Woman's Era*, May 1894; Bruce, *Negro Problem*, 12–13.

42. Quoted in Miller and Pruitt-Logan, *Faithful to the Task at Hand*, 120. Original citation: *Howard University Record* 86 (1923).

43. Madame Katherine Wilson, "Be Beautiful," *Heebie Jeebies*, September 4, 1926, 29.

44. De Knight, *Date with a Dish*, 8.

Chapter 1

1. Crumpler, *A Book of Medical Discourses*, dedication page.

2. Crumpler, 107, 134.

3. Crumpler, 111–12.

4. Disability historian Kim Nielsen also uses the term "civic fitness." Nielsen argues that Helen Keller, despite her gender and disability (two constructs that marginalized her from civic life), asserted her fitness for citizenship through her political writings. She defines civic fitness as "historical and cultural definitions of who is fit for civic life and the relationship of those definitions to our bodies." I make a similar argument that in the early twentieth century, despite racism and sexism, Black women affirmed their fitness for citizenship partly through their participation in physical culture. While I find the concept of civic fitness valuable as Nielsen deploys it, I do not argue

that race or gender are categorically similar to disability. For Nielsen's definition of "civic fitness," see Nielsen, "Helen Keller and the Politics of Civic Fitness," 269.

5. "Whitley Exerciser," RM721.W54, CHM.

6. Sherman, *Civics*, 115-16.

7. Dudley and Kellor, *Athletic Games in the Education of Women*, 37, HJLSCPC.

8. The "strenuous life" refers to a speech given by Theodore Roosevelt discussed later in this chapter.

9. I use the term "aspiring-class" as theorized by Michele Mitchell. See *Righteous Propagation*, xx.

10. Historian Rayford Logan asserted that the post-Reconstruction era was the "nadir of race relations." Logan, *Negro in American Life and Thought*.

11. Historian Mia Bay presents counterarguments that Black leaders made regarding white citizenship, most pertinently civic leader Harvey Johnson, who "argued that white people were a failure as a race and doubted whether they would ever be fit for self-government." Bay, *White Image in the Black Mind*, 106.

12. Historiographical texts that document anti-Black ideologies and the African American struggle for citizenship are numerous. Some of the key scholarship that informs my understanding of fitness, citizenship, and anti-Black racism in the twentieth century includes Gilmore, *Gender and Jim Crow*; M. Jones, *Birthright Citizens*; B. Kelley, *Right to Ride*; Kendi, *Stamped from the Beginning*; and Rosen, *Terror in the Heart of Freedom*.

13. Bruce, *Negro Problem*, 4-5. Alexandra Cornelius's essay alerted me to this source. See Cornelius, "Taste of the Lash of Criticism," 93-109.

14. White writers often used Black physical "deficiencies" (compared with putatively superior white physical characteristics) as justifications for Black subjugation and inequality. Similar to Bruce, Eberhard Hayen, an obscure figure but an apparent white supremacist by virtue of his writings, noted in 1908, "The dark color of skin, the peculiar penetrant odor, the wild, unsteady eye, and the ugly formation of features of the negro are distasteful, if not nauseous, to the white, which no length of time can diminish. He feels the negro is not '*one of us*,' and cannot occupy an equal social position alongside of him" (emphasis in original). Hayen, *Negro Question*, 20. This tendency to delineate Black ugliness, odor, and physical repulsion as the basis of racial difference has a long history and appears in Thomas Jefferson's *Notes on the State of Virginia* published in the 1780s.

15. Bruce, *Negro Problem*, 12-13.

16. F. Hoffman, *Race Traits and Tendencies*, v.

17. F. Hoffman, 171.

18. F. Hoffman, 228.

19. F. Hoffman, 95.

20. F. Hoffman, 95.

21. Fry, *Voice of the Third Generation*, 3.

22. U.S. Const. amend. XV, § 1.

23. Fry, *Voice of the Third Generation*, 7.

24. Fry, 14. Fry cites this quotation in reference to the Lincoln-Douglas debates.

25. "The Negro Problem: How It Appears to a Southern Colored Woman," *Independent*, September 18, 1902, 2222.

26. The idea of the "woman citizen" as both white and morally sound became inextricable by the turn of the twentieth century. White Progressive Era suffragists

argued, for example, that they deserved the franchise and full-fledged citizenship based on their moral attributes. Black suffragists made similar arguments vis-à-vis Black men, but white suffragists built their arguments concerning moral superiority, in part, on anti-Black ideology. Gullett, "Constructing the Woman Citizen"; Terborg-Penn, *African American Women in the Struggle for the Vote.*

27. Giddings, "Last Taboo," 416.

28. J. Hunter, *Nickel and a Dime,* 126.

29. Roosevelt, *Strenuous Life,* 2.

30. Roosevelt, 73.

31. Bederman, *Manliness and Civilization,* 170–216.

32. To accommodate this "strenuous life," the desirable male body shifted from a lean figure to one of muscle and heft. Around the turn of the twentieth century, bodybuilding and exhibition wrestling gained national attention, and muscle-bound showmen like Eugen Sandow achieved a formidable male following.

33. Putney, *Muscular Christianity*; Winter, *Making Men.*

34. Gail Bederman focuses more on the gender aspect of exercise and fitness in *Manliness and Civilization,* noting, "By the 1890s, strenuous exercise and team sports had come to be seen as crucial to the development of powerful manhood. College football had become a national craze; and commentators like Theodore Roosevelt argued that football's ability to foster virility was worth even an occasional death on the playing field." Bederman, *Manliness and Civilization,* 15.

35. Willard, "Physical Culture and Dress Reform," 110.

36. Quoted in Giddings, *Ida,* 266. Original citation in the New York *Voice,* an interview published in 1890. Also quoted in M. Parker, "Desiring Citizenship," 56.

37. Quoted in Giddings, *Ida,* 267.

38. Historians and classicists note that the assumed "whiteness" and beauty of Greek sculpture, which stemmed from the scholarship of eighteenth-century art historian Johann Winckelmann, have been used as "justification for asserting white supremacy" in the nineteenth and twentieth centuries. Many of these sculptures were originally bronze and polychromous. For quotation see Purdy, "The Whiteness of Beauty." Also see Bond, "Why We Need to Start Seeing the Classical World in Color."

39. Plaster casts of Atlas, Venus, and Apollo, for instance, were featured at the Race Betterment Foundation's exhibit at the Panama-Pacific International Exhibition in 1915.

40. Many other white women reformers incorporated physical culture into their campaigns that targeted industrial laborers, schoolchildren, and everyday women after the turn of the century.

41. Fletcher, *Woman Beautiful,* 56, HJLSCPC.

42. A specific instance of this is discussed in chapter 2. See "Live Topics of the Town," *Freeman* (Indianapolis), September 16, 1916, 1.

43. Sargent, "Significance of a Sound Physique," 12.

44. Presidential Committee on Harvard and the Legacy of Slavery, *Harvard and the Legacy of Slavery,* 40.

45. Kasson, *Houdini, Tarzan, and the Perfect Man.*

46. R. E. Wales, "The Most Perfect Girl in the World," *San Francisco Sunday Call,* April 10, 1910, 5.

47. Black newspaper editors considered dress a critical component of race representation. More generally, "dressing well" served as a marker of Black progress and

middle-class sexual politics. See Rhodes, "Pedagogies of Respectability"; and Wolcott, *Remaking Respectability*.

48. Shah, *Contagious Divides*; Stern, *Eugenic Nation*.

49. Macfadden, *Macfadden's Encyclopedia of Physical Culture*, 2416.

50. Macfadden used even more incendiary language about race and ethnicity in *Physical Culture*. In a 1906 issue he stated, "It seems to me that it is about time for the American nation to wake up. . . . Immigration will not continue indefinitely as it has in the past, but even admitting that it will do so, is it right or wise that the 'scum of the earth,' inferior persons of various European and Asiatic nationalities, shall ultimately furnish the moral and physical characteristics of the citizens of the United States? It is about time for us to make known the truth in reference to our physical degeneracy." Bernarr Macfadden, "Are Americans Degenerating?," *Physical Culture*, August 1906, 199, author's collection.

51. Examples of fitness segregation in the twentieth century are innumerable and are included throughout the book, but this small sampling provides support for the premise that physical culture, exercise, "the strenuous life," and the like were both gendered and racialized.

52. Jackson, *Lines of Activity*, 307.

53. Cahn, *Coming on Strong*, 17.

54. "Afro-American Notes," *Pittsburgh Press*, February 10, 1918, 52.

55. A "race woman" or "race man" refers to a publicly recognized person committed to improving the social, economic, and political conditions of African Americans.

56. F. Cooper, "Elevating the Race."

57. Dorsey, "Despite Poor Health."

58. B. Washington, *Up from Slavery*, 101.

59. Herndl, "Invisible (Invalid) Woman," 561.

60. Davidson, "How Shall We Make the Women of Our Race Stronger?"

61. Davidson, 299.

62. The full quotation reads: "Nervous and organic diseases have laid tyrannous hands upon us and are leading us helpless captives away from the highest avenues of usefulness into the darker ways of suffering and too often of selfish narrowness, for though a strong, earnest spirit may rise above, and inspire a weak body, generally the weakness of the body will crop the wings and keep the soul from soaring." Davidson, 299.

63. Davidson, 300.

64. In this way, Davidson continued the work of Sarah Mapps Douglass, a Black science educator who used physiology lessons to challenge theories of Black racial inferiority in the early and mid-nineteenth century. Mapps Douglass believed that anatomy and physiology could edify young Black women by encouraging positive body esteem and Black autonomy in her students. See Haynes, *Riotous Flesh*; and Rusert, *Fugitive Science*. I thank LaKisha Simmons for alerting me to this connection.

65. "Catalogue of the Tuskegee State Normal School at Tuskegee, Alabama for the Academic Year 1885–86," Tuskegee University Archives, Tuskegee, AL.

66. Davidson, "How Shall We Make the Women of Our Race Stronger?," 299.

67. Little biographical information exists on Evans. For information on her work with the Boston NAACP, see Schneider, *Boston Confronts Jim Crow*, 158. Her anti-lynching work was featured in "Anti-Lynchers in Boston," *New York Times*, May 21, 1899.

68. Mary P. Evans, "Health and Beauty from Exercise Paper No. 3," *Woman's Era*, May 1894.

69. Mary P. Evans, "Health and Beauty from Exercise Paper No. 1," *Woman's Era*, May 1894.

70. Race woman Fannie Barrier Williams invoked the term "usefulness" to describe Black women's contribution to racial uplift in 1904. Black feminist scholar Tamara Beauboeuf-Lafontant uses the term "social usefulness" to describe another race woman, Lucy Diggs Slowe, and her aspirations for college women at Howard University in the 1920s and 1930s. See Wolcott, *Remaking Respectability*, 18–19; and Beauboeuf-Lafontant, "New Howard Woman."

71. Camp, "Black Is Beautiful," 677.

72. Elizabeth Johnson, "Women at Home," *Woman's Era*, March 1894, 11.

73. M. Mitchell, *Righteous Propagation*.

74. M. Mitchell, 135.

75. Northrop, Gay, and Penn, *College of Life*, front cover.

76. While the target audience for this text included the entire "colored race," it is not documented who actually read this advice book. Literate, aspiring-class race women and men likely read these works, which did not represent a large swath of African Americans in 1895. Michele Mitchell notes that advice literature authors often targeted Black mothers and fathers so that parents could use the lessons offered to instruct future generations.

77. Harrison and Harrison, *Life and Times of Irvine Garland Penn*, chap. 6, location 1426, Kindle ed.

78. Harrison and Harrison, chap. 6, location 1426, Kindle ed.

79. Northrop, Gay, and Penn, *College of Life*, 294.

80. Northrop, Gay, and Penn, 295.

81. Northrop, Gay, and Penn, 292, 295.

82. I have been unable to locate additional information on Le Zetora, but the caption below the image suggests that she may have been part of a circus act, perhaps in Europe. However, white-dominated circuses in the late nineteenth century rarely, if ever, allowed Black women prominent performer roles. See Childress, "Life beyond the Big Top."

83. In personal correspondence, weightlifting historian David P. Webster estimated that this globe weight is seventy pounds.

84. Northrop, Gay, and Penn, *College of Life*, 301.

85. Northrop, Gay, and Penn, 298.

86. Richings, *Evidences of Progress among Colored People*, iii.

87. Richings, iii–iv.

88. Richings, viii.

89. Richings, 104.

90. "The Working Woman's Health: Rules of Physical Culture to Be Followed by All," *Wisconsin Weekly Advocate*, April 30, 1903, 8.

91. "The Call for the Skillful Negro—Training Women," *Washington Bee*, August 24, 1912, 8.

92. "The Call for the Skillful Negro—Training Women," 8.

93. "Women and Exercise," *Chicago Defender*, December 6, 1913, 8.

94. Leola Lillard, "A Key to Culture: Appropriate Dress," *New York Amsterdam News*, September 5, 1928, 8.

95. Leola Lillard, "Health and Grace," *New York Amsterdam News*, October 5, 1927, 14.

96. E. Elliot Rawlings, "Heading off Sickness," *New York Amsterdam News*, September 28, 1927, 14.

Chapter 2

1. "Manhattan Y.W.C.A. Notes," *New York Amsterdam News*, February 7, 1923, 6.

2. As discussed in the previous chapter, Bernarr Macfadden's attitudes about non-white people were questionable at best and racist at worst. His willingness to deliver a speech at this Black YWCA was highly unusual and reveals Macfadden's complicated relationship with African Americans.

3. Dr. Algernon B. Jackson, "Health as a Factor in the Solution of the Race Problem," *Heebie Jeebies*, August 27, 1929, 11.

4. Jackson, 11.

5. Dr. B. S. Herben, "Are You Strong for the Race?," *Negro World*, April 7, 1923, 3.

6. Several scholars make similar claims about "(un)sanitized citizenship" and "public health citizenship." See Knadler, "Unsanitized Domestic Allegories"; S. Roberts, *Infectious Fear*; and Tomes, *Gospel of Germs*.

7. Roman, "Medical Phase of the South's Ethnic Problem," 151. Roman held prominent roles in medicine throughout his life. He served as president of the National Medical Association, was the founder of the Department of Ophthalmology and Otolaryngology at Meharry Medical College (where he also taught medical history and ethics), and was the director of health at Fisk University, to name a few of his accomplishments.

8. Molina, *Fit to Be Citizens?*, 91–97; S. Roberts, *Infectious Fear*, 42–66; Wailoo, *Dying in the City of the Blues*, 55–83.

9. Mckiernan-González, *Fevered Measures*; Molina, *Fit to Be Citizens?*

10. "The Negro Race Problem," *Health*, January 1908, 52. These predictions were rooted in a century of scientific racism most associated with proslavery scientists like Samuel Cartwright and Josiah Knott. Cartwright and Knott rose to popularity in the mid-nineteenth century and disseminated ideas of enslaved people's biological difference and polygenesis, respectively. Cartwright, a leading American physician, even commented on slaves' health and what happened when they exercised, asserting that "all negroes are not equally black—the blacker the healthier and stronger, and deviation from the black color, in the pure race, is a mark of feebleness or ill health. When heated from exercise, the negro's skin is covered with an oily exudation that gives a dark color to white linen, and has a very strong odor." Samuel A. Cartwright, "Report on the Diseases of and Physical Peculiarities of the Negro Race," *New Orleans Medical and Surgical Journal* 7 (May 1851): 697.

11. *Negro Year Book*, 1914–15, 319, Tuskegee University Archives, Tuskegee, AL.

12. *Negro Year Book*, 321.

13. D. Roberts, *Killing the Black Body*; H. Washington, *Medical Apartheid*.

14. S. Roberts, *Infectious Fear*, 221.

15. In response to this exclusion, Black physicians founded the National Medical Association in 1895. Nonetheless, the exclusion had dire consequences. In 2005, a panel of experts from the American Medical Association investigated its history of segregation. The panel admitted that being barred from membership to prominent medical societies resulted in African Americans' "professional isolation, erosion of

professional skills, and limitations on sources of income." Baker et al., "African American Physicians and Organized Medicine."

16. S. Hoffman, "Progressive Public Health Administration"; McBride, *Integrating the City of Medicine*; S. Roberts, *Infectious Fear*.

17. Byrd and Clayton, *American Health Dilemma*, 15.

18. F. Washington, *Negro in Detroit*, 137.

19. F. Washington, 180.

20. Some African Americans believed that unclean homes were the bane of Black existence. In 1899, African American educator and reformer Lucy C. Laney stated, "There is no greater enemy of the race than these untidy and filthy homes, they bring not only physical disease and death, but they are [the] very incubators of sin, they bring intellectual and moral death." Lucy C. Laney, "The Burden of the Educated Colored Woman," *Southern Workman* 28 (September 1899): 342.

21. Newly arrived European immigrants living in cities had similar experiences with housing in the late nineteenth and early twentieth centuries. They often lived in dilapidated tenement quarters and suffered from poverty and housing-related health issues.

22. McBride, *Integrating the City of Medicine*, 30. According to McBride, infectious diseases were less prevalent among whites than among African Americans in Philadelphia. Between 1910 and 1929, infant mortality rates dropped for both groups, but Black rates were typically double those of white infant mortality numbers.

23. "V. B. Hodges to Neighborhood Union Doctors, 9 August 1924," box 5, folder 18, Neighborhood Union Collection, RWWL.

24. Ellison, *Selected Letters*, 70, letter dated May 27, 1935.

25. Ellison, 72, letter dated June 1, 1935.

26. Ellison, 72, letter dated October 1935.

27. F. Washington, *Negro in Detroit*, 194.

28. Hart, *Health in the City*.

29. Alnutt, "'Negro Excursions'"; Wiltse, *Contested Waters*.

30. The school publicized that "only well prepared and thoroughly qualified young women are accepted." The enrollment was limited to 100 students. "Central School of Hygiene and Physical Education."

31. "Girl Barred from School by 'Y.W.' Rule," *Chicago Defender*, November 22, 1924, 1.

32. "Live Topics of the Town," *Freeman*, September 16, 1916, 1.

33. Like the Central School of Hygiene, the Dudley Sargent School was an elite institution that sought the best students. In 1915, the school enrolled 450 students from all parts of the United States and Canada, and 4,000 students attended the school's summer camp. P. Sargent, *Handbook of the Best Private Schools*, 198.

34. Verbrugge, "Recreation and Racial Politics."

35. "Young Women's Christian Association History of Colored Work," 84, Young Women's Christian Association Records, Arthur and Elizabeth Schlesinger Library on the History of Women in America, Cambridge, MA.

36. Hult and Trekell, *Century of Women's Basketball*, 13.

37. Gwyneth King Roe, "The Woman's Gym for Women and Children," box 6, folder 6, Mss 151, Gwyneth King Roe Papers, Wisconsin Historical Society, Madison.

38. Harvey Green, *Fit for America*, 229.

39. "Electronic Massage Exerciser," *Physical Culture*, July 1900, HJLSCPC.

40. The average worker made only a few dollars a week in 1900. "Sandow's Own Combined Developer," *Physical Culture*, May 1900, HJLSCPC.

41. Hilary Green, *Educational Reconstruction*; Masur, *Example for All the Land*.

42. Clark et al., "Remember the Titans"; Henderson, "Progress and Problems"; Laker, *Beyond the Boundaries of Physical Education*.

43. Du Bois, *Health and Physique of the Negro American*, 90.

44. Du Bois, 90.

45. "Practically Nothing," *Atlanta Independent*, June 14, 1913, 4.

46. "The Kansas Industrial and Educational Institute Begins 25th School Year September 6th 1920," *Topeka Plaindealer*, August 6, 1920, 1.

47. Brochure, Wiley College, *Wiley College 1929–1930*, Marshall, TX, box 19, folder 7, Black Print Culture Collection, MARBL.

48. Verbrugge, *Active Bodies*, 126, 134. Verbrugge cites Hampton and Tuskegee as examples of bifurcated, gender-specific collegiate physical activity. After World War I, all students were expected to take physical education classes. This was a nationwide change precipitated by the high failure rate of military physical fitness tests.

49. This section uses "physical culture" and "physical education" interchangeably. In the context of late nineteenth- and early twentieth-century primary, secondary, and college education, historical actors sometimes used "physical culture" to mean "physical education."

50. "Self-Sacrificing Women," *Freeman*, April 20, 1901, 2.

51. "Self-Sacrificing Women," 2.

52. Knadler, "Unsanitized Domestic Allegories."

53. "Self-Sacrificing Women," 2.

54. Nannie Helen Burroughs, "Anniversary Echoes: Nannie Burroughs," *Southern Workman* 50 (September 1921): 413–14. Burroughs directed this statement to students at Hampton Institute.

55. Advertisements for Burroughs's school, with "physical culture" listed as one of the foci of the school, often appeared in the advertiser section of the *Crisis*. See "Educate Your Girl at the National Training School for Women and Girls," *Crisis*, May 1921, 36. By 1929, the school enrolled 102 students. Lerner, *Black Women in White America*, 133–34.

56. Harley, "Nannie Helen Burroughs"; T. Taylor, "'Womanhood Glorified.'"

57. "Educate Your Girl at the National Training School for Women and Girls," 36.

58. Catalog, Spelman Seminary, *Fifth Annual Catalogue of the Spelman Seminary and Normal School for Women and Girls, 1885–1886*, Atlanta, GA, box 18, folder 11, Black Print Culture Collection, MARBL.

59. Lefever, "The Early Origins of Spelman College," 62.

60. Helen James Chisholm, "Hampton Normal and Agricultural Institute Student Account Book, 1897–1903," box 12, folder 2, Chisholm Family Papers, MARBL.

61. Chisholm's diary also reveals her height and weight. At 5′2″ and 116 lbs., Chisholm's body fell within a "normal" weight range and aligned with burgeoning ideas of thinness, health, and respectability that I explore in the following chapter. Helen James Chisholm, "Standard Diary, 1909," box 14, folder 8, Chisholm Family Papers, MARBL.

62. Captain, "Enter Ladies and Gentlemen of Color."

63. Verbrugge, *Active Bodies*, 163–65.

64. Some of the exercise "habits" listed included basketball, volleyball, four-mile hikes, and folk dances. Olive B. Rowell, Physical Education for Girls 1921–1922, Physical Education Department Collection, Hampton University Archives, Hampton, VA.

65. Quoted in Miller and Pruitt-Logan, *Faithful to the Task at Hand*, 119-20. Original citation: *Howard University Record* 86 (1923).

66. Quoted in Miller and Pruitt-Logan, *Faithful to the Task at Hand*, 202. Original citation: Howard University, Annual Report of the Dean of Women, 1932-1933.

67. Verbrugge, "Recreation and Racial Politics," 1194.

68. Speech delivered January 27, 1922, Irene McCoy Gaines Papers, CHM.

69. Verbrugge, "Recreation and Racial Politics," 1201.

70. Verbrugge, 1201.

71. "Y.W.C.A. Notes," *Philadelphia Tribune*, December 16, 1916, 1.

72. "Brooklyn Y.W.C.A. Working for Gym," *Pittsburgh Courier*, March 23, 1912, 1.

73. "Brooklyn Y.W.C.A. Working for Gym," 1.

74. Addie Hunton, "Negro Womanhood Defended," *Voice of the Negro*, July 1904, 282.

75. "Young Women's Christian Association History of Colored Work," Young Women's Christian Association Records, Arthur and Elizabeth Schlesinger Library on the History of Women in America, Cambridge, MA.

76. As a part of Washington's political ideology, he did not necessarily advocate exercise and health for its own sake but to buttress his stance on a Black laboring underclass. He valued health for what healthy Black workers would mean for the Southern labor and agricultural market. His health activism often sounded like this: "The entire South is dependent, in a large measure, upon the Negro for certain kinds of work. A weak body, a sickly body, is costly to the whole State from an economic view." R. Brown, "National Negro Health Week Movement," 555.

77. R. Brown, "National Negro Health Week Movement."

78. National Negro Health Week brochure, 1925, box 1, folder 1, National Negro Health Week Papers, Tuskegee University Archives, AL.

79. Helen A. Whiting, *Booker T. Washington's Contribution to Education* (Charlotte: Kluttz Mail Advertising Service, 1929), 57-58, box 1, folder 11, Helen Adele Johnson Whiting Papers, Auburn Avenue Research Library on African Culture and History, Atlanta, GA.

80. Rouse, "Legacy of Community Organizing."

81. Neighborhood Union pamphlet, undated, box 2, folder 1, Neighborhood Union Collection, RWWL.

82. Neighborhood Union charter document, 1911, box 2, folder 2, Neighborhood Union Collection, RWWL.

83. Rouse, "Legacy of Community Organizing," 115.

84. Neighborhood Union, "A Survey," 1926, box 2, folder 8, Neighborhood Union Collection, RWWL.

85. Neighborhood Union, "A Survey."

86. "Health Center Report," box 5, folder 22, Neighborhood Union Collection, RWWL. This document has "468" patients typed, but "518" penciled in.

87. T. Hunter, *To 'Joy My Freedom*, 187-218.

88. V. May, "Standardizing the Home?"

89. Neighborhood Union, "A History of the Neighborhood Union," undated, box 2, folder 12, Neighborhood Union Collection, RWWL.

90. Mullins, "Nudes, Prudes, and Pigmies."

91. Ellis, "Status of Health and Physical Education," 141.

92. Ellis, 135.

93. Antoinette, "Straight Shoulder Line Flatters, While Bent One Detracts," *Baltimore Afro-American*, September 12, 1931, 16.

94. Mme. Qui Vive, "Shoulders Tell Tales," *Atlanta Daily World*, September 17, 1935, 2.

95. Mme. Qui Vive, 2.

96. Baron and Boris, "'The Body' as a Useful Category."

97. Minutes of the Second Mothers' Conference Held in Pine Bluff, AR, September 8, 9, and 10, 1894 (Atlanta: Chas. P. Byrd), box 1, folder 14, Adam Knight Spence and John Wesley Work Collection, Auburn Avenue Research Library on African Culture and History, Atlanta, GA.

98. National Association of Colored Women, Inc., "A Closer View," *Synopsis Explaining Organization, Activities, [and] Future Trends*, box 39, folder "Negro Girls and Women, 1930–1933," Alliance for Guidance of Rural Youth Records Collection, David M. Rubenstein Rare Book and Manuscript Library, Duke University, Durham, NC.

99. Ruth Arnett, "Girls Need Physical Education," *Chicago Defender*, December 10, 1921, 10.

100. "Colored Girl Makes Good," *Norfolk New Journal and Guide*, July 14, 1917, 1. This article foreshadowed an observation Du Bois made in 1922: "[The Negro] is beginning to gather himself together . . . he is beginning carefully to train and breed for [brains, efficiency, and beauty] in varying proportions." W. E. B. Du Bois, "Opinion: The Negro," *Crisis*, August 1922, 153.

Chapter 3

1. Madame Sara Washington, "Beauty Secrets: Fight Fat," *New York Amsterdam News*, June 1, 1927, 6. It is unclear if this is the same Sara Washington who founded the Apex News and Hair Company.

2. Maryrose Reeves Allen, "An Outline: The Development of Beauty among College Women through Health and Physical Education," 1938, box 160-4, folder 4, series B, education, Maryrose Reeves Allen Papers, Moorland-Spingarn Research Center, Howard University, Washington, DC.

3. Throughout this chapter, I use the following terms interchangeably while acknowledging that they relay different meanings: middle-class, elite, and professional. These terms are meant to alert the reader to Black women who were educated, lived relatively privileged lives, and maintained social capital within their communities but who were also financially and politically marginalized.

4. See, for example, Gaines, *Uplifting the Race*; White, *Too Heavy a Load*; Hendricks, *Gender, Race, and Politics in the Midwest*; Higginbotham, *Righteous Discontent*; M. Mitchell, *Righteous Propagation*; and Wolcott, *Remaking Respectability*.

5. The scholarship is more attentive to the ways in which white men linked their fit bodies to civilization and modernity. See Bederman, *Manliness and Civilization*; Kasson, *Houdini, Tarzan, and the Perfect Man*; and Putney, *Muscular Christianity*.

6. Mixter, *Health and Beauty Hints*; Pinkham, *Lydia E. Pinkham's Private Text-Book*; Pratt, *Body Beautiful*; Rubinstein, *Art of Feminine Beauty*, HJLSCPC.

7. Peiss, *Hope in a Jar*, 97–98.

8. Pratt, *Body Beautiful*, 19, HJLSCPC.

9. For a discussion of variations of the "New Woman" from the turn of the twentieth century, including "New Negro Women," see Patterson, *Beyond the Gibson Girl.*

10. H. Hancock, *Physical Training for Women*, xi, HJLSCPC.

11. Bernarr Macfadden, "The Editor's Viewpoint," *Physical Culture*, May 1910, 413, HJLSCPC.

12. Bernarr Macfadden, "The Development of Womanly Beauty," *Woman's Physical Development*, October 1900, 14–21, HJLSCPC.

13. Fitness magazines from the early twentieth century greatly influenced ideas about the "perfect" body. According to scholar Mark Whalan, "*Physical Culture* generated a consumer desire in the space between a consumer's self-perception and the visual representation of idealized physiques—the space between the real, and representation that claimed the authority of the 'ideal.'" See Whalan, "'Taking Myself in Hand.'"

14. Macfadden, "Development of Womanly Beauty," 15.

15. Ingelhart, *Press Freedoms*, 223.

16. See "Bernarr Macfadden Guilty: Physical Culture Man Gets Prison Sentence for Mailing Objectionable Matter," *New York Times*, November 12, 1907; and "Saves Macfadden from Jail: President Commutes Sentence of Man Who Ran Brawn and Beauty Shows," *New York Times*, November 18, 1909.

17. For instance, physical culturists H. Van de Velde authored the salacious *Sex Efficiency through Exercise*, which featured a flipbook of half and sometimes fully nude white women performing sexually suggestive exercises. Van de Velde, *Sex Efficiency through Exercise*, HJLSCPC.

18. Several texts have examined African American women's efforts to combat stereotypes of Black women as licentious and wanton. See Hine, "Rape and the Inner Lives of Black Women"; Hendricks, *Gender, Race, and Politics in the Midwest*; and Higginbotham, *Righteous Discontent.*

19. Kern, *Glorious Womanhood*, 4, HJLSCPC.

20. Farrell, *Fat Shame*, 27–32; Grover, *Fitness in American Culture*, 86–122; Oliver, *Fat Politics*; Vertinsky, "'Weighs and Means.'"

21. Peters, *Diet and Health with Key to the Calories*, 12.

22. "Losing 103 Lbs. to Music!," *Cosmopolitan*, December 1922, 145; "Playing Off Pounds," *Good Housekeeping*, May 1922, 195.

23. See Craig, *Ain't I a Beauty Queen?*; Gill, *Beauty Shop Politics*; Peiss, *Hope in a Jar*; and Rooks, *Hair Raising.*

24. This proved true for Black beauty culturists like Madam C. J. Walker.

25. Allen, "An Outline: The Development of Beauty among College Women through Health and Physical Education," Maryrose Reeves Allen Papers, Moorland-Spingarn Research Center, Howard University, Washington, DC.

26. "Exercise Promotes Beauty in Women," *Baltimore Afro-American*, August 23, 1902, 6.

27. W. E. B. Du Bois, "The Problem of Amusement," *Southern Workman* 27 (September 1897): 184.

28. Overton-Hygienic Company, *Encyclopedia of Colored People*, E185 .O9 1921, CHM, 38.

29. Overton-Hygienic Company, 38.

30. Campt, *Image Matters*, 7.

31. See Raiford, *Imprisoned in a Luminous Glare*; and Wallace and Smith, *Pictures and Progress*.

32. Some Black women worried about the aesthetic risks of physical overdevelopment from sport participation. They discouraged "rugged" athletics, believing this kind of physical activity would damage women's grace, femininity, and allure. Ivora King, a sports writer for the *Baltimore Afro-American*, warned, "The girl who is too athletic is on the wrong track to becoming a wife." Maryrose Reeves Allen relayed similar sentiments: "The heavier sports, I feel, have no place in a woman's life: they rob her of her feminine charms." Ivora King, "Women in Sports," *Baltimore Afro-American*, September 19, 1931, 13; Allen, "An Outline: The Development of Beauty among College Women through Health and Physical Education," Maryrose Reeves Allen Papers, Moorland-Spingarn Research Center, Howard University, Washington, DC.

33. Davis, *Blues Legacies and Black Feminism*.

34. Garber, "Gladys Bentley"; Wilson, *Bulldaggers, Pansies, and Chocolate Babies*, 154–91.

35. Cited in Davis, *Blues Legacies and Black Feminism*, 276.

36. Cited in Davis, 281–82.

37. Dan Burley, "Fame and Fortune for Fat Folks!," *New York Amsterdam News*, November 30, 1940, 21. I thank LaShawn Harris for sending me this source.

38. Shaw, *Embodiment of Disobedience*.

39. If these women could afford to take photographs, they may have been financially comfortable, considering the high cost of portraits.

40. Stearns, *Fat History*, 89.

41. Alice Randall, "Black Women and Fat," *New York Times*, May 5, 2012, SR5.

42. See Rockeymoore, "Are Black Women Obese Because We Want to Be?"; Rooks, "Do Black Women Really Want to Be Fat?"; and "Women, Weight and Wellness—Room for Debate."

43. Comments like Randall's have explicit political uses and consequences. Days after the publication of her article, conservative political commentator Rush Limbaugh read Randall's piece at length on his radio show. He applauded her personal responsibility approach to addressing the nation's (and specifically African American) obesity rates and presented her comments as a condemnation of the Affordable Care Act and government intervention more generally. See the May 8, 2012, transcript here: http://www.rushlimbaugh.com/daily/2012/05/08/obesity_it_s_the_state_s_problem_not_yours.

44. "Great Eaters," *Christian Recorder*, February 27, 1864.

45. "Are Fat People Healthy?," *Christian Recorder*, December 12, 1878, and December 19, 1878.

46. Farrell, *Fat Shame*, 25–58; Schwartz, *Never Satisfied*, 47–111.

47. I extracted these terms from weight-related articles published in the *Baltimore Afro-American* and the *Chicago Defender* between 1904 and 1934. This is not meant to be an exhaustive list. Rather, it is a sampling to give the reader an idea of how some African Americans regarded fatness during the period under study.

48. Edwards, *Southern Urban Negro as a Consumer*, 238.

49. The researcher classified the respondents as "professional" Black women.

50. The literature on Black women's clubs has focused on propriety, comportment, clothing, and the like but has not been attentive to middle-class Black women's

concepts of the respectable body and physical culture. See Hendricks, *Gender, Race, and Politics in the Midwest*; Knupfer, *Toward a Tenderer Humanity*; White, *Too Heavy a Load*; and Wolcott, *Remaking Respectability*.

51. "Girls Roll Over to Reduce Flesh," *Savannah Tribune*, February 19, 1910, 3.

52. "Girls Roll Over to Reduce Flesh," 3.

53. Greater Bethel A.M.E. Church, where members constructed the gym, was the "largest Negro church in America." A little over a year after the gymnasium opened, suspected Ku Klux Klan members demolished the church by setting it on fire. See "'Greater Bethel' Burns; Suspect Klan," *Pittsburgh Courier*, October 25, 1924, 1.

54. "The Exercise Habit," *Chicago Defender*, June 2, 1923, 4.

55. All of the Dunbar letters can be found in Metcalf, "Letters of Paul and Alice Dunbar." For an in-depth discussion of their relationship see Alexander, *Lyrics of Sunshine and Shadow*.

56. From the extant correspondence between the two, this is the only letter that mentions that particular instance of domestic violence.

57. Dunbar-Nelson also joked about her use of the gym. As a teacher, she wrote to Paul Laurence Dunbar about a few of the troublesome students she encountered: "After class one large boy who is just my height asked me—'Say Miss Moore [her maiden name], do you go to a gymnasium?' 'Yes,' I answered cheerily, 'and I'm willing to undertake to knock you down if you want.' He declined and departed with respect and admiration beaming all over him." Metcalf, "Letters of Paul and Alice Dunbar," 398-99.

58. It is unclear what Dunbar-Nelson meant by "white looking," but it could refer to her history of racial passing. Hull, *Give Us Each Day*, 91, entry dated October 3, 1921.

59. Hull, 175. Americans began using "calories" as a measurement of food energy around the turn of the twentieth century, and the term became fairly common by the 1920s. At the time Dunbar-Nelson wrote this entry, 1,200 calories rated below the recommended amount of calories adults were expected to consume daily. In *How to Select Foods: What the Body Needs*, published in 1917 by nutrition specialists Caroline L. Hunt and Helen W. Atwater, experts recommended "3,000 calories per man per day." The authors did not break down the caloric intake by gender or age, but they noted that each "family" should consume around 10,000 calories per day, for which Dunbar-Nelson's 1,200 would measure dramatically below government recommendations. Dr. Lulu Hunt Peters in her book *Diet and Health with Key to the Calories*, published in 1918, provided more specific recommendations. According to Peters, women "at rest" should consume 1,800-2,000 calories per day (c/d); those with sedentary jobs, 2,000-2,200 c/d; those with occupations involving manual labor, 2,200-2,500 c/d; and those who did more strenuous work, 2,500-3,000 c/d. Again, as a teacher and writer, Dunbar-Nelson would fit into one of the first two categories, falling at least 600 calories below expert suggestions or as much as 1,000 under the same recommendations. It is also important to note that Dunbar-Nelson's exercise habits would allow her to consume even more calories in a day. A few years after this diary entry, the *Pittsburgh Courier* recommended 2,000-2,200 calories for women who lived sedentary lives; for more active women such as housewives it suggested 2,000-2,500 calories, and for women who performed "muscular work," 2,500-3,000 calories. In order of mention: Hunt and

Atwater, *How to Select Foods*, 5; Peters, *Diet and Health with Key to the Calories*, 27; Dr. B. S. Herben, "Let There Be Health: How Much Should I Eat?," *Pittsburgh Courier*, September 6, 1924, 13.

60. Hull, *Give Us Each Day*, 264, entry dated September 14, 1925.

61. Hull, 57, entry dated August 12, 1921.

62. White-owned companies produced many of these products. Black women, nevertheless, served as viable clientele for weight-loss goods. Aside from the fact that Black newspaper owners and editors made conscious decisions to include these ads in their publications, Black women were significant consumers of beauty products, which this chapter shows included weight-reduction technology.

63. "Fat Fade," *New York Age*, July 2, 1914, 2. A dollar at that time would be worth about twenty-nine dollars in 2022.

64. "My Lady Beautiful," *Cleveland Gazette*, October 15, 1910, 4.

65. At the turn of the twentieth century, Americans became more aware of the relationship between calories and weight, and by 1890, almost a dozen diet products existed on the market. See Schwartz, *Never Satisfied*.

66. "An Easy Way to Reduce Flesh," *Chicago Defender*, June 1, 1918, 10.

67. "A New Way to Get Thin," *Chicago Defender*, November 28, 1925, 10.

68. Mme. Roberta Creditt-Ole, "Beauty Chats," *Pittsburgh Courier*, January 23, 1926, 5; "Ex-Baltimor'an Joins Walker Staff," *Baltimore Afro-American*, April 7, 1928, 18.

69. "Be Graceful," *Baltimore Afro-American*, January 28, 1905, 6.

70. "Garden Work an Aid to Beauty," *Savannah Tribune*, September 30, 1910, 6.

71. John A. Diaz, "How, What, and When to Eat," *New York Amsterdam News*, March 10, 1926, 4.

72. These images were so normative and widespread that companies used them to promote products and services that had nothing to do with African Americans or women in particular, like a San Francisco company that used overweight Black women to advertise "furniture and carpets." Gilbert and Moore Factory, Trade Cards of San Francisco Collection, Bancroft Library, University of California, Berkeley.

73. "More Interest in Race Beauty," *New York Age*, August 20, 1914, 1.

74. Cox, *Dreaming of Dixie*, 34–57; Craig, *Ain't I a Beauty Queen*, 45–64.

75. Blair, *I've Got to Make My Livin'*, 19, 95–97.

76. For a discussion of criminalized Black women and alternative notions of womanhood, see Gross, *Colored Amazons*; and Harris, *Sex Workers, Psychics, and Numbers Runners*.

77. Macfadden printed "Health Is Beauty, Ugliness Is a Sin" on the covers of his *Woman's Physical Development* magazines.

78. Hicks, *Talk with You Like a Woman*; Flowe, *Uncontrollable Blackness*; Muhammad, *Condemnation of Blackness*.

79. Salem Tutt Whitney, "Timely Topics: Where Are You Going?," *Chicago Defender*, June 16, 1928, 7.

80. "Quintard Miller," *Baltimore Afro-American*, November 5, 1927, 7.

81. "Matthews Too Fat in Hospital," *Baltimore Afro-American*, January 3, 1925, 2.

82. "The Worth of Fat," *Baltimore Afro-American*, June 18, 1910, 6.

83. Griffith, *Born Again Bodies*, 146–47.

Chapter 4

1. The school was previously known as the Locust Street Social Settlement for Negroes.

2. Elisha A. Chandler, "School of the Week: Industrial School for Girls Was Dream of Virginia Women," [illegible newspaper title], April 1939, Janie Porter Barrett Collection, Hampton University Archives, Hampton, VA.

3. Chandler, "School of the Week."

4. Bellar et al., "Exercise and Academic Performance."

5. Mrs. Gray, "The Dress of Woman," *Liberator*, December 5, 1851, 196. African American writers sometimes used "active recreation" in less definitional terms and instead provided examples of what it entailed, like hiking or playing golf, tennis, or volleyball. For golf and tennis, see "Car Driving Hard on Feet," *Advocate*, October 7, 1921, 4; for volleyball and hiking, see "Girls Find Happiness in Work and Play with Urban League Advisor," *Pittsburgh Courier*, May 5, 1928, A1.

6. There are many scholarly definitions of "recreation" and overlapping terms like "leisure," "amusement," and "play." "Leisure" is perhaps the most contested, as there is no consensus on the term. It could indicate a certain social class, free time, or a state of mind. Some scholars conceive of leisure as *time* and others as *activity*. See Butsch, *For Fun and Profit*; Cross, *Social History of Leisure*; Hurd and Anderson, *Park and Recreation Professional's Handbook*; and Kando, *Leisure and Popular Culture in Transition*. From my reading of primary sources, historical figures often used "recreation/s" and "leisure" interchangeably and loosely defined these terms as activities one performed outside of work. At times, they combined the terms, such as in Gates's *Health through Leisure-Time Recreation*. "Amusement" could also assume the aforementioned definitions or refer to specific kinds of pastimes that involved spectatorship, like movies and parades. "Play" refers to voluntary and inherently pleasurable activity, usually performed by children. These terms, especially for African Americans, are complicated by the idea that recreation and amusement require choice over one's free time. I therefore use the above terms interchangeably throughout the chapter.

7. Chatelain, *South Side Girls*, 130.

8. Heap, *Slumming*.

9. "Not a Season for Excursions," *Baltimore Afro-American*, June 10, 1905, 4.

10. Charles H. Williams, "Recreation in the Lives of Colored People," *Southern Workman* 46 (February 1917): 99.

11. C. H. Williams, 99.

12. Gallon, "Black Migrant Women and Sexual Pleasure during the Great Depression."

13. Michele Mitchell has interrogated the gendered, racialized, and sexualized meaning of "idleness" for young people during the Depression. While Mitchell is more concerned with labor than leisure, she notes that physical movement in the form of chaperoned dances, hiking, sports, and work projects helped to occupy idle youth. See M. Mitchell, "'Corrupting Influence.'"

14. Currell, *March of Spare Time*, 5.

15. R. Kelley, "'We Are Not What We Seem,'" 84.

16. Camp, *Closer to Freedom*.

17. Jessie Coope to Hollis Burke Frissell, 1895–1897, Physical Education Department Collection, Hampton University Archives, VA. Second quoted statement from Verbrugge, *Active Bodies*, 126.

18. Carolyn Finney makes these observations in *Black Faces, White Spaces*.

19. Verbrugge, "Recreating the Body."

20. F. A. Olds, "A North Carolina 'Possum Hunt," *Outing*, April 1900, 33.

21. Powdermaker, *After Freedom*, 24.

22. Wynne, "Illness Census," 10.

23. Handbook, Illinois Athletic Club, n.d., Illinois Athletic Club Records, CHM.

24. The quote "better American citizenship" is derived from the mission statement included on the official Gads Hill website as of 2016. The information about the gym stems from the organization's archival records. Report, Gads Hill Center, 1908, Gads Hill Center Records, CHM.

25. Drake and Cayton, *Black Metropolis*, 110.

26. Cabán, "Subjects and Immigrants during the Progressive Era."

27. von Borosini, "Our Recreation Facilities and the Immigrant," 144.

28. Fannie Barrier Williams, "Need of Social Settlement Work for the City Negro," *Friend's Intelligencer*, November 19, 1904, 739.

29. Jane Addams disagreed with recreation advocates like Fannie Barrier Williams on issues of perceived social ills and delinquency in Black communities. Although she lamented the "harmful effects of race segregation" and "race animosity" directed toward African Americans, she also charged Black people as complicit in their own destruction. In an article she wrote for the *Crisis* in 1911, Addams compared the "social control" of African American girls to that of Italian girls and hinted at the differences in their recreational lives. She explained that the parents of Italian girls guarded them closely, did not allow them to attend parties, and never left them alone outdoors after dark. On the contrary, the "group of colored girls . . . are quite without this protection" due to lack of "social tradition[s]" and social control. With these assumptions in mind, and with a growing number of African Americans moving to Chicago, Hull House continued to accommodate immigrant populations in the twentieth century without exploring the full possibilities for African Americans. Presumptions about Black families, women, and girls, and their cultural traditions, informed the implementation of recreational programs, reinforced segregation, and had a profound role in restricting leisure opportunities for Black people. See Jane Addams, "Social Control," *Crisis*, January 1911, 22.

30. Hartman, *Wayward Lives*, 21.

31. F. Williams, "Need of Social Settlement Work for the City Negro," 739.

32. Peiss, *Cheap Amusements*, 4–5.

33. Fannie Barrier Williams, "The Colored Girl," *Voice of the Negro*, June 1905, 401.

34. "Compelled to Dance with Negro, She Says," *New York Times*, January 17, 1911.

35. "Compelled to Dance with Negro, She Says."

36. Emmett Scott, "Leisure Time and the Colored Citizen," *Playground* 18, no. 10 (January 1925): 593–94.

37. Pilz, "Beginnings of Organized Play," 60.

38. Quoted in Miller and Pruitt-Logan, *Faithful to the Task at Hand*, 62. Original citation: *M Street Junior High School Review*, November 1921.

39. F. Washington, "Recreational Facilities for the Negro," 272.

40. Washington mentions his previous work on Detroit, *Negro in Detroit*, in the current 1928 study.

41. These passive activities likely held significant value to Washington's respondents and rural African Americans more generally. Black farmers, sharecroppers, domestics, and tobacco factory workers performed arduous labor and worked long hours, and many of them likely enjoyed "sitting down" and "doing nothing" whenever they had the opportunity. Considering their grueling work lives, active recreation may not have seemed appealing. Nonetheless, it is difficult to gauge if active recreation was appealing because, as this chapter shows, even if rural southern African Americans desired more active forms of leisure, it was exceedingly difficult to access.

42. F. Washington, "Recreational Facilities for the Negro," 273.

43. Wolcott, *Race, Riots, and Roller Coasters*.

44. F. Washington, "Recreational Facilities for the Negro," 275.

45. F. Washington, "Recreational Facilities for the Negro," 279.

46. "Community Recreation a Factor in Making Healthful Citizenship," *Norfolk New Journal and Guide*, December 29, 1923.

47. "Progressive Cities Stimulate Recreation for Negroes," *Norfolk New Journal and Guide*, May 24, 1924, 9; "Playground and Recreation Ass'n Big Local Asset," *Norfolk New Journal and Guide*, November 2, 1928, 9.

48. "Girls Find Happiness in Work and Play with Urban League Advisor," A1.

49. "'Gulfside' Dedicated This Week," *Sea Coast Echo*, September 2, 1927, 1, Gulfside Association Scrapbook, MG202, SCRBC.

50. Bishop Wilbur P. Thirkield, "The Gulfside Assembly and Chautauqua," Gulfside Association Scrapbook, MG202, SCRBC.

51. The name of the letter's author is illegible, but it is written on Methodist Episcopal Church letterhead. Letter dated September 2, 1927, Gulfside Association Scrapbook, MG202, SCRBC.

52. A member of the Methodist Episcopal Church wrote that Gulfside was unique because the organization was created "by and for Negroes." The identity of the letter writer is unclear, but this letter is also written on Methodist Episcopal Church letterhead from Galveston, TX. Undated, Gulfside Association Scrapbook, MG202, SCRBC.

53. Letter, undated, Gulfside Association Scrapbook, MG202, SCRBC.

54. Author name illegible, written on Sam Houston College letterhead, March 24, 1927, Gulfside Association Scrapbook, MG202, SCRBC.

55. Quoted in 1927 Gulfside Handbook of Information, Gulfside Association Scrapbook, MG202, SCRBC.

56. White, Bay, and Martin, *Freedom on My Mind*, 516.

57. Milton S. J. Wright, "The Coming of the New Deal," *Service*, April 1940, 43, box 21, folder 6, Chisholm Family Papers, MARBL.

58. R. Wright, *12 Million Black Voices*, xii.

59. "The New Deal Begins," *Pittsburgh Courier*, March 4, 1933, 10.

60. Larkins, *Negro Population of North Carolina*, 46.

61. Quoted in Miller and Pruitt-Logan, *Faithful to the Task at Hand*, 273.

62. Other researchers illuminated the importance of recreation for Black children and adults by centering leisure in their academic work. Graduate students in particular examined the problem of recreation and physical education in Black communities throughout the United States. Between 1932 and 1939, graduate students made active recreation in Black female populations the subjects of their master's degree

theses, charting the effect of the economic crisis on Black physical activity, job prospects, and leisure facilities. See Brandford, "Training and Opportunities for Negro Women in Physical Education"; Wilkinson, "Present Status of Physical Education for Women in Negro Colleges and Universities"; and O. Williams, "Study of the Leisure Activities of Negro Women in Orangeburg County, South Carolina."

63. National Association of Colored Women, Inc., "A Closer View," *Synopsis Explaining Organization, Activities, [and] Future Trends,* box 39, folder "Negro Girls and Women, 1930-1933," Alliance for Guidance of Rural Youth Records Collection, David M. Rubenstein Rare Book and Manuscript Library, Duke University, Durham, NC.

64. National Association of Colored Women, Inc., "A Closer View."

65. Brochure, *Human Needs Essential Social Services,* 1933, box 10, folder 14, Neighborhood Union Collection, RWWL.

66. Brochure, *Human Needs Essential Social Services.*

67. Broadside, "Stop! Look! Listen! Big Shiloh Barbe-Q," box 38, folder 33, Black Print Culture Collection, MARBL.

68. Program, "Program of the May 30th Celebration and Business Directory," box 32, folder 45, Black Print Culture Collection, MARBL.

69. Broadside, "All Nations Barbecue," box 38, folder 35, Black Print Culture Collection, MARBL.

70. Alice M. Richards, "Leisure and the Unemployed Man," *Washington Tribune,* July 8, 1932, 8.

71. Historian Marya McQuirter's work alerted me to this source. McQuirter, "Claiming the City."

72. Baynton, "Disability and the Justification of Inequality"; Burch and Patterson, "Not Just Any Body"; Rose, *No Right to Be Idle.*

73. Quoted in J. Hunter, *Nickel and a Dime,* 150.

74. J. Hunter, 7.

75. "Evaluation Report, 1938," 1-2, box 8, folder 16, Phillis Wheatley Association Records, 1914-1916, Western Reserve Historical Society, Cleveland, OH.

76. "November 1939, E.R.C.," 2, box 8, folder 13, Phillis Wheatley Association Records, 1914-1916, Western Reserve Historical Society, Cleveland, OH.

77. Leah Lewinson, "Report of Miss Leah Lewinson President of the Southwest Harlem Neighborhood Council Inc., at the Hearing of the New York State Temporary Commission on [the] Urban Colored Population," 2, box 1, folder 1, MG245, Southwest Harlem Neighborhood Collection, SCRBC.

78. "Girls' Gymnasium Group, 1939-1940," Urban Archives 30, box 26, folder 166, Wharton Centre Collection, Temple University Libraries, Philadelphia, PA.

79. Grover, *Fitness in American Culture,* 30; L. Jones, *Mama Learned Us to Work,* 130-32.

80. Grover, *Hard at Play,* 225; S. Smith, *Sick and Tired of Being Sick and Tired,* 92-97.

81. Mme. Qui Vive, "Beauty Hints: Physical Education," *Atlanta Daily World,* December 1, 1937, 3.

82. Mme. Qui Vive, 3.

83. Bowers and Hunt, "President's Council on Physical Fitness"; Hunt, "Countering the Soviet Threat in the Olympic Medals Race."

Chapter 5

1. Archer, *Let's Face It*, 40.

2. Archer, 49.

3. Neuhaus, "Way to a Man's Heart"; Nickles, "More Is Better"; C. Smith, "Freeze Frames."

4. E. May, *Homeward Bound*, 157.

5. Greer, *Represented*, 207–8; Weems, *Desegregating the Dollar*, 34–37.

6. E. May, *Homeward Bound*, 9–11; Cohen, *Consumers' Republic*, 227–35.

7. Cohen, *Consumer's Republic*; Coontz, *Way We Never Were*; Nickles, "More Is Better"; E. May, *Homeward Bound*.

8. J. Jones, *Labor of Love*, 210–16.

9. A. Green, *Selling the Race*; Greer, *Represented*; T. Parker, *Department Stores and the Black Freedom Movement*.

10. Greer, *Represented*, 223–24; T. Parker, *Department Stores and the Black Freedom Movement*, 52, 152.

11. J. Chambers, *Madison Avenue and the Color Line*, 41–49; A. Green, *Selling the Race*, 130–77; Greer, *Represented*, 142–88.

12. Jason Chambers makes a similar argument about *Ebony*. See J. Chambers, "Presenting the Black Middle Class."

13. Baron and Boris, "'The Body' as a Useful Category"; Canning, *Gender History in Practice*; Happe and Johnson, *Biocitizenship*.

14. While not singularly focused on the body, historian Tanisha Ford interrogates Black women's diasporic body politics through sartorial performance, soul aesthetics, and embodied activism in the second half of the twentieth century. See Ford, *Liberated Threads*.

15. Bowers and Hunt, "President's Council on Fitness."

16. Creadick, *Perfectly Average*, 22.

17. Virginia Kachan, "Wives' Help Needed to Reduce 'Softies' Total," *Norfolk New Journal and Guide*, October 15, 1955, 7; Joan Hanauer, "Saving Bulging Males Wives' Job, Says Expert," *Chicago Defender*, June 26, 1957, 14.

18. Earley writes of Black Wacs' physical and psychological fitness being "carefully screened" before they deployed for duty overseas. Earley, *One Woman's Army*, 122.

19. "Colored WACs Tributed during Negro History Week," *Norfolk New Journal and Guide*, February 22, 1947, B13.

20. Bolzenius, *Glory in Their Spirit*, 23.

21. Giddings, *When and Where I Enter*, 237.

22. "Charlotte Moton Given Fine Atlanta Reception," *Atlanta Daily World*, April 21, 1942, 5.

23. "Miss Purnell Made Queen at Cheyney," *Norfolk New Journal and Guide*, May 22, 1943, 9.

24. Meyer, "Creating G.I. Jane."

25. U.S. War Department, *W.A.C. Field Manual*, 1.

26. E. May, *Homeward Bound*, 70–72.

27. Meyer, "Creating G.I. Jane," 583–86.

28. Anderson, "Last Hired, First Fired," 84; Honey, *Bitter Fruit*, 7.

29. U.S. War Department, *W.A.C. Field Manual*, 1.

30. U.S. War Department, 2.

31. U.S. War Department, 4.

32. In the immediate postwar period, ordinary white women received messages from the government, beauty authorities, and insurance companies about remaining fit in order to rebuild the country. Matelski, *Reducing Bodies*, 76–78.

33. U.S. War Department, *W.A.C. Field Manual*, 1.

34. U.S. War Department, 10.

35. "Make with the Muscles Boys, There's Going to Be a Fitness Drive," *Philadelphia Tribune*, August 7, 1941, 9.

36. "Make with the Muscles Boys, There's Going to Be a Fitness Drive," 9.

37. Melancholy Jones, "Office of Civilian Defense to Make U.S. Virile, Healthy Nation via Physical Fitness Idea 'Hale America,'" *Atlanta Daily World*, March 12, 1942, 5.

38. Brooks, *Defining the Peace*; Klinkner and Smith, *Unsteady March*; Krebs, *Fighting for Rights*; Lentz-Smith, *Freedom Struggles*; Rosenberg, *How Far the Promised Land?*; Singh, *Black Is a Country*; C. L. Williams, *Torchbearers of Democracy*.

39. "New Negroes," *Pittsburgh Courier*, May 10, 1941, 14.

40. "Make with the Muscles Boys, There's Going to Be a Fitness Drive," 9.

41. Bradley, "Some Health Education Implications of the Physical Examinations of Negroes in World War II," 150.

42. Bradley, 153.

43. Bradley, 154.

44. Lentz-Smith, *Freedom Struggles*, 7.

45. "Dusky Belles Parade in Negro Contest," *Des Moines Register*, March 21, 1937, 66.

46. Earlier contests focused on *facial* beauty.

47. E. Brown, "Black Models and the Invention of the U.S. Negro Market."

48. Haidarali, "Polishing Brown Diamonds," 24.

49. This might not be surprising considering that modeling programs were in the business of keeping bodies in shape. Nevertheless, the training these models received trickled down to everyday Black women through print culture. Modeling school owners stressed appearance, grooming, social graces, and weight maintenance, including Barbara M. Watson's "Charm Clinic" and the DeVore School of Charm. *Ebony*, *Our World*, and *Jet* magazines featured women who enrolled in these schools.

50. Mabel Alston, "Mabel Alston's Charm School," *Baltimore Afro-American*, January 27, 1940, 15.

51. "Exercise for a Ballerina Figure," *Jet*, March 26, 1953, 33.

52. "Exercise for a Ballerina Figure," 33–34. Evidence suggests that Black women celebrities and models began to favor gym exercise over "in home" physical activity in the mid-twentieth century. Dancer and physical trainer Jeni LeGon helped Black Hollywood actors become "screen ready" through gym exercises. Actors like Pearl Reynolds and Mary Louis prepared for their roles in *House of Flowers* by "trying out facilities at the Harlem YWCA's new health and recreation center." One *Jet* pinup model explained, "When I am tired and feel no vim, I simply work out at the local gym." See "Film Formula for Glamour," *Ebony*, June 1948, 32; "Keeping in Shape," *Jet*, March 10, 1955, 61; "Jet's 1960 Calendar Pin-Ups," *Jet*, January 7, 1960, 31.

53. Perhaps Black print culture emphasized Black women's physicality as a precondition for desire more than African Americans did in real life. In a 1957 study of dating behaviors among African American students at a North Carolina college, corporal signifiers scored surprisingly low in how respondents rated potential mates. The top five

qualities included values like "friendliness," "self-confidence," and "dependability," while more aesthetic values like "smoothness in manner and appearance" and "sex appeal" ranked seventh and seventeenth, respectively, out of twenty-eight values. See Anderson and Himes, "Dating Values and Norms on a North Carolina Campus," 227.

54. Haidarali, "Polishing Brown Diamonds."

55. David Sullivan, "A Catalogue of Don'ts," *Negro Digest*, June 1943, 49–51. Sullivan also published this advice in *Sales Management* and admonished white businesses to avoid depicting African American women as "buxom, broad-faced grinning mammies and Aunt Jemimas" since "Negroes have no monopoly on size."

56. The Miss Fine Brown Frame contest took place in 1946, but print outlets reported on the event the following year.

57. "Miss Fine Brown Frame: Darkest Girl in Contest Wins First Prize," *Ebony*, May 1947, 47–48. Craig's *Ain't I a Beauty Queen?* alerted me to this source.

58. "Miss Fine Brown Frame," 47.

59. "Miss Fine Brown Frame," 47.

60. "The Truth about Beauty Contests," *Jet*, February 26, 1953, 28.

61. Scholars have analyzed several disturbing contradictions within the pageant, *Ebony*'s coverage of the story, and Sanders's win. One example includes the half-page advertisement for "Beauty Star Skin Whitener," a skin lightening cream, on the opposite page of the Sanders story in *Ebony*. More alarmingly, the magazine decided to bear Sanders's image in an enlarged photograph of her body and its measurements, with her head removed from the picture. In that headless photo, the magazine featured measurements of Sanders's thighs, calves, and ankles, in addition to her bust-waist-hip measurements. *Ebony* readers did not learn much else about Sanders except that she was twenty-four years of age, was an aspiring model, and called Freeport, Long Island, her hometown (several other print outlets reported her age as seventeen). Her body seemed to serve as a proxy for her talents and personality. For more on the paradoxes of the contest, particularly her disembodiment, see Craig, *Ain't I a Beauty Queen?*, 56–57; and Matelski, "(Big and) Black Is Beautiful."

62. All of the major Black newspapers reported on this pageant. The May 1947 issue in which *Ebony* reported the story sold more copies than any previously published *Ebony* magazine. Greer, *Represented*, 165.

63. "Fine Browns In on 'Fine Brown Frame Contest,'" *Cleveland Call and Post*, November 30, 1946, 6B.

64. John E. Fuster, "No Ohio Girls in Fine Brown Frame Finals at Philadelphia," *Cleveland Call and Post*, December 20, 1947, 12B.

65. "N.Y. Girl Picked for Finest 'Body' in National Finals," *Baltimore Afro-American*, January 11, 1947, 7; "Buddy Johnson to Fight 'Miss America' Color Bar," *Baltimore Afro-American*, December 28, 1946, 7.

66. "Joe Louis, Lena Horne Judges for 'Fine Brown Frame' Contest," *Norfolk New Journal and Guide*, November 23, 1946, 14.

67. "'Miss Fine Brown Frame' Runners-Up Attack Sponsor," *New York Amsterdam News*, August 23, 1947, 17.

68. "Applause for Wrong Girl Lands Man into Court," *Norfolk New Journal and Guide*, July 20, 1946, A1.

69. "Letters to the Editor: Fine Brown Frame," *Ebony*, August 1947, 4. Some letters were not congratulatory and expressed dismay at the revealing nature of the images.

NOTES TO PAGES 150–55

70. Balogun, "Cultural and Cosmopolitan"; Banet-Weiser, *Most Beautiful Girl in the World*; Barnes, "Face of the Nation"; Kozol, "Miss Indian America."

71. Greer, *Represented*.

72. Craig, *Ain't I a Beauty Queen?*, 5.

73. Greer, *Represented*, 3.

74. Banet-Weiser, "Miss America," 71.

75. "Beauty Queens to Vie in Brown Frame Contest," *Atlanta Daily World*, December 11, 1947, 3.

76. "N.Y. Drama Student Wins Right to National Contest," *Baltimore Afro-American*, June 22, 1946, 6.

77. Sparrow, "'Buying Our Boys Back.'"

78. "Buddy Johnson to Fight 'Miss America' Color Bar," *Baltimore Afro-American*, December 28, 1946, 7.

79. "How Evelyn Gets and Keeps Her Prize-Winning Frame," *Ebony*, May 1947, 49.

80. Lowe, *Looking Good*, 38–39.

81. U. Taylor, *Promise of Patriarchy*, 44–50.

82. White women are often the assumed subjects in the historiography on American dieting. See Schwartz, *Never Satisfied*; Stearns, *Fat History*; and Vester, "Regime Change."

83. Opie, *Hog and Hominy*, xi.

84. Williams-Forson, *Building Houses Out of Chicken Legs*, 136.

85. Walker, "Mighty Matriarchs Kill It with a Skillet," 121.

86. Psyche Williams-Forson also discusses food resistance in *Building Houses Out of Chicken Legs*, although she uses the fictional text *Say Jesus Come to Me* in order to historicize this impulse to, for instance, "[refuse] the largest piece of chicken." Doris Witt highlights Black women's appetite suppression in the fiction works of Gloria Naylor and Alice Walker. See Williams-Forson, *Building Houses Out of Chicken Legs*, 159; Witt, *Black Hunger*.

87. Historical scholarship chronicles the types of food that African Americans have used to distinguish themselves as good citizens based on class, education, and region. See Wallach, *Every Nation Has Its Dish*; and Zafar, *Recipes for Respect*.

88. Biltekoff, *Eating Right in America*, 51.

89. U.S. Department of Agriculture, *National Food Guide*, 1.

90. U.S. Department of Agriculture, *Food for Fitness*.

91. For "civic-minded citizens" reference, see "The Grand Rapids Study Club," fundraising letter, February 5, 1942, box 4, folder 2, Grand Rapids Study Club Records, Grand Rapids Public Library and Special Collections, Grand Rapids, MI. For nutrition reference, see Grand Rapids Study Club Meeting Minutes, March 12, 1942, box 1, vol. 3, Grand Rapids Study Club Records.

92. "Friendly Inn Board Meeting May 1942," 1, box 1, folder 1, Friendly Inn Social Settlement Records, Western Reserve Historical Society, Cleveland, OH.

93. Richard, *Lena Richard's Cook Book*, 40, preface, Janice Bluestein Longone Culinary Archive, University of Michigan Special Collections, Ann Arbor, MI.

94. Biltekoff, *Eating Right in America*, 60.

95. U.S. Department of Agriculture, *Home Demonstration Agent*, 30.

96. Dirks and Duran, "African American Dietary Patterns."

97. Biltekoff, *Eating Right in America*, 55.

98. U.S. Department of Agriculture, *Home Demonstration Agent*, 30.

99. Biltekoff, *Eating Right in America*; Veit, *Modern Food*; Vester, *Taste of Power*.

100. U.S. Department of Agriculture, *Home Demonstration Agent*, 15.

101. Schwartz, *Never Satisfied*, 252-68.

102. Elta Arnold, "Diet Plus Exercise Will Take Off Pounds," *Baltimore Afro-American*, June 17, 1950, A7.

103. "Attention Diet Watchers," *Chicago Defender*, March 8, 1960, A15.

104. "You're Finding Your Diet Fun, and Plenty Filling," *Chicago Defender*, June 19, 1956, 16.

105. "Get on the Mark! Diet with a Fat Girl and Lose a Pound a Day," *Chicago Defender*, June 12, 1956, 14.

106. "Health Hints: Weight Control," *Crisis*, March 1950, 190.

107. Toki Schalk-Johnson, "'You Can Lose Weight,' Says Busy Pittsburgher," *Pittsburgh Courier*, September 13, 1947, 8.

108. Schalk-Johnson, 8.

109. Some considered overweight individuals poor members of the expanding consumer economy. Presumably, they *overconsumed* and could not self-regulate in the marketplace of abundance. While Americans were driven into consumerism through the purchase of practical items for the home, they were discouraged from decadent consumption and opulent living, and the overweight body read as just that. As one white health expert explained, "The [physically] unfit are both bad producers and bad consumers." For more on decadent spending, see E. May, *Homeward Bound*, 157-59. For quotation see Josephine Robertson, "Theater Cashier, 23, Wins Title of 'Norma,' Besting 3,863 Entries," *Cleveland Plain Dealer*, September 23, 1945, 1, 4. Creadick's *Perfectly Average* alerted me to this source.

110. Actress Dorothy Dandridge made a similar comment in 1952: "Boredom can sabotage any beauty program. When a woman is bored, she often starts eating, and when she starts eating . . . well, look out. She's spreading!" "Glamour Can Be Manufactured!," *Jet*, July 17, 1952, 32-33.

111. "What AFRO Dieters Say," *Baltimore Afro-American*, November 1, 1952, A13.

112. "What AFRO Dieters Say," A13.

113. "What AFRO Dieters Say," A13.

114. M. C. Jones, *Eating for Health*, Janice Bluestein Longone Culinary Archive, University of Michigan Special Collections, Ann Arbor.

115. M. C. Jones, 22.

116. M. C. Jones, 14.

117. M. C. Jones, 9.

118. De Knight, *Date with a Dish*, 8.

119. According to De Knight, she targeted the book to average cooks, housewives, "business-wives," and those who were not "naturals" in cooking.

120. Several scholars have written about De Knight's efforts to redefine Black food culture: A. Green, *Selling the Race*, 169-71; Theophano, *Eat My Words*, 52-60; and Zafar, *Recipes for Respect*, 56-58.

121. "Goodbye Mammy, Hello Mom," *Ebony*, March 1947, 36-37; Pierce, "This Book Is for Us and by Us."

122. De Knight, *Date with a Dish*, xiii.

123. De Knight, 9.

124. Archer, *Let's Face It*, 39.

Epilogue

1. Historian Jeanne Theoharis contends that there may be too much emphasis on walking in the dominant narratives about the boycott (especially in Hollywood), and that carpools accounted for the boycott's success. I posit that we may benefit from critically analyzing the walking required of boycotters and its political meaning. Theoharis, *More Beautiful and Terrible History*, 196.

2. As a political act, walking incurred its own version of racialized insults, as white aggressors would harass and attack Black pedestrians whom they assumed were participating in the boycott.

3. Parks, "'Tired of Giving In,'" 64, 72.

4. Alderman, Kingsbury, and Dwyer, "Reexamining the Montgomery Bus Boycott," 179.

5. In order of "held high," "while praying," and "with God" references: Art Carter, "'We'll Walk 'til Victory Is Complete,' Say Boycotters: 4,000 Vow to Walk 'til Bitter End," *Baltimore Afro-American*, May 5, 1956, 1; "Montgomery Minister Talks at Wilberforce," *Cleveland Call and Post*, April 14, 1956, 3D; Rufus Wells, "'God Walks with Us,' King Tells Teachers," *Baltimore Afro-American*, November 10, 1956, 17.

6. P. Bernard Young Jr., "Some of the People Who Lead and Support Montgomery Bus Boycott," *Norfolk New Journal and Guide*, April 14, 1956, 13.

7. Al Sweeny, "42,000 Walk: Brave the Rain in Protest Pilgrimage," *Baltimore Afro-American*, March 3, 1956, 1.

8. Hill-Collins, *Black Feminist Thought*, 76–106.

9. "Welfare Queen Becomes Issue in Reagan Campaign," *New York Times*, February 15, 1976, 51.

10. Kandaswamy, *Domestic Contradictions*.

11. Political scientist Ange-Marie Hancock posits that ideas about race, gender, and class conspired to create a "politics of disgust" directed toward African American women. Lawmakers, taxpayers, politicians, and the media felt *disgusted* with Black welfare recipients. They stitched together the public identity of the "welfare queen" that was, and still is, a target of extreme contempt and inspired the 1996 changes in welfare policies. See A. Hancock, *Politics of Disgust*.

12. Black magazines like *Jet* also stoked anti-welfare sentiment with news stories about Black "welfare queens." *Jet* initially reported on Linda Taylor, designating her a "welfare queen" in 1974. See "Alleged 'Welfare Queen' Is Accused of $154,000 Ripoff," *Jet*, December 19, 1974, 16. For similar stories, see "'Welfare Queen' Found Guilty by Illinois Court," *Jet*, April 14, 1977, 24; "'Welfare Queen' Sentenced to Eight-Year Prison Term," *Jet*, January 25, 1979, 48; "Calif. Woman Earns 'Welfare Queen' Title," *Jet*, March 12, 1981, 8.

13. Kwate and Threadcraft, "Perceiving the Black Female Body"; Sanders, "Color of Fat"; Strings, "Obese Black Women as 'Social Dead Weight.'"

14. Retha Powers, "Fat Is a Black Women's Issue," *Essence*, October 1989, 75, 78, 134, 136.

15. Georgiana Arnold, "Fat War: One Woman's Battle to Control Her Weight," *Essence*, July 1990, 52–53, 104–5, 109.

16. Some Black women, including Black feminist writers and thinkers, framed food as an addictive substance with dire consequences for Black women at the same time that rising fat hostility was transpiring in the 1980s and early 1990s. For more, see Witt, "What (N)Ever Happened to Aunt Jemima."

17. Bass, "On Being a Fat Black Girl in a Fat-Hating Culture," 227.

18. Sanders, "Color of Fat," 298.

19. Cited in Oldenburg, "Rush Limbaugh Attacks Michelle Obama's Diet."

20. Stephanie Houston Grey's work alerted me to this source. Grey, "Contesting the Fit Citizen." Also see Breitman, "Fox Doc Steps Up FLOTUS Grilling." Original quote featured on timestamp 1:18–2:10, https://www.youtube.com/watch?v=_jhHVml9nxc.

21. Ayee et al., "White House, Black Mother," 462.

22. "Achievements."

23. The White House: Office of the First Lady, "Remarks by the First Lady at the White House Kitchen Garden Dedication."

24. Here I am thinking of historian Stephanie Y. Evans's concept of "historical wellness." See Evans, *Black Women's Yoga History*.

Bibliography

Primary Sources

MANUSCRIPT AND SPECIAL COLLECTIONS

Arthur and Elizabeth Schlesinger Library on the History of Women in America, Cambridge, MA
    Young Women's Christian Association Records
Auburn Avenue Research Library on African Culture and History, Atlanta, GA
    Adam Knight Spence and John Wesley Work Collection
    Helen Adele Johnson Whiting Papers
Bancroft Library, University of California, Berkeley
    Trade Cards of San Francisco Collection
Chicago History Museum, IL
    Chicago Daily News Negatives Collection
    Gads Hill Center Records
    Illinois Athletic Club Records
    Irene McCoy Gaines Papers
David M. Rubenstein Rare Book and Manuscript Library, Duke University, Durham, NC
    Alliance for Guidance of Rural Youth Records Collection
Dolph Briscoe Center for American History, University of Texas at Austin
    Black Texas Women Collection
Grand Rapids Public Library and Special Collections, MI
    Grand Rapids Study Club Records
Hampton University Archives, VA
    Janie Porter Barrett Collection
    Physical Education Department Collection
    Physical Education Photographs Collection
H. J. Lutcher Stark Center for Physical Culture and Sports, University of Texas at Austin
Library of Congress, Washington, DC
    Frances Benjamin Johnston Collection
    Office of War Information Photograph Collection
Manuscripts, Archives, and Rare Books Library, Emory University, Atlanta, GA
    Black Print Culture Collection
    Chisholm Family Papers
Moorland-Spingarn Research Center, Howard University, Washington, DC
    Maryrose Reeves Allen Papers
National Archives and Records Administration, College Park, MD
    Harmon Foundation Collection
Robert W. Woodruff Library, Atlanta University Center, GA
    Atlanta University Photograph Collection
    Neighborhood Union Collection

Schomburg Center for Research in Black Culture, New York, NY
    General Research and Reference Division
    Gulfside Association Scrapbook
    Southwest Harlem Neighborhood Collection
Temple University Urban Archives, Philadelphia, PA
    Wharton Centre Collection
Tuskegee University, AL
    National Negro Health Week Papers
    Tuskegee University Archives
University of Michigan Special Collections, Ann Arbor
    Janice Bluestein Longone Culinary Archive
Western Reserve Historical Society, Cleveland, OH
    Friendly Inn Social Settlement Records
    Phillis Wheatley Association Records
Wisconsin Historical Society, Madison
    Gwyneth King Roe Papers

GOVERNMENT DOCUMENTS AND REPORTS

Hunt, Caroline L., and Helen W. Atwater. *How to Select Foods: What the Body Needs.* Washington, DC: United States Department of Agriculture, 1917.

U.S. Department of Agriculture. *Food for Fitness: A Daily Food Guide.* Washington, DC: U.S. Government Printing Office, 1958.

———. *The Home Demonstration Agent.* Misc. pub. no. 602. Washington, DC: U.S. Government Printing Office, 1946.

———. *National Food Guide.* Washington, DC: U.S. Government Printing Office, 1946.

U.S. War Department. *W.A.C. Field Manual: Physical Training.* Washington, DC: U.S. Government Printing Office, 1943.

NEWSPAPERS AND MAGAZINES

Advocate	*Heebie Jeebies*
Atlanta Daily World	*Independent*
Atlanta Independent	*Jet*
Baltimore Afro-American	*Liberator*
Chicago Defender	*Ms. Magazine*
Christian Recorder	*Negro Digest*
Cleveland Call and Post	*Negro World*
Cleveland Gazette	*New Orleans Medical and*
Cleveland Plain Dealer	*Surgical Journal*
Cosmopolitan	*New York Age*
Crisis	*New York Amsterdam News*
Des Moines Register	*New York Times*
Ebony	*Norfolk (VA) New Journal*
Essence	*and Guide*
Freeman (Indianapolis)	*Outing*
Friend's Intelligencer	*Philadelphia Tribune*
Good Housekeeping	*Physical Culture*
Health	*Pittsburgh Courier*

Pittsburgh Press
Playground
La Prensa
San Francisco Sunday Call
Savannah Tribune
Southern Workman

Topeka Plaindealer
Voice of the Negro
Washington Bee
Washington Tribune
Wisconsin Weekly Advocate
Woman's Era

BOOKS, REPORTS, THESES, AND ARTICLES

Anderson, Charles S., and Joseph S. Himes. "Dating Values and Norms on a North Carolina Campus." *Marriage and Family Living* 21, no. 3 (1959): 227-29.

Archer, Elsie. *Let's Face It: A Guide to Good Grooming for Negro Girls*. Philadelphia: J. B. Lippincott, 1959.

Bradley, Gladyce H. "Some Health Education Implications of the Physical Examinations of Negroes in World War II." *Journal of Negro History* 16, no. 2 (1947): 148-54.

Brandford, Pat A. "Training and Opportunities for Negro Women in Physical Education." MA thesis, State University of Iowa, 1939.

Brown, Roscoe C. "The National Negro Health Week Movement." *Journal of Negro Education* 6, no. 3 (1937): 553-64.

Bruce, William Cabell. *The Negro Problem*. Baltimore: John Murphy and Co., 1891.

"The Central School of Hygiene and Physical Education." *American Physical Education Review* 29 (1924): 625.

Cooper, Anna Julia. *A Voice from the South*. Xenia, OH: Aldine Printing House, 1892.

Crumpler, Rebecca. *A Book of Medical Discourses: In Two Parts*. Boston: Keating and Co. Printers, 1883.

Davidson, Olivia A. "How Shall We Make the Women of Our Race Stronger?" In *The Booker T. Washington Papers Volume II: 1860-1889*, edited by Booker T. Washington and Louis R. Harlan, 298-305. Urbana: University of Illinois Press, 1972. Original speech delivered in 1886.

De Knight, Freda. *A Date with a Dish: A Cook Book of American Negro Recipes*. New York: Hermitage Press, 1948.

Drake, St. Clair, and Horace R. Cayton. *Black Metropolis: A Study of Negro Life in a Northern City*. Chicago: University of Chicago Press, 1970. Originally published in 1945.

Du Bois, W. E. B. *The Health and Physique of the Negro American*. Atlanta: Atlanta University Press, 1906.

Dudley, Gertrude, and Frances Kellor. *Athletic Games in the Education of Women*. New York: Henry Holt, 1909.

Edwards, Paul K. *The Southern Urban Negro as a Consumer*. College Park, MD: McGrath, 1969. Originally published in 1932.

Ellis, A. W. "The Status of Health and Physical Education for Women in Negro Colleges and Universities." *Research Quarterly* 10 (1939): 135-41.

Fletcher, Ella Adelia. *The Woman Beautiful*. New York: Brentano's Publishers, 1901.

Fry, Henry Peck. *The Voice of the Third Generation: A Discussion of the Race Question for the Benefit of Those Who Believe That the United States Is a White Man's Country and Should Be Governed by White Men*. Chattanooga: MacGowan-Cooke, 1906.

Gates, Edith. *Health through Leisure-Time Recreation*. New York: Woman's Press, 1931.

Hancock, H. Irving. *Physical Training for Women by Japanese Methods*. New York: G. P. Putnam's Sons, 1904.

Hayen, Eberhard. *The Negro Question: An Essay*. Baltimore: Eberhard Hayen, 1908.

Henderson, Edwin B. "Progress and Problems in Health and Physical Education among Colored Americans." *Journal of Health and Physical Education* 6, no. 6 (1935): 9, 55.

Hoffman, Frederick L. *Race Traits and Tendencies of the American Negro*. New York: American Economic Association/Macmillan Company, 1896.

Hunter, Jane Edna. *A Nickel and a Dime*. Cleveland: Elli Kani, 1940.

Jones, Marvene Constance. *Eating for Health: Food Facts and Recipes for Pleasant Eating and Better Health*. Nashville: Southern Publishing Association, 1947.

Kern, John Hewins. *Glorious Womanhood*. New York: Charles Renard, 1925.

Larkins, John R. *The Negro Population of North Carolina: Social and Economic*. Raleigh: North Carolina State Board of Charities and Public Welfare, 1944.

Macfadden, Bernarr. *Macfadden's Encyclopedia of Physical Culture*. New York: Physical Culture, 1920.

Macfadden, Bernarr, and Marion Malcolm. *Health-Beauty-Sexuality: From Girlhood to Womanhood*. New York: Physical Culture, 1904.

Mixter, Margaret. *Health and Beauty Hints*. New York: Cupples and Leon, 1910.

Northrop, Henry Davenport, Joseph R. Gay, and Irvine Garland Penn. *College of Life or Practical Self-Educator: A Manual of Self-Improvement for the Colored Race*. Chicago: Chicago Publication and Lithograph, 1895.

Olcott, Jane. *The Work of Colored Women*. New York: Colored Work Committee War Work Council, 1919.

The Overton-Hygienic Company. *Encyclopedia of Colored People*. Chicago: Overton-Hygienic, 1921.

Peters, Lulu Hunt. *Diet and Health with Key to the Calories*. Chicago: Reilly and Lee, 1918.

Pinkham, Lydia E. *Lydia E. Pinkham's Private Text-Book*. Lynn, MA: Lydia E. Pinkham's Medicine Company, 1910.

Pratt, Nannette Magruder. *The Body Beautiful: Common Sense Ideas on Health and Beauty without Medicine*. New York: Baker and Taylor, 1902.

Richard, Lena. *Lena Richard's Cook Book*. New Orleans: Rogers Printing, 1947.

Richings, G. F. *Evidences of Progress among Colored People*. 11th ed. Philadelphia: Geo. S. Ferguson, 1904.

Roman, C. V. "The Medical Phase of the South's Ethnic Problem." *Journal of the National Medical Association* 8, no. 3 (1916): 150–52.

Roosevelt, Theodore. *The Strenuous Life: Essays and Addresses*. Mineola, NY: Dover, 2009. Originally published in 1900.

Rubinstein, Helena. *The Art of Feminine Beauty*. New York: Horace Liverwright, 1930.

Sargent, Dudley Allen. "The Significance of a Sound Physique." *Annals of the American Academy of Political and Social Science* 34, no. 1 (1909): 9–15.

Sargent, Porter. *A Handbook of the Best Private Schools of the United States and Canada*. Boston: Press of Geo. M. Ellis, 1915.

Sherman, Waldo H. *Civics: Studies in American Citizenship*. New York: Macmillan, 1905.

Van de Velde, H. *Sex Efficiency through Exercise: Special Physical Culture for Women*. London: William Heinemann, 1933.

von Borosini, Victor. "Our Recreation Facilities and the Immigrant." *Annals of the American Academy of Political and Social Science* 35, no. 2 (1910): 141–51.

Washington, Booker T. *Up from Slavery: An Autobiography*. West Berlin, NJ: Townsend Press, 2004. Originally published in 1901.

Washington, Forrester B. *The Negro in Detroit: A Survey of the Conditions of a Negro Group in a Northern Industrial Center during the War Prosperity Period*. Detroit: Research Bureau Associated Charities of Detroit, 1920.

———. "Recreational Facilities for the Negro." *Annals of the American Academy of Political and Social Science* 140 (1928): 272–82.

Wilkinson, Lula. "The Present Status of Physical Education for Women in Negro Colleges and Universities: A Study of Thirty-Eight Colleges and Universities." MA thesis, New York University, 1932.

Willard, Frances E. "Physical Culture and Dress Reform." Minutes of the National Woman's Christian Temperance Union at the Eighteenth Annual Meeting, November 13–18, 1891. Chicago: Woman's Temperance Publication Association, 1891.

Williams, Ophelia. "A Study of the Leisure Activities of Negro Women in Orangeburg County, South Carolina." MA thesis, Pennsylvania State College, 1939.

Woodson, Carter G. "Fifty Years of Negro Citizenship as Qualified by the United States Supreme Court." *Journal of Negro History* 6, no. 1 (1921): 1–53.

Wright, Richard. *12 Million Black Voices*. New York: Basic Books, 2002. Originally published in 1941.

Wynne, Shirley W. "Illness Census." *Monthly Bulletin of the Department of Health in the City of New York* 8, no. 1 (January 1918): 1–17.

Secondary Sources
ARTICLES AND BOOK CHAPTERS

Alderman, Derek H., Paul Kingsbury, and Owen J. Dwyer. "Reexamining the Montgomery Bus Boycott: Toward an Empathetic Pedagogy of the Civil Rights Movement." *Professional Geographer* 65, no. 1 (2013): 171–86.

Alnutt, Brian E. "'The Negro Excursions': Recreational Outings among Philadelphia African Americans, 1876–1926." *Pennsylvania Magazine of History and Biography* 129, no. 1 (2005): 73–104.

Anderson, Karen Tucker. "Last Hired, First Fired: Black Women Workers during World War II." *Journal of American History* 69, no. 1 (1982): 82–97.

Ayee, Gloria Y. A., Jessica D. Johnson Carew, Taneisha N. Means, Alicia M. Reyes-Barriéntez, and Nura A. Sedige. "White House, Black Mother: Michelle Obama and the Politics of Motherhood as First Lady." *Politics and Gender* 15 (2019): 460–83.

Bacchi, Carol Lee, and Chris Beasley. "Citizen Bodies: Is Embodied Citizenship a Contradiction in Terms?" *Critical Social Policy* 22, no. 2 (2002): 324–52.

Baker, Robert B., Harriet A. Washington, Ololade Olakanmi, Todd L. Savitt, Elizabeth A. Jacobs, Eddie Hoover, and Matthew K. Wynia. "African American Physicians and Organized Medicine, 1846–1968: Origins of a Racial Divide." *JAMA* 300, no. 3 (2008): 306–13.

Balchin, Ross, Jani Linde, Dee Blackhurst, H. G. Laurie Rauch, and Georg Schönbächler. "Sweating Away Depression? The Impact of Intensive Exercise on Depression." *Journal of Affective Disorders* 200 (2016): 218–21.

Balogun, Oluwakemi M. "Cultural and Cosmopolitan: Idealized Femininity and Embodied Nationalism in Nigerian Beauty Pageants." *Gender and Society* 26, no. 3 (2012): 357–81.

Banet-Weiser, Sarah. "Miss America, National Identity, and the Identity Politics of Whiteness." In *There She Is, Miss America: The Politics of Sex, Beauty, and Race in America's Most Famous Pageant*, edited by Elwood Watson and Darcy Martin, 67–89. New York: Palgrave Macmillan, 2004.

Barnes, Natasha B. "Face of the Nation: Race, Nationalisms and Identities in Jamaican Beauty Pageants." *Massachusetts Review* 35, no. 3 (1994): 471–92.

Baron, Ava, and Eileen Boris. "'The Body' as a Useful Category for Working-Class History." *Labor* 4, no. 2 (2007): 23–43.

Bass, Margaret K. "On Being a Fat Black Girl in a Fat-Hating Culture." In *Recovering the Black Female Body: Self-Representations by African American Women*, edited by Michael Bennett and Vanessa D. Dickerson, 219–30. New Brunswick, NJ: Rutgers University Press, 2001.

Baynton, Douglas C. "Disability and the Justification of Inequality in American History." In *The New Disability History: American Perspectives*, edited by Paul K. Longmore and Lauri Umansky, 33–57. New York: New York University Press, 2001.

Beauboeuf-Lafontant, Tamara. "The New Howard Woman: Dean Lucy Diggs Slowe and the Education of a Modern Black Femininity." *Meridians* 17, no. 1 (2018): 25–48.

Bellar, David, Lawrence W. Judge, Jeffrey Petersen, Ann Bellar, and Charity L. Bryan. "Exercise and Academic Performance among Nursing and Kinesiology Students at U.S. Colleges." *Journal of Education and Health Promotion* 3, no. 9 (2014): 48–52.

Bowers, Matthew T., and Thomas M. Hunt. "The President's Council on Physical Fitness and the Systematisation of Children's Play in America." *International Journal of the History of Sport* 28, no. 11 (2011): 1496–511.

Brown, Elsa Barkley. "Negotiating and Transforming the Public Sphere: African American Political Life in the Transition from Slavery to Freedom." *Public Culture* 7, no. 1 (1994): 107–46.

———. "Polyrhythms and Improvisation: Lessons for Women's History." *History Workshop* 31 (1991): 85–90.

Brown, Elspeth. "Black Models and the Invention of the U.S. Negro Market, 1945–1960." In *Inside Marketing: Practices, Ideologies, Devices*, edited by Detlev Zwick and Julien Cayla, 185–211. New York: Oxford University Press, 2011.

Burch, Susan, and Lindsey Patterson. "Not Just Any Body: Disability, Gender, and History." *Journal of Women's History* 25, no. 4 (2013): 122–37.

Cabán, Pedro. "Subjects and Immigrants during the Progressive Era." *Discourse* 23, no. 3 (2001): 24–51.

Camp, Stephanie. "Black Is Beautiful: An American History." *Journal of Southern History* 81, no. 3 (2015): 675–90.

Captain, Gwendolyn. "Enter Ladies and Gentlemen of Color: Gender, Sport, and the Ideal African American Manhood and Womanhood during the Late Nineteenth and Early Twentieth Centuries." *Journal of Sport History* 18, no. 1 (1991): 81–102.

Chambers, Jason. "Presenting the Black Middle Class: John H. Johnson and *Ebony* Magazine, 1945–1974." In *Historicizing Lifestyle: Mediating Taste, Consumption, and Identity from the 1900s to 1970s*, edited by David Bell and Joanne Hollows, 54–69. London: Ashgate, 2006.

Childress, Micah. "Life beyond the Big Top: African American and Female Circusfolk, 1860–1920." *Journal of the Gilded Age and Progressive Era* 15 (2016): 176–96.

Clark, Langston, Marcus W. Johnson, Latrice Sales, and LaGarrett King. "Remember the Titans: The Lived Curriculum of Black Physical Education Teacher Education Scholars in the U.S." *Sport, Education, and Society* 25, no. 5 (2020): 507–17.

Cooper, Frederick. "Elevating the Race: The Social Thought of Black Leaders, 1827–50." *American Quarterly* 24, no. 5 (1972): 604–25.

Cornelius, Alexandra. "A Taste of the Lash of Criticism: Racial Progress, Self-Defense, and Christian Intellectual Thought in the Work of Amelia E. Johnson." In *Toward an Intellectual History of Black Women*, edited by Mia Bay, Farah J. Griffin, Martha S. Jones, and Barbara D. Savage, 93–109. Chapel Hill: University of North Carolina Press, 2015.

Dirks, Robert T., and Nancy Duran. "African American Dietary Patterns at the Beginning of the 20th Century." *Journal of Nutrition* 131, no. 7 (2001): 1881–89.

Dorsey, Carolyn. "Despite Poor Health: Olivia Davidson Washington's Story." *Sage* 2, no. 2 (1985): 69–72.

Elliot, Charlene D. "Big Persons, Small Voices: On Governance, Obesity, and the Narrative of the Failed Citizen." *Journal of Canadian Studies* 41, no. 3 (2007): 134–49.

Farmer, Ashley D. "In Search of the Black Women's History Archive." *Modern American History* 1, no. 2 (2018): 289–93.

Francis, Kennon T. "The Role of Endorphins in Exercise: A Review of Current Knowledge." *Journal of Orthopaedic and Sports Physical Therapy* 4, no. 3 (1983): 169–73.

Gallon, Kim. "Black Migrant Women and Sexual Pleasure during the Great Depression." *Journal of African American History* 105, no. 3 (2020): 424–51.

Garber, Eric. "Gladys Bentley: The Bulldagger Who Sang the Blues." *Out/Look: National Lesbian and Gay Quarterly* 1 (1988): 52–61.

Giddings, Paula. "The Last Taboo." In *Words of Fire: An Anthology of African-American Feminist Thought*, edited by Beverly Guy-Sheftall, 414–28. New York: The New Press, 1995.

Grey, Stephanie Houston. "Contesting the Fit Citizen: Michelle Obama and the Body Politics of *The Biggest Loser*." *Journal of Popular Culture* 49, no. 3 (2016): 564–81.

Gullett, Gayle. "Constructing the Woman Citizen and Struggling for the Vote in California, 1896–1911." *Pacific Historical Review* 69, no. 4 (2000): 573–93.

Haidarali, Laila. "Polishing Brown Diamonds: African American Women, Popular Magazines, and the Advent of Modeling in Postwar America." *Journal of Women's History* 17, no. 1 (2005): 10–37.

Hammonds, Evelynn M. "Toward a Genealogy of Black Female Sexuality: The Problematic of Silence." In *Feminist Theory and the Body: A Reader,* edited by Janet Price and Margrit Shildrick, 93–104. New York: Routledge, 2010.

Harley, Sharon. "Nannie Helen Burroughs: 'The Black Goddess of Liberty.'" *Journal of African American History* 81, no. 4 (1996): 62–71.

Hartog, Hendrik. "The Constitution of Aspiration and 'The Rights That Belong to Us All.'" *Journal of American History* 74, no. 3 (1987): 1013–34.

Herbenick, Debby, and J. Dennis Fortenberry. "Exercise-Induced Orgasm and Pleasure among Women." *Sexual and Relationship Therapy* 26, no. 4 (2011): 373–88.

Herndl, Diane Price. "The Invisible (Invalid) Woman: African-American Women, Illness, and Nineteenth-Century Narrative." *Women's Studies* 24, no. 6 (1995): 553–72.

Hicks, Cheryl. "'Bright and Good Looking Colored Girl': Black Women's Sexuality and 'Harmful Intimacy' in Early-Twentieth-Century New York." *Journal of the History of Sexuality* 18, no. 3 (2009): 418–56.

Hine, Darlene Clark. "Rape and the Inner Lives of Black Women in the Middle West." *Signs* 14, no. 4 (1989): 912–20.

Hoffman, Steven J. "Progressive Public Health Administration in the Jim Crow South: A Case Study of Richmond, Virginia, 1907–1920." *Journal of Social History* 35, no. 1 (2001): 175–94.

Hunt, Thomas M. "Countering the Soviet Threat in the Olympic Medals Race: The Amateur Sports Act of 1978 and American Athletics Policy Reform." *International Journal of the History of Sport* 24, no. 6 (2007): 796–818.

Kelley, Robin D. G. "'We Are Not What We Seem': Rethinking Black Working-Class Opposition in the Jim Crow South." *Journal of American History* 80, no. 1 (1993): 75–112.

Kerber, Linda K. "The Meanings of Citizenship." *Journal of American History* 84, no. 3 (1997): 833–54.

Knadler, Stephen. "Unsanitized Domestic Allegories: Biomedical Politics, Racial Uplift, and the African American Risk Narrative." *American Literature* 85, no. 1 (2013): 93–119.

Kozol, Wendy. "Miss Indian America: Regulatory Gazes and the Politics of Affiliation." *Feminist Studies* 31, no. 1 (2005): 64–94.

Kwate, Naa Oyo A., and Shatema Threadcraft. "Perceiving the Black Female Body: Race and Gender in Police Constructions of Body Weight." *Race and Social Problems* 7, no. 3 (2015): 213–26.

Kymlicka, Will, and Wayne Norman. "Return of the Citizen: A Survey of Recent Work on Citizenship Theory." *Ethics* 104, no. 2 (1994): 352–81.

Lefever, Harry G. "The Early Origins of Spelman College." *Journal of Blacks in Higher Education* 47 (2005): 60–63.

Liberti, Rita. "'We Were Ladies, We Just Played Basketball Like Boys': African American Womanhood and Competitive Basketball at Bennett College, 1928–1942." *Journal of Sport History* 26, no. 3 (1999): 567–84.

Marshall, T. H. "Citizenship and Social Class." In *The Citizenship Debates: A Reader,* edited by Gershon Shafir, 93–112. Minneapolis: University of Minnesota Press, 1998. Originally published in 1950.

Matelski, Elizabeth. "(Big and) Black Is Beautiful: Body Image and Expanded Beauty Ideals in the African American Community." *Essays in History* 45 (2012): 1–33.

May, Vanessa. "Standardizing the Home? Women Reformers and Domestic Service in New Deal New York." *Journal of Women's History* 23, no. 2 (2011): 14–38.

Meyer, Leisa D. "Creating G.I. Jane: The Regulation of Sexuality and Sexual Behavior in the Women's Army Corps during World War II." *Feminist Studies* 18, no. 3 (1992): 581–601.

Mitchell, Michele. "'A Corrupting Influence': Idleness and Sexuality during the Great Depression." In *Interconnections: Gender and Race in American History*, edited by Carol Faulkner and Alison M. Parker, 187–228. Rochester: University of Rochester Press, 2012.

———. "Silences Broken, Silences Kept: Gender and Sexuality in African-American History." *Gender and History* 11, no. 3 (1999): 433–44.

Morgan, Joan. "Why We Get Off: Moving Towards a Black Feminist Politics of Pleasure." *Black Scholar* 45, no. 4 (2015): 36–46.

Mullins, Greg. "Nudes, Prudes, and Pigmies: The Desirability of Disavowal in 'Physical Culture.'" *Discourse* 15, no. 1 (1992): 27–48.

Neuhaus, Jessamyn. "The Way to a Man's Heart: Gender Roles, Domestic Ideology, and Cookbooks in the 1950s." *Journal of Social History* 32, no. 3 (1999): 529–55.

Nickles, Shelley. "More Is Better: Mass Consumption, Gender, and Class Identity in Postwar America." *American Quarterly* 54, no. 4 (2002): 581–622.

Nielsen, Kim. "Helen Keller and the Politics of Civic Fitness." In *The New Disability History: American Perspectives*, edited by Paul K. Longmore and Lauri Umansky, 268–92. New York: New York University Press, 2001.

Parker, Meagan. "Desiring Citizenship: A Rhetorical Analysis of the Wells/Willard Controversy." *Women's Studies in Communication* 31, no. 1 (2008): 56–78.

Parks, Rosa. "'Tired of Giving In': The Launching of the Montgomery Bus Boycott." In *Sisters in the Struggle: African-American Women in the Civil Rights–Black Power Movement*, edited by Bettye Collier-Thomas and V. P. Franklin, 61–74. New York: New York University Press, 2001.

Pierce, Donna. "'This Book Is for Us and by Us': Freda De Knight and Postwar Black Cooking." *Repast* 24, no. 2 (2013): 16–18.

Pilz, Jeffrey J. "The Beginnings of Organized Play for Black America: E. T. Attwell and the PRAA." *Journal of African American History* 70, no. 3 (1985): 59–72.

Purdy, Daniel. "The Whiteness of Beauty: Weimar Neo-Classicism and the Sculptural Transcendence of Color." In *Colors 1800/1900/2000: Signs of Ethnic Difference*, edited by Birgit Tautz, 83–99. Amsterdam: Rodopi, 2004.

Rhodes, Jane. "Pedagogies of Respectability: Race, Media, and Black Womanhood in the Early 20th Century." *Souls* 18 (2016): 201–14.

Rouse, Jacqueline A. "The Legacy of Community Organizing: Lugenia Burns Hope and the Neighborhood Union." *Journal of African American History* 69, no. 3 (1984): 114–33.

Russell, Thaddeus. "The Color of Discipline: Civil Rights and Black Sexuality." *American Quarterly* 60, no. 1 (2008): 101–28.

Sanders, Rachel. "The Color of Fat: Racializing Obesity, Recuperating Whiteness, and Reproducing Injustice." *Politics, Groups, and Identities* 7, no. 2 (2019): 287–304.

Scully, Deirdre, John Kremer, Mary M. Meade, Rodger Graham, and Katrin Dudgeon. "Physical Exercise and Psychological Well Being: A Critical Review." *British Journal of Sports Medicine* 32, no. 2 (1998): 111–20.

Simmons, Christina. "'I Had to Promise . . . Not to Ask "Nasty" Questions Again': African American Women and Sex and Marriage Education in the 1940s." *Journal of Women's History* 27, no. 1 (2015): 110-35.

Simmons, LaKisha Michelle. "'To Lay Aside All Morals': Respectability, Sexuality and Black College Students in the United States in the 1930s." *Gender and History* 24, no. 2 (2012): 431-55.

Smith, Christopher Holmes. "Freeze Frames: Frozen Foods and Memories of the Postwar American Family." In *Kitchen Culture in America: Popular Representations of Food, Gender, and Race,* edited by Sherrie A. Inness, 175-209. Philadelphia: University of Pennsylvania Press, 2001.

Sparrow, James T. "'Buying Our Boys Back': The Mass Foundations of Fiscal Citizenship in World War II." *Journal of Policy History* 20, no. 2 (2008): 263-86.

Stanton, Amelia M., Ariel B. Handy, and Cindy M. Meston. "The Effects of Exercise on Sexual Function in Women." *Sexual Medicine Reviews* 6, no. 4 (2018): 548-57.

Strings, Sabrina. "Obese Black Women as 'Social Dead Weight': Reinventing the 'Diseased Black Woman.'" *Signs* 41, no. 1 (2015): 107-30.

Taylor, Traki L. "'Womanhood Glorified': Nannie Helen Burroughs and the National Training School for Women and Girls, Inc., 1909-1961." *Journal of African American History* 87 (2002): 390-403.

Thorén, Peter, John S. Floras, Pavel Hoffmann, and Douglas R. Seals. "Endorphins and Exercise: Physiological Mechanisms and Clinical Implications." *Medicine and Science in Sports and Exercise* 22, no. 4 (1990): 417-28.

Todd, Jan. "Bernarr Macfadden: Reformer of Feminine Form." *Journal of Sport History* 14, no. 1 (1987): 61-75.

———. "Reflections on Physical Culture: Defining Our Field and Protecting Its Integrity." *Iron Game History* 13, nos. 2-3 (2015): 1-8.

Verbrugge, Martha H. "Recreating the Body: Women's Physical Education and the Science of Sex Differences in America, 1900-1940." *Bulletin of the History of Medicine* 71, no. 2 (1997): 273-304.

———. "Recreation and Racial Politics in the Young Women's Christian Association of the United States, 1920s-1950s." *International Journal of the History of Sport* 27, no. 7 (2010): 1191-218.

Vertinsky, Patricia. "'Weighs and Means': Examining the Surveillance of Fat Bodies through Physical Education Practices in North America in the Late Nineteenth and Early Twentieth Centuries." *Journal of Sport History* 35, no. 3 (2008): 449-68.

Vester, Katharina. "Regime Change: Gender, Class, and the Invention of Dieting in Post-Bellum America." *Journal of Social History* 44, no. 1 (2010): 39-70.

Walker, Jessica Kenyatta. "Mighty Matriarchs Kill It with a Skillet: Critically Reading Popular Representations of Black Womanhood and Food." In *Dethroning the Deceitful Pork Chop: Rethinking African American Foodways from Slavery to Obama,* edited by Jennifer Jensen Wallach, 121-35. Fayetteville: University of Arkansas Press, 2015.

Whalan, Mark. "'Taking Myself in Hand': Jean Toomer and Physical Culture." *Modernism/Modernity* 10, no. 4 (2003): 597-616.

Witt, Doris. "What (N)Ever Happened to Aunt Jemima: Eating Disorders, Fetal Rights, and Black Female Appetite in Contemporary American Culture." *Discourse* 17, no. 2 (1994): 98-122.

BOOKS AND DISSERTATIONS

Alexander, Eleanor. *Lyrics of Sunshine and Shadow: The Courtship and Marriage of Paul Laurence Dunbar and Alice Ruth Moore*. New York: Penguin, 2004.

Baldwin, Davarian. *Chicago's New Negroes: Modernity, the Great Migration, and Black Urban Life*. Chapel Hill: University of North Carolina Press, 2007.

Banet-Weiser, Sarah. *The Most Beautiful Girl in the World: Beauty Pageants and National Identity*. Berkeley: University of California Press, 1999.

Bay, Mia. *The White Image in the Black Mind: African-American Ideas about White People, 1830–1925*. New York: Oxford University Press, 2000.

Bederman, Gail. *Manliness and Civilization: A Cultural History of Gender and Race in the United States, 1880–1917*. Chicago: University of Chicago Press, 1996.

Bell, Christopher M., ed. *Blackness and Disability: Critical Examinations and Cultural Interventions*. East Lansing: Michigan State University Press, 2012.

Berrey, Stephen. *The Jim Crow Routine: Everyday Performances of Race, Civil Rights, and Segregation in Mississippi*. Chapel Hill: University of North Carolina Press, 2015.

Berry, Daina Ramey, and Leslie M. Harris, eds. *Sexuality and Slavery: Reclaiming Intimate Histories in the Americas*. Athens: University of Georgia Press, 2018.

Biltekoff, Charlotte. *Eating Right in America: The Cultural Politics of Food and Health*. Durham: Duke University Press, 2013.

Black, Jonathan. *Making the American Body: The Remarkable Saga of the Men and Women Whose Feats, Feuds, and Passions Shaped Fitness History*. Lincoln: University of Nebraska Press, 2013.

Blair, Cynthia M. *I've Got to Make My Livin': Black Women's Sex Work in Turn-of-the-Century Chicago*. Chicago: University of Chicago Press, 2010.

Bloom, John. *To Show What an Indian Can Do: Sports at Native American Boarding Schools*. Minneapolis: University of Minnesota Press, 2000.

Bolzenius, Sandra M. *Glory in Their Spirit: How Four Black Women Took On the Army during World War II*. Urbana: University of Illinois Press, 2018.

Brooks, Jennifer E. *Defining the Peace: World War II Veterans, Race, and the Remaking of Southern Political Tradition*. Chapel Hill: University of North Carolina Press, 2004.

Brown, Jayna. *Babylon Girls: Black Women Performers and the Shaping of the Modern*. Durham: Duke University Press, 2008.

Butsch, Richard. *For Fun and Profit: The Transformation of Leisure into Consumption*. Philadelphia: Temple University Press, 1990.

Byrd, W. Michael, and Linda A. Clayton. *An American Health Dilemma: The Medical History of African Americans and the Problem of Race, Beginnings to 1900*. New York: Routledge, 2000.

Cahn, Susan K. *Coming on Strong: Gender and Sexuality in Twentieth-Century Women's Sports*. Cambridge, MA: Harvard University Press, 1998.

Camp, Stephanie M. H. *Closer to Freedom: Enslaved Women and Everyday Resistance in the Plantation South*. Chapel Hill: University of North Carolina Press, 2004.

Campt, Tina. *Image Matters: Archive, Photography, and the African Diaspora in Europe*. Durham: Duke University Press, 2012.

Canaday, Margot. *The Straight State: Sexuality and Citizenship in Twentieth-Century America*. Princeton: Princeton University Press, 2009.

Canning, Kathleen. *Gender History in Practice: Historical Perspectives on Bodies, Class, and Citizenship*. Ithaca: Cornell University Press, 2006.

Chambers, Jason. *Madison Avenue and the Color Line: African Americans in the Advertising Industry*. Philadelphia: University of Pennsylvania Press, 2008.

Chambers, John Whiteclay. *The Tyranny of Change: America in the Progressive Era, 1890–1920*. New Brunswick: Rutgers University Press, 2000.

Chapman, Erin D. *Prove It on Me: New Negroes, Sex, and Popular Culture in the 1920s*. New York: Oxford University Press, 2012.

Chatelain, Marcia. *South Side Girls: Growing Up in the Great Migration*. Durham: Duke University Press, 2015.

Cohen, Lizabeth. *A Consumers' Republic: The Politics of Mass Consumption in Postwar America*. New York: Alfred A. Knopf, 2003.

Coontz, Stephanie. *The Way We Never Were: American Families and the Nostalgia Trap*. New York: Basic Books, 2016.

Cooper, Brittney. *Beyond Respectability: The Intellectual Thought of Race Women*. Urbana: University of Illinois Press, 2017.

Cox, Karen L. *Dreaming of Dixie: How the South Was Created in American Popular Culture*. Chapel Hill: University of North Carolina Press, 2011.

Craig, Maxine Leeds. *Ain't I a Beauty Queen? Black Women, Beauty, and the Politics of Race*. New York: Oxford University Press, 2002.

Creadick, Anna. *Perfectly Average: The Pursuit of Normality in Postwar America*. Amherst: University of Massachusetts Press, 2010.

Cross, Gary S. *A Social History of Leisure since 1600*. State College, PA: Venture, 1990.

Currell, Susan. *The March of Spare Time: The Problem and Promise of Leisure in the Great Depression*. Philadelphia: University of Pennsylvania Press, 2005.

Davis, Angela Y. *Blues Legacies and Black Feminism: Gertrude "Ma" Rainey, Bessie Smith, and Billie Holiday*. New York: Vintage, 1999.

Dworkin, Shari L., and Faye Linda Wachs. *Body Panic: Gender, Health, and the Selling of Fitness*. New York: New York University Press, 2009.

Earley, Charity Adams. *One Woman's Army: A Black Officer Remembers the WAC*. College Station: Texas A&M University Press, 1996.

Ellison, Ralph. *The Selected Letters of Ralph Ellison*. Edited by John F. Callahan and Marc C. Conner. New York: Random House, 2019.

Evans, Stephanie Y. *Black Women's Yoga History: Memoirs of Inner Peace*. Albany: State University of New York Press, 2021.

Farrell, Amy E. *Fat Shame: Stigma and the Fat Body in American Culture*. New York: New York University Press, 2011.

Finney, Carolyn. *Black Faces, White Spaces: Reimagining the Relationship of African Americans to the Great Outdoors*. Chapel Hill: University of North Carolina Press, 2014.

Flowe, Douglas J. *Uncontrollable Blackness: African American Men and Criminality in Jim Crow New York*. Chapel Hill: University of North Carolina Press, 2020.

Ford, Tanisha C. *Liberated Threads: Black Women, Style, and the Global Politics of Soul*. Chapel Hill: University of North Carolina Press, 2015.

Fuentes, Marisa J. *Dispossessed Lives: Enslaved Women, Violence, and the Archive*. Philadelphia: University of Pennsylvania Press, 2016.

Gaines, Kevin K. *Uplifting the Race: Black Leadership, Politics, and Culture in the Twentieth Century*. Chapel Hill: University of North Carolina Press, 1996.

Giddings, Paula. *Ida: A Sword among Lions: Ida B. Wells and the Campaign against Lynching*. New York: Harper Collins, 2008.

———. *When and Where I Enter: The Impact of Black Women on Race and Sex in America*. New York: William Morrow Paperbacks, 2007.

Gill, Tiffany M. *Beauty Shop Politics: African American Women's Activism in the Beauty Industry*. Urbana: University of Illinois Press, 2010.

Gilmore, Glenda Elizabeth. *Gender and Jim Crow: Women and the Politics of White Supremacy in North Carolina, 1896-1920*. Chapel Hill: University of North Carolina Press, 1996.

Glenn, Evelyn Nakano. *Unequal Freedom: How Race and Gender Shaped American Citizenship and Labor*. Cambridge, MA: Harvard University Press, 2002.

Green, Adam. *Selling the Race: Culture, Community, and Black Chicago, 1940-1955*. Chicago: University of Chicago Press, 2007.

Green, Harvey. *Fit for America: Health, Fitness, Sport and American Society*. Baltimore: Johns Hopkins University Press, 1988.

Green, Hilary. *Educational Reconstruction: African American Schools in the Urban South, 1865-1890*. New York: Fordham University Press, 2016.

Greer, Brenna Wynn. *Represented: The Black Imagemakers Who Reimagined African American Citizenship*. Philadelphia: University of Pennsylvania Press, 2019.

Griffith, R. Marie. *Born Again Bodies: Flesh and Spirit in American Christianity*. Berkeley: University of California Press, 2004.

Gross, Kali N. *Colored Amazons: Crime, Violence, and Black Women in the City of Brotherly Love, 1880-1910*. Durham: Duke University Press, 2006.

Grover, Kathryn. *Hard at Play: Leisure in America, 1840-1940*. Amherst: University of Massachusetts Press, 1992.

———, ed. *Fitness in American Culture: Images of Health, Sport, and the Body, 1830-1940*. Amherst: University of Massachusetts Press, 1990.

Hancock, Ange-Marie. *The Politics of Disgust: The Public Identity of the Welfare Queen*. New York: New York University Press, 2004.

Happe, Kelly E., and Jenell Johnson, eds. *Biocitizenship: The Politics of Bodies, Governance, and Power*. New York: New York University Press, 2018.

Harris, LaShawn. *Sex Workers, Psychics, and Numbers Runners: Black Women in New York City's Underground Economy*. Urbana: University of Illinois Press, 2016.

Harrison, Joanne K., and Grant Harrison. *The Life and Times of Irvine Garland Penn*. Philadelphia: Xlibris, 2000. Kindle.

Hart, Tanya. *Health in the City: Race, Poverty, and the Negotiation of Women's Health in New York City, 1915-1930*. New York: New York University Press, 2015.

Hartman, Saidiya. *Wayward Lives, Beautiful Experiments: Intimate Histories of Riotous Black Girls, Troublesome Women, and Queer Radicals*. New York: W. W. Norton, 2019.

Haynes, April R. *Riotous Flesh: Women, Physiology, and the Solitary Vice in Nineteenth-Century America*. Chicago: University of Chicago Press, 2015.

Heap, Chad. *Slumming: Sexual and Racial Encounters in American Nightlife, 1885-1940*. Chicago: University of Chicago Press, 2010.

Hendricks, Wanda A. *Gender, Race, and Politics in the Midwest: Black Club Women in Illinois*. Bloomington: Indiana University Press, 1998.

Hicks, Cheryl D. *Talk with You Like a Woman: African American Women, Justice, and Reform in New York, 1890-1935*. Chapel Hill: University of North Carolina Press, 2010.

Higginbotham, Evelyn Brooks. *Righteous Discontent: The Women's Movement in the Black Baptist Church, 1880-1920*. Cambridge, MA: Harvard University Press, 1994.

Hill-Collins, Patricia. *Black Feminist Thought: Knowledge, Consciousness, and the Politics of Empowerment*. New York: Routledge, 2009.

Honey, Maureen, ed. *Bitter Fruit: African American Women in World War II*. Columbia: University of Missouri Press, 1999.

Hull, Gloria T. *Give Us Each Day: The Diary of Alice Dunbar Nelson*. New York: W. W. Norton, 1986.

Hult, Joan S., and Marianna Trekell, eds. *A Century of Women's Basketball: From Frailty to Final Four*. Reston, VA: American Alliance for Health, Physical Education, Recreation and Dance, 1991.

Hunter, Tera W. *To 'Joy My Freedom: Southern Black Women's Lives and Labors after the Civil War*. Cambridge, MA: Harvard University Press, 1998.

Hurd, Amy R., and Denise M. Anderson. *The Park and Recreation Professional's Handbook*. Champaign, IL: Human Kinetics, 2010.

Ingelhart, Louis Edward. *Press Freedoms: A Descriptive Calendar of Concepts, Interpretations, Events, and Court Actions, from 4000 BC to the Present*. Santa Barbara: Greenwood, 1987.

Jackson, Shannon Patricia. *Lines of Activity: Performance, Historiography, Hull-House Domesticity*. Ann Arbor: University of Michigan Press, 2001.

Jones, Jacqueline. *Labor of Love, Labor of Sorrow: Black Women, Work, and the Family, from Slavery to the Present*. New York: Basic Books, 2010.

Jones, Lu Ann. *Mama Learned Us to Work: Farm Women in the New South*. Chapel Hill: University of North Carolina Press, 2002.

Jones, Martha. *Birthright Citizens: A History of Race and Rights in Antebellum America*. Cambridge: Cambridge University Press, 2018.

Kandaswamy, Priya. *Domestic Contradictions: Race and Gendered Citizenship from Reconstruction to Welfare Reform*. Durham: Duke University Press, 2021.

Kando, Thomas M. *Leisure and Popular Culture in Transition*. St. Louis: C. V. Mosby Company, 1975.

Kasson, John F. *Houdini, Tarzan, and the Perfect Man: The White Male Body and the Challenge of Modernity in America*. New York: Hill and Wang, 2001.

Kelley, Blair L. M. *Right to Ride: Streetcar Boycotts and African American Citizenship in the Era of Plessy v. Ferguson*. Chapel Hill: University of North Carolina Press, 2010.

Kelley, Robin D. G. *Race Rebels: Culture, Politics, and the Black Working Class*. New York: Free Press, 1996.

Kendi, Ibram X. *Stamped from the Beginning: The Definitive History of Racist Ideas in America*. New York: Nation Books, 2016.

Klinkner, Philip A., and Rogers M. Smith. *The Unsteady March: The Rise and Decline of Racial Equality in America*. Chicago: University of Chicago Press, 2002.

Knupfer, Anne. *Toward a Tenderer Humanity and a Nobler Womanhood: African American Women's Clubs in Turn-of-the-Century Chicago*. New York: New York University Press, 1997.

Krebs, Ronald R. *Fighting for Rights: Military Service and the Politics of Citizenship*. Ithaca: Cornell University Press, 2006.

Laker, Anthony. *Beyond the Boundaries of Physical Education: Educating Young People for Citizenship and Social Responsibility*. New York: Routledge, 2000.

LeFlouria, Talitha. *Chained in Silence: Black Women and Convict Labor in the New South*. Chapel Hill: University of North Carolina Press, 2015.

Lentz-Smith, Adriane. *Freedom Struggles: African Americans and World War I*. Cambridge, MA: Harvard University Press, 2011.

Lerner, Gerda. *Black Women in White America: A Documentary History*. New York: Vintage Books, 1992.

Logan, Rayford Whittingham. *The Negro in American Life and Thought: The Nadir, 1877–1901*. New York: Dial Press, 1954.

Lowe, Margaret A. *Looking Good: College Women and Body Image, 1875–1930*. Baltimore: Johns Hopkins University Press, 2003.

Masur, Kate. *An Example for All the Land: Emancipation and the Struggle over Equality in Washington, D.C.* Chapel Hill: University of North Carolina Press, 2012.

Matelski, Elizabeth M. *Reducing Bodies: Mass Culture and the Female Figure in Postwar America*. New York: Routledge, 2017.

May, Elaine Tyler. *Homeward Bound: American Families in the Cold War Era*. New York: Basic Books, 2017.

McBride, David. *Integrating the City of Medicine: Blacks in Philadelphia Health Care, 1910–1965*. Philadelphia: Temple University Press, 1989.

McKenzie, Shelly. *Getting Physical: The Rise of Fitness Culture in America*. Lawrence: University Press of Kansas, 2013.

Mckiernan-González, John. *Fevered Measures: Public Health and Race at the Texas-Mexico Border, 1848–1942*. Durham: Duke University Press, 2012.

McQuirter, Marya. "Claiming the City: African Americans, Urbanization, and Leisure in Washington, D.C., 1902–1957." PhD diss., University of Michigan, 2000.

Metcalf, Eugene Wesley. "The Letters of Paul and Alice Dunbar: A Private History." PhD diss., University of California Irvine, 1973.

Miller, Carroll L. L., and Anne S. Pruitt-Logan. *Faithful to the Task at Hand: The Life of Lucy Diggs Slowe*. Albany: State University of New York Press, 2012.

Mitchell, Koritha. *Living with Lynching: African American Lynching Plays, Performance, and Citizenship, 1890–1930*. Urbana: University of Illinois Press, 2011.

Mitchell, Michele. *Righteous Propagation: African Americans and the Politics of Racial Destiny after Reconstruction*. Chapel Hill: University of North Carolina Press, 2004.

Molina, Natalia. *Fit to Be Citizens? Public Health and Race in Los Angeles, 1879–1939*. Berkeley: University of California Press, 2006.

———. *How Race Is Made in America: Immigration, Citizenship, and the Historical Power of Racial Scripts*. Berkeley: University of California Press, 2014.

Moran, Rachel Louise. *Governing Bodies: American Politics and the Shaping of the Modern Physique*. Philadelphia: University of Pennsylvania Press, 2018.

Muhammad, Khalil Gibran. *The Condemnation of Blackness: Race, Crime, and the Making of Modern Urban America*. Cambridge, MA: Harvard University Press, 2010.

Ngai, Mae M. *Impossible Subjects: Illegal Aliens and the Making of Modern America*. Princeton: Princeton University Press, 2014.

Nielsen, Kim. *A Disability History of the United States*. Boston: Beacon Press, 2013.

Oliver, Eric. *Fat Politics: The Real Story behind America's Obesity Epidemic*. New York: Oxford University Press, 2005.

Opie, Frederick Douglass. *Hog and Hominy: Soul Food from Africa to America*. New York: Columbia University Press, 2010.

Parker, Traci. *Department Stores and the Black Freedom Movement: Workers, Consumers, and Civil Rights from the 1930s to the 1980s*. Chapel Hill: University of North Carolina Press, 2019.

Patterson, Martha. *Beyond the Gibson Girl: Reimagining the American New Woman, 1895–1915*. Urbana: University of Illinois Press, 2005.

Peiss, Kathy. *Cheap Amusements: Working Women and Leisure in Turn-of-the-Century New York*. Philadelphia: Temple University Press, 1986.

———. *Hope in a Jar: The Making of America's Beauty Culture*. Philadelphia: University of Pennsylvania Press, 1998.

Powdermaker, Hortense. *After Freedom: A Cultural Study in the Deep South*. New York: Viking, 1939.

Putney, Clifford. *Muscular Christianity: Manhood and Sports in Protestant America, 1880–1920*. Cambridge, MA: Harvard University Press, 2001.

Raiford, Leigh. *Imprisoned in a Luminous Glare: Photography and the African American Freedom Struggle*. Chapel Hill: University of North Carolina Press, 2011.

Roberts, Dorothy. *Killing the Black Body: Race, Reproduction, and the Meaning of Liberty*. New York: Vintage Books, 1998.

Roberts, Samuel. *Infectious Fear: Politics, Disease, and the Health Effects of Segregation*. Chapel Hill: University of North Carolina Press, 2009.

Rooks, Noliwe M. *Hair Raising: Beauty, Culture, and African American Women*. New Brunswick, NJ: Rutgers University Press, 1996.

Rose, Sarah F. *No Right to Be Idle: The Invention of Disability, 1840s–1930s*. Chapel Hill: University of North Carolina Press, 2017.

Rosen, Hannah. *Terror in the Heart of Freedom: Citizenship, Sexual Violence, and the Meaning of Race in the Postemancipation South*. Chapel Hill: University of North Carolina Press, 2009.

Rosenberg, Jonathan. *How Far the Promised Land? World Affairs and the American Civil Rights Movement from the First World War to Vietnam*. Princeton: Princeton University Press, 2005.

Rusert, Britt. *Fugitive Science: Empiricism and Freedom in Early African American Culture*. New York: New York University Press, 2017.

Russell, Emily. *Reading Embodied Citizenship: Disability, Narrative, and the Body Politic*. New Brunswick, NJ: Rutgers University Press, 2011.

Schneider, Mark. *Boston Confronts Jim Crow, 1890–1920*. Boston: Northeastern University Press, 1997.

Schwartz, Hillel. *Never Satisfied: A Cultural History of Diets, Fantasies, and Fat*. New York: Doubleday, 1990.

Shah, Nayan. *Contagious Divides: Epidemics and Race in San Francisco's Chinatown*. Berkeley: University of California Press, 2001.

———. *Stranger Intimacy: Contesting Race, Sexuality and the Law in the North American West*. Berkeley: University of California Press, 2012.

Shaw, Andrea Elizabeth. *The Embodiment of Disobedience: Fat Black Women's Unruly Political Bodies*. New York: Lexington Books, 2006.

Singh, Nikhil Pal. *Black Is a Country: Race and the Unfinished Struggle for Democracy*. Cambridge, MA: Harvard University Press, 2005.

Smith, Susan L. *Sick and Tired of Being Sick and Tired: Black Women's Health Activism in America, 1890–1950*. Philadelphia: University of Pennsylvania Press, 1995.

Smith, Virginia. *Clean: A History of Personal Hygiene and Purity*. New York: Oxford University Press, 2007.

Spires, Derrick R. *The Practice of Citizenship: Black Politics and Black Print Culture in the Early United States*. Philadelphia: University of Pennsylvania Press, 2019.

Stage, Sarah, and Virginia B. Vincenti, eds. *Rethinking Home Economics: Women and the History of a Profession*. Ithaca: Cornell University Press, 1997.

Stearns, Peter N. *Fat History: Bodies and Beauty in the Modern West*. New York: New York University Press, 2002.

Stern, Alexandra Minna. *Eugenic Nation: Faults and Frontiers of Better Breeding in Modern America*. Berkeley: University of California Press, 2015.

Taylor, Ula. *The Promise of Patriarchy: Women and the Nation of Islam*. Chapel Hill: University of North Carolina Press, 2017.

Terborg-Penn, Rosalyn. *African American Women in the Struggle for the Vote, 1850–1920*. Bloomington: Indiana University Press, 1998.

Theoharis, Jeanne. *A More Beautiful and Terrible History: The Uses and Misuses of Civil Rights History*. Boston: Beacon Press, 2018.

Theophano, Janet. *Eat My Words: Reading Women's Lives through the Cookbooks They Wrote*. New York: Palgrave MacMillan, 2003.

Thuesen, Sarah Caroline. *Greater Than Equal: African American Struggles for Schools and Citizenship in North Carolina, 1919–1965*. Chapel Hill: University of North Carolina Press, 2013.

Todd, Jan. *Physical Culture and the Body Beautiful: Purposive Exercise in the Lives of American Women, 1800–1875*. Macon: Mercer University Press, 1999.

Tomes, Nancy. *The Gospel of Germs: Men, Women, and the Microbe in American Life*. Cambridge, MA: Harvard University Press, 1998.

Veit, Helen Zoe. *Modern Food, Moral Food: Self-Control, Science, and the Rise of Modern American Eating in the Early Twentieth Century*. Chapel Hill: University of North Carolina Press, 2015.

Verbrugge, Martha H. *Able-Bodied Womanhood: Personal Health and Social Change in Nineteenth-Century Boston*. New York: Oxford University Press, 1988.

———. *Active Bodies: A History of Women's Physical Education in Twentieth-Century America*. New York: Oxford University Press, 2012.

Vester, Katharina. *A Taste of Power: Food and American Identities*. Berkeley: University of California Press, 2015.

Wailoo, Keith. *Dying in the City of the Blues: Sickle Cell Anemia and the Politics of Race and Health*. Chapel Hill: University of North Carolina Press, 2001.

Wallace, Maurice O., and Shawn Michelle Smith, eds. *Pictures and Progress: Early Photography and the Making of African American Identity*. Durham: Duke University Press, 2012.

Wallach, Jennifer Jensen. *Every Nation Has Its Dish: Black Bodies and Black Food in Twentieth-Century America*. Chapel Hill: University of North Carolina Press, 2019.

Warren, Kim Cary. *The Quest for Citizenship: African American and Native American Education in Kansas, 1880–1935*. Chapel Hill: University of North Carolina Press, 2010.

Washington, Harriet A. *Medical Apartheid: The Dark History of Medical Experimentation on Black Americans from Colonial Times to the Present*. New York: Broadway Books, 2006.

Weems, Robert E. *Desegregating the Dollar: African American Consumerism in the Twentieth Century*. New York: New York University Press, 1998.

White, Deborah Gray. *Too Heavy a Load: Black Women in Defense of Themselves, 1894–1994*. New York: W. W. Norton, 1999.

White, Deborah Gray, Mia Bay, and Waldo E. Martin Jr. *Freedom on My Mind: A History of African Americans*. Boston: Bedford/St. Martin's, 2013.

Whorton, James C. *Crusaders for Fitness: The History of American Health Reformers*. Princeton: Princeton University Press, 1982.

———. *Nature Cures: The History of Alternative Medicine in America*. New York: Oxford University Press, 2004.

Williams, Chad L. *Torchbearers of Democracy: African American Soldiers in the World War I Era*. Chapel Hill: University of North Carolina Press, 2010.

Williams-Forson, Psyche. *Building Houses Out of Chicken Legs: Black Women, Food, and Power*. Chapel Hill: University of North Carolina Press, 2006.

Wilson, James F. *Bulldaggers, Pansies, and Chocolate Babies: Performance, Race, and Sexuality in the Harlem Renaissance*. Ann Arbor: University of Michigan Press, 2011.

Wiltse, Jeff. *Contested Waters: A Social History of Swimming Pools in America*. Chapel Hill: University of North Carolina Press, 2010.

Winter, Thomas. *Making Men, Making Class: The YMCA and Workingmen, 1877–1920*. Chicago: University of Chicago Press, 2002.

Witt, Doris. *Black Hunger: Soul Food and America*. Minneapolis: University of Minnesota Press, 2004.

Wolcott, Victoria W. *Race, Riots, and Roller Coasters: The Struggle over Segregated Recreation in America*. Philadelphia: University of Pennsylvania Press, 2012.

———. *Remaking Respectability: African American Women in Interwar Detroit*. Chapel Hill: University of North Carolina Press, 2001.

Zafar, Rafia. *Recipes for Respect: African American Meals and Meaning*. Athens: University of Georgia Press, 2019.

WEB-BASED SOURCES

"Achievements." Let's Move! Accessed May 13, 2021. https://letsmove .obamawhitehouse.archives.gov/achievements.

Bond, Sarah E. "Why We Need to Start Seeing the Classical World in Color." *Hyperallergic*, June 7, 2017. https://hyperallergic.com/383776/why-we-need-to -start-seeing-the- classical-world-in-color/.

Breitman, Kendall. "Fox Doc Steps Up FLOTUS Grilling." *Politico*, August 13, 2014. https://www.politico.com/story/2014/08/fox-keith-ablow-michelle-obama-109985.

"History." YMCA. Accessed July 20, 2018. http://www.ymca.net/history/1800–1860s.html.

"History." YWCA. Accessed July 20, 2018. http://www.ywca.org/site/c.cuIRJ7NTKrLaG/b.7515891/k.C524/History.htm.

Oldenburg, Ann. "Rush Limbaugh Attacks Michelle Obama's Diet." *USA Today*, February 21, 2011. http://content.usatoday.com/communities/entertainment/post/2011/02/rush-limbaugh-attacks-michelle-obamas-diet/1?loc=interstitialskip#.W3NV99VKjIU.

Presidential Committee on Harvard and the Legacy of Slavery. "Harvard and the Legacy of Slavery." Harvard University. Accessed June 11, 2022. https://legacyofslavery.harvard.edu/.

Randall, Alice. "Black Women and Fat." *New York Times*, May 5, 2012. https://www.nytimes.com/2012/05/06/opinion/sunday/why-black-women-are-fat.html.

Rockeymoore, Maya. "Are Black Women Obese Because We Want to Be?" *Huffington Post*, May 8, 2012. https://www.huffpost.com/entry/black-women-and-obesity_b_1498145.

Rooks, Noliwe M. "Do Black Women Really Want to Be Fat?" *Time*, May 14, 2012. https://ideas.time.com/2012/05/14/do-black-women-really-want-to-be-fat/.

The White House: Office of the First Lady. "Remarks by the First Lady at the White House Kitchen Garden Dedication." Speech delivered October 5, 2016. https://obamawhitehouse.archives.gov/the-press-office/2016/10/05/remarks-first-lady- white-house-kitchen-garden-dedication.

"Women, Weight and Wellness—Room for Debate." *New York Times*, May 7, 2012. https://www.nytimes.com/roomfordebate/2012/05/07/women-weight-and-wellness.

"Wrestling with Respectability in the Age of #blacklivesmatter: A Dialogue." *For Harriet*, October 13, 2015. http://www.forharriet.com/2015/10/wrestling-with-respectability-in-age-of.html.

Index

Page numbers in italics refer to illustrations.